The Book of
LEIGH & BRANSFORD

COMPILED BY MALCOLM SCOTT

ON BEHALF OF THE PARISH COUNCIL

HALSGROVE

First published in Great Britain in 2002

This book is dedicated to all those who value parish life.

Frontispiece photograph: *Marriage of Thomas Henry Jones and Gladys Elizabeth Mary Banner, 22 April 1914.* Left to right, back row: *Walter Banner, Dolly Hill, Fanny Winkett (?), Ted Jones, Thomas Henry Jones, Gladys Elizabeth Mary Banner, George Banner, Sarah Banner, Elsie Ball, Henry Jones (father of Thomas Jones);* front row: *?, Laura Ethel Banner, Susan Jones, Grace Boulter.* (CORAL CLARKE, CONNIE TOHTZ)

British Library Cataloguing-in-Publication Data
A CIP record for this title is available from the British Library

ISBN 1 84114 178 X

HALSGROVE

Halsgrove House
Lower Moor Way
Tiverton, Devon EX16 6SS
Tel: 01884 243242
Fax: 01884 243325
email: sales@halsgrove.com
website: www.halsgrove.com

Printed and bound in Great Britain by Bookcraft Ltd, Midsomer Norton

FOREWORD

It has taken just over a year for this book to grow from 'a good idea' to a fully illustrated, comprehensive record of historical value. At a time when country life and values are undergoing rapid evaluation and change there can be no better way of reminding us locals and 'newcomers' alike of the heritage now entrusted to us by our forebears. The Parish Council is hugely indebted to Malcolm Scott for his energy and drive in bringing this project to fruition.

CAROLINE ORGEE
CHAIRMAN OF LEIGH & BRANSFORD PARISH COUNCIL

Leigh and Bransford Horticultural Show, held at the Memorial Hall, c.1930.
This photograph shows the Children's Fancy Dress Competition. In the picture are: Maude Smith, Gwen Taylor, Barbara James, Peggy Johnson, Eileen Weaver, Edna Phillips, Harold Portman, Raymond Dyson, Reg Powell, Hilda Smith, Eileen Bowcott, Doreen Jones, Freda Spencer, Connis Dance, Bernice Rolph.
(DOREEN ROWLEY)

Leigh Court Station around 1900. Clearly some special event is taking place, because everyone is dressed in their best clothes. (GEOFF SMITH)

Bransford garage before it had a canopy over the forecourt. (DOROTHY DYSON)

Cherry orchard in Brockamin, 1958. Left to right (children): *Brian Salter, Richard Beard and David Salter.* (RUTH BEARD)

CONTENTS

Left: *Hop stacking at Leigh Court, 1955.*
(WRO/SERGEANT)

Below: *Workers at the Great House, c.1920.*
Included are: Tom Johnson (with fox), ?,
Arthur Emson, Herbert Leeke (with dog).
(OLIVE BISHOP)

Bottom picture: *The Gabb family transport*
around 1910. William Henry Gabb in the trap
with his wife Jessie and daughter Monica.
(The pony was called Tinker.) (SALLY STEWART)

ACKNOWLEDGEMENTS

Collecting the material for this pictorial history has been fascinating, and has involved the collaboration of a large number of people, without whom it could not have been written. The majority are present or past parishioners but, in addition, there have been valuable contributions from people unconnected with the parish. Some people have given photographs or information, others have spent an hour or so – and sometimes much more – reminiscing and being questioned.

Given the number of contributors, it may be unwise to single out individuals, but there are four people who have spent more time than most in helping to prepare this book. The first is Sheila Cridland, who has spent tens of hours listening to tape-recorded interviews and transcribing them. The second is Caroline Rees, a freelance editor, who has read and commented on the whole manuscript. The third is Michael Stedman, a military historian, whose original contribution 'Leigh at War' has formed a major part of the first two chapters. Finally, there is Geoff Wright, whose own volumes on our parish history have been invaluable, who has also commented on the whole manuscript, and who has been both helpful and encouraging throughout.

The present parishioners who have contributed to this book are: Les and Florence Alford, Bernard Atkinson, Harry and Dorothy Banner, Bill Banner, Geoffrey Bartlett, Olive Bishop, Andrew Bullock, Julian Burton, Valda Cane, Rosemary Chidlow, Des and Coral Clarke, Ivy Coley, Fred Covins, Edna Davies, Ken Davies, Cecil and Pat Dee, Graham Froggatt, Geoff and Mary Fynn, Gill and Mary Gale, Martin and Helena Gloster, John and Brenda Guise, Beryl and Peter Gwinnett, Nora Hadley, Vi Handy, John and Pauline Harcombe, Roy Hill, Wendy Howard, Anne Jackson, Lillian Jauncey, Nora Jay, Graham and Susan Jones, Ken Jones, Muriel 'Bib'

Hop picking at Castle Green Farm in the 1920s. The busheller is Ned Pole, and his wife Beatrice is the woman in the hat. The two girls in front are Doreen Lewis (Eileen Kebby's cousin) and Eileen Kebby. The rest of the children are the Poles, known to Eileen (who lived next door) as 'the gang'. (EILEEN KEBBY)

Jones, Gwen Jones, Eileen Kebby, Norman Kimber, John Lapworth, Richard Lewis, Patrick Mills, Jeremy Morfey, Lilian Morris, Peter Norbury, Tom Norbury, Caroline Orgee, Christopher Phillips, Pauline Phillips, Dr A.J. Popert, Elizabeth Portman, Harold and Elsie Portman, George Price, Eileen Purvis, Jeremy Roberson, John Roberts, June Robinson, Doreen Rowley, Ronald Simcock, Geoff and Kate Smith, Eva Smith, Lillian Somervaille, Thelma Spencer, Patricia Stevens, Barclay and Sally Stewart, John Swindell, Des Symonds, Shirley Tasker, Tom Teague, Connie Tohtz, Will Tooby, Eric Vine, John Wenden, Sheila Wright and John Young.

The former parishioners, together with those unconnected with the parish who have helped, are: Kevin Allen, Valerie Allfrey, Chris Almgill (Partnership Housing Group), Emmie Bagley, John Banner, Ruth Beard, Pat Bowers, Stella Braithwaite, Liz Carlin (Bank House Hotel), Hazel Chambers, David Chaundy, Eddie Clarke, Judi Creed-Newton, Maureen Croall, Simon Croall, Tony Cubberley (King's School), Harry Davies, Jimmy Davies, Mowey Davies, Dorothy Dyson, Jill Ellard, Shirley Ellis, Eunice Emery, Douglas and Peggy Emson, Paul and June Etheridge, John Farr, Alan Garness, Peter Gill, David Grant, Vera (Connie) Green, John Griffin, Noel Griffin, Janet Griffiths, Mike Grundy (*Worcester Evening News*), Gwen Hawkins, Beryl Hope, Dorothy Hughes, Joseph Hughes, Ronald Hunt, Brian Iles, Carol Irons, Ray Jackson, Kathleen Jauncy, Sue Jones, Ivy Keeling, Catherine Lees, Neil Leighton (*Western Daily Press*), Janet Long, Malvern Public Library, Jean McGowan, Glenda Merrell, Ann Moore, Lilian Morris, Deborah Overton (Worcestershire Archaeological Service), Mervyn Philpott, Colin Portman, David and Merle Portman, Gordon and Dorothy Portman, Aubrey and Cecilia Pritchard, Mike Pryce (*Worcester Evening News*), Mike Quarrell (Worcestershire Record Office), Sue Rickuss, Marc Ridley, Caroline Roslington (King's School), Brian Savage, Marion Simmons, Paul Simmons (Partnership Housing Group), Max Sinclair, Margaret Staplehurst (Archivist, Countess of Huntingdon's Connexion), David Steel, Robert Stone (King's School), Jim Stubbs, Paul Thompson (King's School), Kenneth Wadley, Basil and Jackie Wadley, Barbara Wall, Bertha Weaver, Mrs D. West, Prue Wilesmith, Mick Wilks, Worcestershire Countryside Service.

Finally, in a book covering such a wide spectrum of activities and range of time, there will inevitably be errors. Most will be mine. For these I can only apologise, and hope that they do not spoil your reading.

MALCOLM SCOTT
AUBRETIA COTTAGE, LEIGH
JULY 2002

Pictorial Acknowledgements

In brackets below each picture are one or two names. The first name is the person providing the picture. Where it simply gives 'WRO' this is the Worcestershire Record Office. If there is a second name, this is the copyright holder, whose permission has been given for publication. We are particularly grateful to *Newsquest Ltd (Berrows Journal)* for allowing us to publish their pictures from whatever source.

Test loading the new bridge at Bransford, c.1925. (WRO/COUNTY SURVEYOR)

Chapter One

HISTORY & DEVELOPMENT

*Celtic one quarter stater gold coin of the Dobunni tribe, 50BC, found at Brockamin by Paul Dunmall.
This tribe lived down the Severn, from Worcestershire down to beyond Bristol.*

Introduction

This is the pictorial history of two parishes, Bransford and Leigh, in Worcestershire. Leigh, the larger of the two, includes the villages of Leigh and Leigh Sinton. Although the two parishes have retained some of their identity by having separate annual Parish Meetings, since 1971 they have been served by a common Parish Council, Leigh and Bransford.

So 'Leigh' can be either the parish or the village, and 'parish' can mean either Leigh or Bransford. To simplify the text, we will use the term 'parish' to mean the area served by the Parish Council. When we need to make finer distinctions we will refer to 'Bransford Parish' or ' Leigh Parish', or will name the village concerned.

Leigh has been variously spelled in ancient documents as Leah, Leyghe, Lega and Ley. The word 'Leah' in Saxon English means 'a woodland clearing or glade'. The earliest mention of Leigh is in three tenth-century charters recording grants of land. In one of these, dated AD972, King Edgar granted land at Leigh to Pershore Abbey, and defined the parish boundaries.

Leigh Sinton has a wider range of name variants, including Lye Sinton, Sodyngton and Syddington. However, the number of variations is clearly limited, because in 1714 a magistrate quashed an order on an Ann Guise because 'there be no such place as Leye-Shinton.' Bransford, on the other hand, has always been fairly recognisable – Bradnesforde, Brainesford, Braunceford and Braynesford being some of the spellings, the 'ford' ending relating to being able to cross the River Teme there.

Early History

Like most parishes in England, the earliest written history relating to Leigh and Bransford is in the Domesday Book, which was produced in 1086. Before that one can only conjecture about our history,

9

Above: *Neolithic (4000 to 2500*BC*)
flint arrowhead found at Little
Brockamin Farm by Paul Dunmall.*

Left: *The Roman tile kiln at Lower
Sandlin Farm, 1961.*
(WRO/A. PANTRY-WHITE)

based on archaeological finds. The parish is, however, rich in these. The earliest ones are from Neolithic times – 4000BC to 2500BC – a flint arrowhead being found at Brockamin, and a stone axe head at Sherridge, so there has been human activity in the parishes for up to 6,000 years.

So far nothing has been found in the parish relating to the Bronze and Iron Ages which followed, although one coin from pre-Roman Britain has been discovered. However, once one gets to the period of the Roman occupation (43BC to AD409) there is abundant evidence of a wide range of activities. A significant find has been at Upper Sandlin Farm, Leigh Sinton, where a Roman tile-making kiln was unearthed in 1961 by a local research group attached to the University of Birmingham. Fragments around the kiln showed that local clay was used to make roof tiles and bricks.

In a 1954 report of earlier excavations at the site, pottery fragments found were dated as being late-second century AD. The same report found possible evidence of iron smelting, showing that the Romans were well established locally. Indeed, somebody who is familiar with the range of Roman objects

found in Leigh Parish believes that there could have been up to three farms there.

The Worcestershire County Archaeological Department's records show that there have been Roman pottery finds all over the parish. For example, there is an abundance of pottery shards south of Stocks Lane, Bransford, which has been identified as a site of Roman occupation. Pottery fragments have also been found around the old Leigh Court Station, by the Old Clay Pits at Smith End Green and near Bransford Manor.

Pottery finds are usually of small fragments, requiring reconstruction by an expert or a vivid imagination to excite a lay person. In contrast, metal items are often intact and readily recognisable. A large number of Roman coins have also been found. One of the most striking non-military finds was of a bracelet in Stock Wood, Bransford. Instead of being found after painstaking digging it was found at the entrance to a rabbit burrow, excavated by a rabbit! Another interesting find has been of a key handle at Leigh. There are also finds relating to the Roman military occupation.

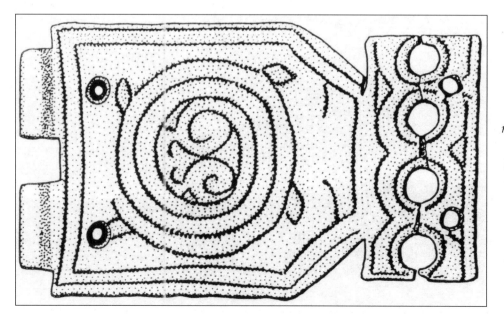

*First-century
AD Roman
military buckle,
66mm long,
found at Bank
Farm by Paul
Dunmall.*
DRAWING BY
ANDY ISHAM.

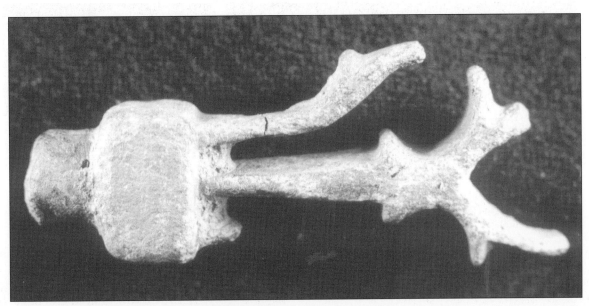

Roman bronze key handle, of uncertain date, found on Bank Farm, Leigh, by Paul Dunmall. The key itself was made of iron, and has rusted away.

Above, left: *A Nero Claudius Drusus silver denarius found by Paul Dunmall at Brockamin. These coins were minted by Nero's son between AD41 and AD54, in memory of his father, who died in 9BC. One of these was the weekly pay for a Roman soldier.*

Above, right: *Roman bracelet found at the entrance to a rabbit burrow in Leigh Sinton. A similar find in Colchester dates it from AD320–450. Made from Roman silver it is 65–70mm in diameter and 4mm wide.* (KEN DAVIES)

Left: *Roman military buckle from the first century AD, found at Bank Farm, Leigh, by Paul Dunmall.*

The period between the end of the Roman occupation, in AD409, and the Norman Conquest by William in 1066, is amazingly poor in archaeological remains – nothing has been found in the parish. This was a period of great turmoil nationally, so it is perhaps not surprising that there are few written records relating to the parish. In his famous (though somewhat colourful) *History of Worcestershire*, Revd Treadway Russell Nash, who was the rector of Leigh from 1792 to 1811, describes the misery and chaos during this period:

After the Romans left this island the inhabitants being much oppressed by the Picts and Scots called in the Saxons to their assistance, who, about the year 443 or 450 AD began to settle here. They afterwards divided the island into seven kingdoms... The last kingdom they established [which included Worcestershire] was that of Mercia.

Then, speaking of a period 500 years or so later, he paints a similar picture:

About the year 990, and for many years after, the Danes by their invasion and plunderings much oppressed the island... The English did not submit easily, and Worcestershire was frequently the scene of sharp and bloody actions!

'The Dark Ages' between the Roman occupation and the coming of the Normans were a time of brutality, and records are non-existent. The most likely source of any parish records during this period, Pershore Abbey, was burnt down several times, notably in 1000, 1223 and 1287. Treadway Nash notes that: 'In one of these fires the register containing an account of the estates, and all the customs and privileges of the abbey was destroyed.'

Even the little which does survive about the parishes is sometimes ambiguous. For example, speaking about Bransford Manor, one account says that it belonged to the Abbey of Pershore at the time of Edward the Confessor (AD1042–66), whilst another claims that it was given to the Abbey at Evesham in AD716.

The Domesday Book

The earliest detailed historical facts about the parish came with the production of the Domesday Book, in 1086. This is an amazing record in many ways. It is an inventory of the spoils of war, a record of the King's tax base and a record of the changes of land ownership. As one writer put it:

Nothing else gives us so vivid or so real a picture of the effects of the Conquest: nothing shows so clearly the way England had to submit to the yoke of the Conqueror.

Equally amazing was the very thorough way the information was compiled. Commissioners were appointed for each county. For Worcestershire they were the Bishop of Lincoln, the Earl of Buckingham, the Lord of Tutbury and Adam Fitz Hubert, the brother of one of King William's stewards. The Bishop of Worcester and the Prior of Pershore Abbey both sent representatives. The Commissioners called over 50 witnesses, who are all named, and included William Beauchamp, William of Leigh, Rand Priest of Leigh, and Maurice his son. These gave evidence relating to land ownership, occupancy and human and material resources.

Three groups of people owned land in that time – the King, the Church and a handful of laymen. In Worcestershire, a large proportion of land was owned by the Church, the three Benedictine houses at Evesham, Pershore and Worcester owning 70,000 acres, of which Pershore had about 10,000.

So what does the Domesday Book say about Leigh and Bransford? A translation of the Latin entry is as follows:

The Church itself held at LEIGH 3 hides which pay tax. Of these, the Abbot [of Pershore] has 1 hide in lordship. He has 2 ploughs; 12 villagers and 32 smallholders with 29 ploughs. 2 slaves. 2 mills at 10s.9d.; meadow, 30 acres; woodland 3 leagues long and 2 leagues wide.
Value before 1066 £20; now £16.

Of the said land two riders held 1¹/₂ hides. Now Urso the Sheriff holds them. He has 2 ploughs; 2 villagers, 11 smallholders and 1 Frenchman; between them they have 4 ploughs, 2 slaves.
A mill at 4s.
Value 50s.

Urso also holds a third hide of this land at BRANSFORD.
He has 1 plough in lordship; 9 smallholders with 4 ploughs.
A mill at 20s.
Value £4.
Of this hide the County states that it was the Church of Pershore's before 1066; however, the Abbot of Evesham held it on the day of King Edward's death, but they do not know how.

Although this sounds very precise, trying to unravel it is very difficult, not least because the measures used varied around the country, and the exact significance of some terms has been lost. However, let us try to shed a little light on our own entry. A 'hide' was about a 120 acres of land, a 'league' was possibly three miles, and a 'plough' was a measure of the amount of land under cultivation – although how much is not certain. Its significance is that the total area farmed was either ploughed (i.e. cultivated), pasture (for grazing) or meadow (for hay).

View of the tithe barn before restoration. Sketch by Charles Grant from his book Village Sketches, *Orphans Press, Leominster, 1990.* (REPRODUCED BY PERMISSION OF DAVID GRANT.)

Above: *The Leigh Court tithe barn shrouded in plastic during its restoration, 1987–88.*
(MIKE GRUNDY/BERROWS)

Right: *View of the tithe barn taken from the top of the tower of St Edburga's Church in 1995.* (MALCOLM SCOTT)

A hide 'held in lordship' meant that this was land for the named person's use (his 'demesne', or domain). 'Villagers' were people who worked for the land-owner, whereas 'smallholders' had their own plot of land and could graze their animals on common land. The significance of a 'mill' is that the smallholders and villagers had to pay to have their corn ground, so a mill was a source of income. The area of 'meadow' was important, because it was used to make hay for winter feed. If there was not enough, then the animals died. Indeed, it was customary to kill some animals before winter set in, so that there was enough hay to over-winter the breeding animals. These were hard times! Finally, the area of woodland was important, simply because it provided both fuel and building materials.

Although the size of the parishes has changed over the centuries, at the time of the Domesday Book it was probably more than 7,000 acres. The broad-brush picture of Leigh Parish is therefore of a heavily wooded area with 300 to 400 acres of farmed land principally owned by Pershore Abbey, over 100 acres being worked for the Abbot himself. Urso the Sherriff (Urso of Abetot, the Sherriff of Worcestershire and the King's representative) held a further 200 acres. Urso also had over 100 acres of farmed land in Bransford, some of which was farmed for him. A total of 71 people are listed in the two parishes. They would all be households, so the total population could have been 300 to 400.

Urso of Abetot was one of the people who replaced the pre-Conquest tenants when the Normans confiscated their land. He was infamous for acquiring over 2,000 acres in Worcestershire,

Interior of the tithe barn, 2000. Built in the 1300s to house the tithes for the monks of Pershore Abbey, it is considered to be England's largest and most significant cruck structure, measuring 150 feet by 34 feet (45.7m by 10.4m). (MALCOLM SCOTT)

much of it by simple seizure, either from the Church or from the tenants. Whether he got the land in Leigh 'legally' is not recorded, but it is believed that it was at Braces Leigh. Certainly the manor at Braces Leigh passed down through his descendants, the Beauchamps through his daughter, Emiline.

The links between Leigh and Pershore Abbey were strong ones. The abbots are believed to have stayed in Leigh from time to time, and in 1289 one of them (Henry de Caldwell) died there. The lasting memorial to this connection is, of course, the tithe barn at Leigh Court, a Grade I listed building and an awe-inspiring architectural gem. Built in the 1300s, it is England's largest and most significant cruck structure, measuring 150 feet by 34 feet (45.7m by 10.4m). Made up of nine enormous full-cruck roof trusses, with two large entrance bays, it was in use until the 1980s. By then, 700 years had taken their toll, and it needed complete renovation. However, the cost of undertaking this was enormous, and the owners of Leigh Court, Barclay and Sally Stewart, negotiated for several years for a grant to meet the cost of the restoration. It was eventually funded by English Heritage, who are now guardians.

The restoration cost about £500,000 and took two years. The barn was opened to the public by the chairman of English Heritage, Lord Montagu of Beaulieu, and the Duke of Gloucester in June 1990. Although infrequently used for functions, its size and magnificence make it a superb setting for occasional church and village events. It can be visited from 1 April until 30 September between 10.00a.m. and 6.00p.m. from Thursday to Sunday.

After the Domesday Book

The coming of the Normans brought relative stability and a definable administrative structure to society. It also started a period of intense building activity nationally, both of castles – to defend their new conquests – and of churches. Old Anglo-Saxon buildings, mainly of wood, were demolished to make way for new, stone ones. For example, the building of the present Leigh church started during the 1100s, as did that of the churches in the surrounding parishes of Cradley and Mathon. The Dark Ages were over!

Nevertheless, although there are records of what happened both nationally and locally, the miseries brought about by wars were not over. The Normans had conquered the English but not the Welsh. William the Conqueror therefore set about creating Herefordshire as a military buffer zone, a semi-independent region ruled by his own nobles. However, the influence of the Herefordshire lords did not ensure peace. Shortly after the Norman Conquest the country slipped back into a period of brutal civil wars. Extracts from the contemporary chronicle of Henry, Archdeacon of Huntingdon (c.1080–1160), gives us a picture of how life in Leigh must have seemed to its inhabitants at the time:

At this period [during the reign of King Stephen, 1135 to 1154] *England was in a very disturbed state; on the one hand, the king and those who took his part grievously oppressed the people, on the other frequent turmoils were raised by the Earl of Gloucester, and, what with the tyranny of the one, and the turbulence of the other, there was universal turmoil and desolation. Some, for whom their country had lost its charms, chose rather to make their abode in foreign lands; others drew to the churches for protection, and constructing mean hovels in their precincts, passed their days in fear and trouble.*

Food being scarce, for there was a dreadful famine throughout England, some of the people disgustingly devoured the flesh of dogs and horses; others appeased their insatiable hunger with the garbage of uncooked herbs and roots; many, in all parts, sunk under the severity of the famine and died in heaps; others with their whole families went sorrowfully into voluntary banishment and disappeared...

The 'motte and bailey' fortifications which can still be seen at Castle Green Farm (called 'Castle Leigh' in old documents) probably dates from this period. A 'motte' is a circular mound on which a lookout or a defensible tower was situated, and a 'bailey' is the fortified enclosure next to it, where the inhabitants could shelter. The base of the Castle Leigh motte is approximately 30 metres in diameter, dropping to 22 metres at the top. It is roughly 6 metres high and surrounded by a substantial moat. Located to the south of the motte there is also a round bailey platform, only three metres high but some 40 metres across.

Leigh Castle was less substantial than other structures of the same period. It was probably not built by royal licence, but to protect its occupier from warring lords. The castle's broad moat was fed from the nearby stream, and its position allowed it to dominate the surrounding arable land.

In 1200, Stephen Devereux (Stephen d'Evereux) obtained a licence from the Abbot of Pershore Abbey to have a private chapel at Leigh Castle, to be served on three days a week by the 'chaplain of the mother church', at Leigh. By the second half of the thirteenth century, Leigh Castle was in the hands of the powerful Pembridge family, who originated from Herefordshire. Henry de Pembridge, 'son of Henry de Cleyhongre', is described in the *Victoria County History of Worcestershire* as 'engaged in lawless acts during the Barons' War', but noted as having died before 1279. In the words of the *Victoria History*:

Henry lost his lands by his depredations after the peace concluded at Winchester in 1265, when his

Plan of the motte and bailey castle at Castle Green Farm.

N

Motte

Bailey

40 metres

Artist's impression of Leigh Castle.
(ANDREW KNEEN, REPRODUCED WITH PERMISSION)

Above: *Engraved medieval gold ring with a sapphire stone, found by Paul Dunmall in Leigh.* (MALCOLM SCOTT)

lands in Leigh were given to Matthew de Gamages. His son Henry in 1272 claimed the restoration of his lands by virtue of the dictum of Kenilworth, and recovered Leigh from the Gamages. Henry died before 1279, and was succeeded by his son Fulk, who was alive in 1282. There is no further mention of this family in connection with Leigh until 1344–5, when the manor of Castle Leigh was granted by Thomas de Compton and John de Middelham to Peter de Montfort for life, with remainder to Alice wife of Richard de Noners for her life, and remainder on her death to Robert de Pembridge and his heirs. In 1384–5 peaceable possession of the manor of Castle Leigh was secured by the Abbot and convent of Pershore by Robert Forstall of Leigh, Isabella his wife and Richard their son. It was subordinate to the abbey's manor of Leigh till the Dissolution.

For much of his life Sir Richard Pembridge was away from this area on military service, taking part in Edward III's naval victory at Sluys (24 June 1340), and at the battles of Crecy (26 August 1346) and Poitiers (19 September 1356). It is very likely that men from the vicinity of Leigh were present with him at each of these conflicts.

Although not the principal dwelling of the Pembridge family, Leigh Castle provided a good place from which to manage their manors on the borders of Hereford and Worcestershire. They retained Leigh Castle almost continuously until 1384–5, after which it was held by tenants of Pershore Abbey – initially the Forstall family – until the Dissolution of the Monasteries, during the reign of Henry VIII.

Memorial to William Coles in St Edburga's, Leigh. (MALCOLM SCOTT)

Soon after the Dissolution, the manor of Leigh was divided and, in 1553, William Colles, who had been its bailiff, leased the house and the land around St Edburga's Church for 67 years. However, the original house was almost certainly to the east of St Edburga's, and not where Leigh Court is now. This older site may also have been where an even earlier monastery was situated. As we shall see, the original house was burnt down during the civil wars, some of its remains being unearthed in the 1860s and '70s, during the excavations for the Worcester to Leominster railway. According to 'Stroller', who wrote in the *Worcester Herald* in the 1920s, the finds suggested that the house was so totally destroyed as to be irreparable. This would explain why the present Leigh Court was built on a different site.

William Colles then passed the lease to his son, Edmund. Edmund enlarged the estate, buying a third of the Leigh Sinton Manor estate in 1575, and the rest of it later. There are still traces of a moated grange at Moat House Farm. Built much later than Leigh Castle, it was probably more typical of the moated half-timbered manor houses built in the fifteenth and sixteenth centuries. The family also bought Leigh Castle and its lands from the Earl of Leicester in 1605.

Edmund Colles died in 1606, aged 76, and his memorial is in Leigh church. It shows this extraordinary man, who had extensive property in Worcestershire, in civilian attire. He was a Catholic who paid the assessed fine as a recusant, somebody who refused to change from the Catholic Church to the Church of England. He was very active in the county, being a Deputy Lieutenant, a Justice, a Sheriff, and an MP, as well as being a Member of the Council of the Marches of Wales. It is therefore clear that during the Elizabethan era, at least in this part of Worcestershire, politically compliant Catholics were allowed considerable freedom.

Well before he died, Edmund passed control of the whole enlarged estate to his son William in 1583, when the latter married Mary Palmer. When she died, in 1602, he erected the splendid memorial which is in St Edburga's, his name being added when he died in 1615. Sadly, however, under William and his son Edmund the family got very seriously into debt, and the debt and the interest on it were so crippling that the whole estate had to be sold. As one commentator put it:

Leigh being so surcharged with debt, which (like a snowball rolling down from the Malvern Hills gathers greatness) increased with huge usery, as for the discharge thereof Leigh was sold.

This dramatic change in the fortunes of the Colles family is associated with a ghost story. It has been widely, and variously, retold, the version below being reproduced with permission from *Curiosities of Worcestershire: a County Guide to the Unusual* by Ann Moore:

The manor of Leigh was granted by Elizabeth I to Edmund Colles whose handsome memorial lies in the church opposite. There is, however, a ghost story, well-known locally, concerning his grandson, also Edmund.

One Christmas Eve after his father's death, Edmund was drinking with John Leitchcroft, his friend from schooldays and now Godfather to his children, when he confessed that being bankrupt, he feared he must sell Leigh Court. John, anxious to help, rode off to Worcester to collect some of his own money.

But Edmund could not face accepting his friend's charity. Drunk now, he hid in the churchyard waiting for John's return. As Leitchcroft passed, Colles sprang out, and clutching the horse's bridle, demanded the money which hung at his friend's waist. Leitchcroft drew his sword, slashing out at his attacker, and then rode on home. Arriving in the light at the stable, he was sickened to find that a hand, severed at the wrist, still clung to the horse's bridle, but worse, one finger wore a ring which he recognised as belonging to Edmund.

Next morning Leitchcroft went to visit his friend, by now huddled in his room nursing the injured arm which he refused to let anyone tend. When they were alone John told Edmund that he knew the truth and forgave the by now abject and frightened man. The next day Edmund disappeared and was never seen alive again. Only his ghost continued to haunt Leigh at Christmas time. It is said that, driving a coach drawn by four charging horses, he careers frantically through the lanes, to take flight finally over the Tithe barn and disappear beneath the nearby waters of the River Teme.

Twelve years after Colles' death exorcism was tried in an attempt to release his troubled spirit. Twelve parsons gathered at a midnight service with an inch of candle, conjuring the ghost to rest. As the wick guttered, the lighted candle was thrown, with the ghost, into a local pond which, it is said, was then filled in.

In 1617 the manor and its rights were bought by Sir Walter Devereux who, in 1646, inherited the title of Viscount Hereford. It was, of course, during this period that the Civil War was fought, and both parishes were heavily involved. We will, however, look at this period separately, in Chapter Two.

When Sir Walter Devereux died in 1649, his younger son, Leicester, inherited the manor. On Leicester's death, in 1676, the inheritance then passed in succession through his unmarried sons, Leicester and Edward (who both died young) to their married sister Anne Martin. Her daughter and only child, Elizabeth, married a cousin, Price Devereux, who became the Ninth Viscount Hereford in 1740. Although this brought back the name of Devereux to Leigh, it was only for a short time. Elizabeth died in 1740, and the estate was sold in 1742 to James Cocks.

The Cocks family owned Leigh Court until 1898, when Lady Henry Somerset from Eastnor (Isabelle Caroline Somers Cocks) sold it to William Henry Gabb. Inasmuch as the title of Baron Somers had been awarded to Charles Cocks in 1784, with his son being made an Earl, the end of the Cocks' family ownership was also the end of a titled connection with Leigh. It could be said that this heralded the changes which were to come in the parish in the twentieth century, since William Henry Gabb was described by 'Stroller' as 'a successful hop grower and a representative of a local yeoman family of old standing.'

However, like most of the earlier owners, William Henry Gabb did not live at Leigh Court. He continued to live at Beauchamp Court, moving to Hopton Court towards the end of his life. His son, William Hubert Gabb, lived there until he died suddenly in 1932. After that it was tenanted until his daughter, Sally Stewart, inherited it in 1960. In 1995 Sally and Barclay Stewart sold Leigh Court itself but retained the land, which is farmed from Church Cottage by their son Duncan.

Leigh Manor was, of course, adjacent to the site of St Edburga's Church, and the owners held the living for the rector. St Edburga's is the only church in the two parishes, since Bransford Chapel was always attached to it. Leigh is also the site of the tithe barn, and the parish of Leigh has always been larger than Bransford.

Perhaps for these reasons, Leigh has assumed more

The Gabb family outside Beauchamp Court, where Sally Stewart's grandparents lived before retiring to Hopton Court. Left to right, back row: Henry Cole Gabb (was at Bank Farm, Leigh), George Raymond Gabb, Jessica (Jessie) Gabb, née Hughes (from Pigeon House Farm, Leigh), Mrs Holmes, William Henry Gabb (Sally Stewart's grandfather), Mr Holmes (the tenant at Leigh Court), William Hubert Gabb (Sally Stewart's father); front row: Olive Mary Gabb (Henry Cole Gabb's wife), Henry Roland Gabb (next to his mother), Monica Holmes, Rachel Holmes, Monica Jessie Gabb. (SALLY STEWART)

importance than Bransford in historical records, and this is possibly why the history of the land in Bransford is not very well documented. We have seen that, at the time of the Domesday Book, Urso the Sherriff held one and a half hides (about 180 acres) around what is believed to be Braces Leigh, and a further hide in Bransford at an unknown location. According to the *Victoria History*, the hide of land in Bransford was augmented by William Beauchamp, Urso's decendant, and stayed with the Beauchamp family until the fourteenth century. Leaping to 1608, the manor of Bransford was granted to William Worfield, and it meandered through that family until into the 1700s. After that the ownership of both the manorial rights and the land in Bransford became increasingly fractured.

Although it was important at the time of the Domesday, the house and lands at Braces Leigh are similar to those in Bransford in lacking a coherent ownership history. Braces Leigh passed from Urso the Sherriff through his descendants the Beauchamps, and they retained overall rights until into the 1630s. The Bracy family were there from the mid 1200s, and it is first mentioned as a separate manor in 1316, during the time of Robert de Bracy, being linked to the manor at Madresfield. In 1620 it was sold, and then passed through a succession of owners, one of whom (Charles Grenville) lost it because of his refusal to convert from Catholicism to the Church of England, which was a statutory offence from about 1570 until 1791.

In the early 1800s Braces Leigh was bought by Lady Beauchamp, and stayed in that family until around 1911. In the 1970s the farm was bought by the Guinness Company, who farmed it for hops. They demolished the original (very old and beautiful) house and built a new one. Gerald Jones (b.1917) remembers the old house well, and called it a 'scandal' that it somehow escaped being a listed building.

Growth in the Parish

Because the parish is predominantly rural, growth was slow up until after the Second World War. There were no great building booms, as there were in larger towns and cities accompanying industrial development. The parish did not have groups of houses (the word 'estate' gives the wrong impression) until after the First World War, although a terrace of six houses was built in Leigh Sinton in the late 1800s. In the 1920s, small groups of houses were built both by the council and privately, mainly for agricultural workers. They were at Dragons Cross and further down into Leigh Sinton, at Suffield and at Post Office Lane (on the A4103), along the Suckley Road (Ednoll Cottages), and at Winsgrave, on the Alfrick Road. As an aside, the Winsgrave, Post Office Lane and Suckley Road houses give an insight into life in those days, since they were built with pigsties adjacent to the outside toilets.

Since the Second World War, however, looking at small groups of houses rather than in-filling, development in the three villages has been very different. In the case of Bransford, a further dozen houses were built beside Ednoll Cottages, and a similar number at Suffield, where three blocks of four flats were also added later. The installation of a sewage system in Bransford, in 1971, meant that Martley Rural District Council could consider development on the three-acre site which it had owned on the Suckley Road since 1954. Schemes were invited which would provide a mixture of sheltered housing, housing for sale at normal prices and some for sale at a subsidised price.

Wimpey won the contract, and Orchard Way was built, with 34 houses for sale (12 at a subsidised price) and the Bensfield sheltered housing complex. The latter had 24 one-person bedsitting flatlets, six two-person one-bedroomed flats, warden accommodation and a range of communal facilities – a common room, laundry room, drying room and two guest rooms. This was opened in July 1973 by the Lord Lieutenant of Worcester, Viscount Cobham.

Although extremely well received at the time, Bensfield slowly ceased to be attractive to older people, and the Elgar Housing Association, who took over its management from the Malvern Hills District

Right: *Somers Terrace, Leigh Sinton, in the early 1920s. Left to right: Granny Rowley with Albert ('Ben') Rowley, Elsie Davies, Mrs Powell, Mrs Annie Haggitt, Granny Davis, Mrs Dutson.* (BEN ROWLEY)

Left: *Cover of the brochure marking the opening of Bensfield on 21 July 1973.* (CHRIS ALMGILL)

Below: *Aerial photograph of Leigh, taken around 1983, from St Edburga's Church to just above Bank Farm.* (CLARE HAMPSON)

Leigh Sinton, taken from a helicopter, 12 March 2002. (Simon Croall)

Council, wanted to redevelop the site. In order to influence this, in 1999 the Parish Council undertook a housing-needs survey, which showed that there was a local demand for low-cost housing, as well as for rented accommodation. (Incidentally, it also showed that there were a dozen or so houses without running hot water, and similar numbers with only outside toilets and/or with no bath or shower.)

Following this survey, two members of the Parish Council sat on a development steering group, along with the representatives of the Elgar Housing Association and the Malvern Hills District Council. The final outcome was that ten houses were built and were occupied in 2002, of which six are rented and four have shared ownership. (The shared-ownership scheme allows young people to get a foot on the housing ladder, by purchasing half the house and paying rent for the rest.)

Housing changes in Leigh have been totally different from either Bransford or Leigh Sinton. There have been some new houses built on the sites of old cottages, and a few built on new sites. But the numbers are small. On the other hand, 27 dwellings have resulted from barn conversions, the most recent being at Leigh Court. The only other areas of the parish with large numbers of barn conversions are Sandlin, with 11, and the Norbury farms, with just under 20.

It is Leigh Sinton which has borne the brunt of the development in the parish. After the Second World War, Somers Close was the first small estate to be built by the council. Then followed a private development, Lynn Close, with three dozen or so houses and bungalows. Hooper's Close and Hop Pole Green added over 30 more. Then came Nash Green and Kiln Way, with about 60, and smaller developments at Corbetts and behind the Old Chapel – a total of about 180 houses in estates of varying sizes. On the most recent site to be developed, the former garage, there are nine starter homes, three with a Section 106 agreement on them (restricting their use to parishioners). Given the scale of this development it is not surprising that there is a very strong feeling indeed that there has been enough!

Chapter Two

LEIGH IN THE WARS

Aerial view of St Edburga's Church, Leigh Court, Leigh Court barns and Church Farm, May 2000. (MALCOLM SCOTT)

We have seen that the parish was, like the rest of the country, affected by wars and upheavals for centuries. There are, however, three wars whose effects have probably been the most dramatic. The first is the Civil War. Not only did the Royalist and Commonwealth armies fight in and around the parish, but the proportion of the population killed nationally was greater than in either of the two World Wars.

The second was the First World War, when the carnage affected most households, either directly or indirectly. Finally, there was the Second World War. Even though there were far fewer deaths amongst parishioners, it affected life locally, and its aftermath brought about a period of rapid social change.

The Civil War, 1642–51

The Civil War has left a legacy of half-truth and legend in the parish. Leigh was important because it lay at the confluence of Leigh Brook and the River Teme, and because there was a ferry across the Teme, whilst Bransford had a bridge.

For centuries these two river crossings gave access to Worcester from the south-west. Because much of the Royalist support was in Wales, control of this route was therefore of vital importance to them. Furthermore, St Edburga's Church, Leigh Court and the adjacent tithe barn formed a defensible strong-point. If necessary, the ferry across the Teme at Leigh Court would have allowed a tactical withdrawal to Cotheridge Court, where Sir Rowland Berkeley was a notable and active Royalist. This defensibility, combined with the vantage point of the church tower, made the Leigh Court complex very attractive to forces holding the city.

However, whilst most of the local landed gentry were Royalist, Sir Walter Devereux at Leigh Court was a Parliamentarian. We will see that the close proximity of two important landowners who were on opposite sides in the Civil War had cruel consequences for both families.

To understand the impact of the Civil War locally it is essential to know something of the intrigue that surrounded the ownership of the manor of Leigh. In 1617 it was bought by Sir Walter Devereux, a cousin of Robert Devereux, the Third Earl of Essex (whose father was beheaded by Elizabeth I when he was ten). Sir Walter Devereux then became the MP for

21

Worcester in 1625, and was Sheriff of the county during 1625–6.

However, just as the Civil War started, the Devereux family's life in Leigh was shattered by the untimely death of Walter's eldest son, Essex Devereux, who was drowned, along with his friend George Freke, whilst crossing the River Teme on 20 February 1639. His memorial is in Leigh church. As a result, Walter's second son, Leicester, became his heir.

In the Bishops' War of 1639 and 1640, which preceded the Civil War, Charles I tried to impose Anglican reforms upon the Scottish churches. The issue of funding military operations against the Scots gave rise to tensions between Charles and his Parliament, which was reluctant to grant funds without a debate. After an abortive attempt to coerce Parliament, by attempting to arrest members, Charles left London and raised his standard at Nottingham in August 1642.

At this stage many of Worcester's people were against the Royalist cause. The city's merchants were reluctant to allow Royalist recruiting in the city, and in early September the citizens petitioned the Mayor, Edward Solley, complaining that:

Cavaliers and soldiers in divers parts of the kingdom (where they come) have plundered the towns, bloodily killing the king's peaceable subjects, rifling their houses, and violently taking away of their goods and in some places deflowered women.

To oppose Charles, Walter Devereux's cousin, Robert Devereux, the Third Earl of Essex, was made the Lord General of the Parliamentary army in 1642, although ill health and a less than distinguished military record forced him to relinquish command in 1645. In view of Walter Devereux's close family ties to the leader of the Parliamentary forces he was, quite naturally, a Parliamentary sympathiser. This fact soon attracted the attentions of the Worcester Royalists after the opening skirmishes of the Civil War at Powick on 23 September 1642, not least because the following day Robert Devereux took Worcester for the Parliamentary side, and occupied the city until November.

Thus began a period, lasting almost a decade, during which the armies of both sides harassed and plundered the local communities. Indeed, communities became so desperate that they formed armed, but neutral, groups to try to limit the damage done to them – the 'Clubmen Movements'. As we shall see, however, their success was very limited.

The Royalists reoccupied Worcester in November 1642, and subsequently resisted a Parliamentary siege in the early summer of 1643. Realising that the Parliamentary armies were a force to be reckoned with, the Worcester Royalists later raided Leigh Court:

In February [1645], local men ('Clubmen') twice surprised troops of Royalists ransacking Leigh Court.

Each time the looters were brought before the Governor of Worcester, but it was the captors who were rebuked – for interfering with the King's troops in the execution of their duty.

Even though they were surprised by local Clubmen, the damage to Leigh Court was very severe. Sir Walter Devereux's house at Cowleigh was also burnt, the total damage to both houses being some £20,000 – a small fortune! Later in 1645, Leigh Court was garrisoned by Royalist troops, and became part of the ring of outer defences around Worcester. The Royalist supporters sent to Leigh would have crossed the Teme from Sir Rowland Berkeley's manor at Cotheridge, and some were probably his retainers.

During 1645, the Scots army, which at this time was fighting for the Parliamentary cause, passed through Worcestershire in an orgy of looting and church desecrations. The Clubmen were again determined to practise armed neutrality, and formed a mutual league for each other's defence in the face of what one local leader, Charles Nott of Shelsley, described as the:

... utter ruin [caused] by the outrages and violence of the soldier; threatening to fire our houses; endeavouring to ravish our wives and daughters, and menacing our persons.

However, the presence of heavily-armed Royalists in Leigh Court meant that hopes of reducing this suffering were in vain.

The year of 1646 had begun with Parliamentary forces laying siege to the outlying Royalist defences of Worcester, the two most important of which were at Leigh Court and Madresfield House. Facing Leigh, huge numbers of Parliamentary troops from Gloucester, Hereford and Evesham were billeted in the area to the west of the village, around Alfrick and Lulsley. These villages suffered immensely from the plundering undertaken by these soldiers. By this time, however, Charles was isolated and had insufficient loyal forces, so he had fled north.

On 10 June, Charles, who had been taken prisoner by the Scots and held in Newcastle, issued an order to those Royalist garrisons still holding out that they should 'quit those towns, castles and forts entrusted to you by us, and to disband all the forces under your several commands.' The terms of this surrender did not reach Worcester until 25 June 1646. Four weeks later, on 19 July, Worcester's Mayor and Corporation accepted the Parliamentary forces' terms. The Worcester garrison was disbanded and promised never to take up arms against Parliament again. All arms and ammunition were surrendered and, in return, there was no plundering of the city by the Parliamentarians.

The Earl of Essex, who had been Lord General of the Parliamentary army, died on 14 September 1646.

With him the family Earldom of the Devereux expired, but the Viscounty of Hereford passed to Sir Walter Devereux, who spent the remainder of his life at Westminster. He never returned to Leigh. On his memorial in Leigh church, Sir Walter Devereux is shown, beside his wife, as a recumbent knightly figure armed with sword and dressed in armour. This beautifully detailed effigy reflects the affluence and position of the Devereux family in national life. However, in historical terms, the armour depicted on the memorial is outdated, and not appropriate to the period.

The surrender of Worcester in July 1646 ended the first phase of the English Civil War, but there was more to come. Even in defeat Charles continued to negotiate, promising the Scots Church reform in return for their support. As a result, in 1648 the Scots marched south, marking the start of the second English Civil War. This ended swiftly with the defeat of the Scots army at Preston in August of that year. The Parliamentary standing army then took events into their own hands, purging Parliament of Royalist MPs and trying Charles I for treason. He was beheaded on 30 January 1649, and a perilous peace followed after Oliver Cromwell led the army in putting down revolts in Ireland and Scotland.

Two years later, in January 1651, Charles II was crowned King of Scotland and then laid claim to the English throne. He marched with a new Scots army on England and, although beaten by Cromwell at Dunbar, continued south towards Worcester. By the time they reached Worcester many of the Scots were ill, and morale was at a low ebb, the men having realised that they were resented as 'foreigners'. Nevertheless, when Charles arrived at Worcester, on 23 August, his forces began to expand and strengthen the city's fortifications. Royalist troops were sent out on Monday 25 August to destroy the bridges across the Severn at Bewdley and Upton, as well as those across the Teme, the object being to create an island of defence against the anticipated arrival of Cromwell's forces.

The route to Wales across the bridge at Bransford was initially left intact and under the control of Scots, as a possible escape route for the Royalists. This was a mistake. Whilst the defences were being strengthened, Charles attempted to muster Royalist support in the city. One of the small groups that answered his call to arms was Sir Rowland Berkeley of Cotheridge. But the truth that Charles now had to face was that he was dependent upon a much-resented foreign army – his forces had very few Englishmen. Within days, Cromwell

The memorial to Walter Devereux in St Edburga's, Leigh.
(MALCOLM SCOTT)

gradually reduced the ability of the Scottish troops in Leigh and Bransford to manoeuvre, or to receive reinforcements. A column of Cromwell's New Model Army horse and militia was sent westward to Bransford Bridge, in order to prevent the Royalist forces escaping. Although this move was not seen by the Scots as a prelude to all-out combat, they nevertheless partially destroyed the bridge at Bransford on the evening of Monday 1 September. Unfortunately for them, the damage to the bridge did not stop Cromwell's dragoons from crossing, which they did on 3 September. These cavalry regiments were then able to prevent Royalist forces from fleeing westwards, and the beaten Scots were driven back towards Worcester.

Within Leigh itself the fighting left evidence that turned up much later, both in fable and in a series of grisly discoveries in the 1870s. A local farmer, Mr George Bearcroft Essex, is quoted in a nineteenth-century tract saying that, 'a fight took place in Dead Loons [a field at Sherridge], and the blood was so plentiful that it ran down the furrows.'

Jabez Allies records that a number of human bones as well as canon balls were found around Dead Loons, suggesting that there may be some truth in the idea that Dead Loons is a reference to the burial of Scots. Further evidence of Civil War events was uncovered in the mid-nineteenth century, when new drains and paths were being constructed in the gardens of Leigh Court. Workmen came across:

> ... several skeletons at a depth of about two feet below the surface. The corpses had evidently been hurriedly buried, for they were laid in various directions. When a family vault was being made... no less than 29 skulls were disinterred.

Some cannon balls and complete skeletons were also found on the same site.

A Civil War Postscript

The Civil War threw neighbour against neighbour, and father against son. There could be no winners. Sir Walter Devereux's Cotheridge neighbour, Sir Rowland Berkeley, later claimed that he had never attended the King's muster on Pitchcroft before the Battle of Worcester. Berkeley tried to explain his participation by claiming that he had been seized by cavalry acting on the King's orders, and that he then spent the rest of the day dodging the fighting. Parliament was not convinced by his excuses, and he received the third largest fine amongst the Worcestershire gentry, of £2,030, for his alleged part in the battle.

Ironically, in 1660, having succeeded his father Sir Walter as the Sixth Viscount Hereford, Leicester Devereux was one of the six peers chosen to invite the exiled Charles II to return to England – the Restoration of the English monarchy!

The First World War

Information about any local people who served during the Napoleonic campaigns, in the Crimea, or in South Africa during the Boer War, has proved impossible to find. The numbers involved nationally were small, and it is quite possible that nobody from the parish was involved. However, the twentieth century was a violent and cruel period in human history. Conscription ensured that those eligible could not escape involvement. Even without this, the volunteer armies which fought, for example, at the Somme in 1916, were recruited in an atmosphere of intense patriotism, and men were under very great pressure to enlist.

The war memorials in St Edburga's Church and in Leigh and Bransford Memorial Hall make tracing the effects of both wars easier. A total of 30 men from the parish were killed during the First World War. Casualty figures for this war showed that for every man killed at least three were wounded. So about 120 men from the parish were either killed or injured. Some of the wounded recovered from their wounds, or gassings, and were able to resume normal life after the war. Others were less fortunate and were permanently disabled. Geoff Bartlett (who lives in Leigh Sinton) and Janet Griffiths (who lived at Winsgrave) are two of the parishioners whose fathers were disabled and unable to follow their original occupations. It was, however, rare for members of either group to talk about what they had seen and suffered – 'Best not talked about', as William Weaver from Orchard Cottage, Leigh, used to say to his daughters. Their stoicism and resilience can only be admired.

The work of the Commonwealth War Graves Commission makes it easier to find more details about those who died. They have details about many of the men's origins and an outline of how they died, information which is now available on the internet.

Behind the names on the First World War memorials are the stories of those concerned. Unfortunately, some entries contain errors relating to either the theatre of war or the year of death. In correcting the record for the families concerned we also establish a poignant link between individuals and the reality of the war. We list here the actual entry on the church memorial (name, place and year of death) in bold, with any corrections or the additional information overleaf.

Above: *Suffield House, c. 1910. John Hall, Ernie Hall, Aunt Edith, John Hall's wife.* (MURIEL 'BIB' JONES)

Right: *Solid silver badge from the First World War, 33mm diameter, found by Paul Dunmall at Leigh Sinton.* DRAWING BY ANDY ISHAM.

Above: *Ernest J. Hall's grave in Contray Cemetery, France. Ernest was a lay reader for 'Woodbine Willie' (Revd Studdart Kennedy), a Forces chaplain who lived in Worcester, and who got his nickname for handing out Woodbines to the troops).* (MURIEL 'BIB' JONES)

Some of the Queen's Own Worcestershire Hussars (the Worcestershire Yeomanry) during the First World War. Thomas Jones is on the left of the saddle. (CONNIE TOHTZ)

Left: *Coloured lace on a postcard sent by William Jauncey to his mother during the First World War.* (GLENDA MERRELL)

Left: *Frederick Jauncey.* (GLENDA MERRELL)

Right: *Card sent by William Jauncey to his mother during the First World War.* (GLENDA MERRELL)

Below: *Inside of a First World War memorial card for William Jauncey.* (GLENDA MERRELL)

In health and strength he left his home,
Not thinking death so near,
Death came without a warning given,
And bade him meet his God in heaven.

His King and Country called him,
The call was not in vain;
On Britain's roll of honour
You will find our loved ones name.

We think of him in silence,
And his name we oft' recall;
Though there's nothing left to answer,
But his photo on the wall.

In Loving Memory
OF MY DEAR SON
Pte. William Jauncey,
(1st Worcestershire Regiment),
Who was killed in action in France
August 18th, 1917,
AGED 27 YEARS.

Ever remembered by his Parents, Brothers & Sisters.

James Andrew Amphlett – Pozieres, 1916.

James Amphlett was killed on the first day of the Battle of the Somme, 1 July 1916. He was serving with 1/8th Battalion of the Royal Warwickshire Regiment, not at Pozieres, but further north between Mailly Maillet and the village of Serre. He has no known grave and is commemorated on the Thiepval Memorial to the Missing.

James Bowen – France, 1918.

James Bowen was killed on 23 March 1918. This was the third day of the German spring offensive that year, an offensive that came close to turning the tide of war in Germany's favour. James was serving with the 1st Battalion of the Worcestershire Regiment. He was originally buried in the Croix-Molignaux German Military Cemetery, but his grave was subsequently lost. He is now commemorated on a special memorial at Ham British Cemetery.

William Bowers – St Quentin, 1918.

Frederick Walter Cross – France, 1918.

Alfred George Davies – France, 1918.

Sergeant Alfred Davies served with the 7th Battalion of the Worcestershire Regiment. He died on Monday 12 August 1918 and is buried at Bransford Chapel.

John Devereux – UK, 1915.

Arthur Fitzer – France, 1917.

Lance Corporal Arthur Fitzer served with the 1/8th Battalion of the Worcestershire Regiment. He died on Monday 27 August 1917 on the Passchendaele battlefield. He has no known grave and is commemorated upon the panels of the memorial at Tyne Cot Cemetery below Passchendaele village in Belgium.

George William Fitzer – France, 1917.

Sergeant George Fitzer also served with the 1/8th Battalion of the Worcestershire Regiment. We do not know if he was Arthur's father. Like Arthur, he has no known grave and is commemorated at Tyne Cot Cemetery.

Arthur Grubb – France, 1914.

Arthur was the son of Thomas and Mary Grubb of Sandlin. He was 29 years old when he died on Monday 21 September 1914 whilst serving with the 3rd Battalion of the Worcestershire Regiment. He has no known grave and is commemorated on the memorial at La Ferte-Sous-Jouarre.

Ernest John Hall – France, 1916.

Ernest was the son of John and Emma Hall from Worcester. He was serving with the 3rd Battalion of the Worcestershire Regiment during the 1916 Somme battles. He died, on Saturday 14 October 1916, at the Casualty Clearing Station at Contay along the road towards Amiens and is buried in the British Military Cemetery. He was aged 25.

George Haywood – La Bassee, 1918.

James Hughes – Contalmaison, 1916.

James Hughes was the son of Joseph and Alice Hughes of Holy Well in Leigh. He was serving with the 1st Battalion of the Worcestershire Regiment when he died, aged 26, on Monday 10 July 1916. His unit were fighting for the village of Contalmaison along the main German Second Positions across the Somme battlefield. He has no known grave and is commemorated on the Thiepval Memorial to the Missing.

Thomas Frank Hunt – Cambrai, 1918.

Archibald Alfred Hyde – Salonika, 1917.

Archibald was serving in Northern Greece when he died on Wednesday 9 May 1917. His unit was the 11th Battalion of the Worcestershire Regiment. He is buried at Doiran Military Cemetery near to the south-east shore of Lake Doiran.

William Jackson – India, 1915.

William Jauncey – Dardanelles, 1915.

William Jauncey died whilst serving with the 9th Battalion of the Worcestershire Regiment at Gallipoli.

His date of death was Friday 31 December 1915. He has no known grave and is commemorated on the Helles Memorial on the tip of the Gallipoli peninsula.

William Jauncey – France, 1917.

This William was the son of Henry and Elizabeth Jauncey of Lower Sandlin. William was serving with the 2/8th Battalion of the Worcestershire Regiment when he died on Thursday 16 August 1917, aged 25. His unit was fighting during the battles for Passchendaele and, like many others engaged there, has no known grave. He is commemorated on the Tyne Cot Memorial.

Frederick Thomas Jauncey – France, 1918.

Frederick was not with a Worcestershire unit but was serving, at the time of his death, with the 2/5th Battalion of the East Lancashire Regiment. He died on Friday 5 April 1918 and is buried in the military extension to the cemetery at St Sever, Rouen.

Edwin John Jones – Dardanelles, 1915.

Edwin was the son of Henry Jones from Clifton-upon-Teme and husband to Elizabeth. Whilst serving with the Queen's Own Worcestershire Hussars (the Worcestershire Yeomanry) he was wounded and evacuated from the fighting on the Gallipoli peninsula. Edwin died at Malta on Friday 3 September 1915, and is buried in Pieta Military Cemetery.

Ernest Reubin Kinnard – La Bassee, 1914.

Ernest was the son of Mrs Ellen Kinnard of Chirkenhill Cottage. Serving as a Lance Sergeant with the 1st Battalion of the Duke of Cornwall's Light Infantry, Ernest died on Wednesday 21 October 1914, aged 31. He has no known grave and is commemorated on the walls of Le Touret Memorial near to the Bethune-Armentieres road.

Frederick Joseph Lane – Armentieres, 1917.

Frederick was the son of Thomas and Emma Lane of the Norrest, Malvern, and had married a Welsh girl, May. Frederick was serving with the 14th Battalion of the Welsh Regiment when he died on Wednesday 5 December 1917. He is buried at the Cite Bonjean Military Cemetery in Armentieres.

Arthur Freeman Payne – Egypt, 1915.

Lance Corporal Arthur Freeman Payne, like Edwin Jones above, served with the Worcestershire Hussars. Arthur was the son of Edward Richard and Helen Bennie Freeman Payne, originally from The Rhea, Bromyard. Arthur was wounded at Gallipoli in 1915, whilst serving with the Egyptian Expeditionary Force. He died from his wounds on Sunday 23 April 1916, aged 22. He is commemorated on the Jerusalem Memorial at the north end of the Mount of Olives, outside the City of Jerusalem.

George Ernest Portman – France, 1916.

George was the son of Charles and Ellen Portman of Chapel Cottage, Leigh Sinton. He died, aged 23, on Wednesday 18 October 1916, whilst serving with the 4th Battalion of the Worcestershire Regiment and is buried at Bancourt British Military Cemetery, three miles east of Bapaume.

William Powell – France, 1914.

William had been married to Annie Jane Powell. The Commonwealth War Graves Commission records suggest that Annie Jane (now Haggitt) subsequently remarried and was living at 4 Somers Terrace, Leigh Sinton. William died on Saturday 31 October 1914, aged 27, and has no known grave. He is commemorated on the walls of the Menin Gate in Ypres, from where, with the exception of the period 1939–45, the notes of the Last Post have been sounded every evening since the memorial gate was completed in the early 1930s.

John Walter Prichard – France, 1918.

Lieutenant John Prichard was just 25 years of age when he died on Wednesday 18 September 1918. The son of John and Jane Prichard, he had lived at Brockamin House in Leigh before the war. John served with the 4th Battalion of the Royal Welsh Fusiliers and is buried in Ste Emilie Valley Cemetery, Villers-Faucon, near to where he was killed in the final few weeks of the war during the British Army's Advance to Victory.

Alfred Ernest Smith – France, 1918.

Sidney Stanley – Belgium, 1919.

George Edward Stevens – France, 1917.

George Stevens died during the Battle of Arras on 30 May 1917. He served with the 4th Battalion of the Worcestershire Regiment and has no known grave. He is commemorated on the walls of the Arras Memorial, which forms part of the Faubourg-d'Amiens Cemetery outside Arras. Adjacent to the memorial and cemetery is the Citadel, within whose walls the Gestapo executed many members of the French Resistance during the Second World War.

Luke George Terry – France, 1917.

Luke Terry was 18 years of age when he died on Saturday 17 March 1917. He was a member of the Coldstream Guards' 3rd Battalion and the son of Richard and Matilda Terry of Leigh. He is buried in the British Military Cemetery in a beautiful location on the banks of the River Somme at Sailly-Saillisel. Although a great many 18-year-olds were sent to France later in the war, during 1918, Luke Terry was under military service age throughout his all too brief time within the Armed Forces.

Ernest Ward – Dardanelles, 1915.

Ernest is the last named of the First World War's casualties on the memorial in Leigh church. He was the son of Thomas and Susan Ward, of Coles Green. He died on Friday 6 August 1915 during the fighting along the Gallipoli peninsula and has no known grave. He is therefore commemorated on the Helles Memorial, on the tip of the peninsula looking out across the warm waters of the Aegean Sea.

To this list we should add two more. Although not a parishioner, Frederick Wareham, the head of Leigh Sinton School for decades, also lost two of his sons.

The Second World War

In contrast to the 30 from the parish who were killed in the First World War, only five were killed in the Second World War. Again, the list follows, the church entry being in bold with additional details below.

Corporal Douglas Vincent Fullerton

Douglas was the son of Aubrey and Hazel Fullerton from Worcester. He served with the 4th Battalion of the Suffolk Regiment and died on Tuesday 27 July 1943, aged 25. He is buried in Thanbyuzayat War Cemetery. This is one of a number of cemeteries along the notorious Burma-Siam railroad which now form the last resting place of many thousands of men who died at the hands of Japanese guards and labour marshals, who treated British and American prisoners with cruelty and inhuman forms of punishment.

J. Gregory
G. Hill

Lionel Dennis Palmer

Son of William and Edith Palmer of Bransford Bridge, Lionel was an Able Seaman serving aboard the naval sloop, HMS *Lapwing*. His vessel was escorting an Arctic convoy to Russia (JW85) when it was torpedoed and sunk in the Kola inlet by a German submarine, *U968*, on 20 March 1945. With no known grave he is commemorated at the Plymouth Naval Memorial in Devon.

Stephen Powell

Stephen Powell served with the 1st Battalion of the Herefordshire Regiment, King's Shropshire Light Infantry. He died on Tuesday 15 August 1944, aged 18. Stephen is buried at Banneville-la-Campagne War Cemetery at Calvados between Caen and Pont l'Eveque in Normandy.

The memorial in Leigh church only records those members of the Armed Forces who died in the two World Wars, but the wooden plaques in the Memorial Hall list not only those who died but also those who served. In the case of the Second World War, the list of those who served includes 12 women.

Left: *Inspection of members of the Queen's Own Worcestershire Hussars (the Worcestershire Yeomanry) who served in the First World War by Queen Elizabeth II in 1957. She was accompanied by Lt Col R.A. Wiggin. Thomas Jones is third from the right, wearing a cap.* (CONNIE TOHTZ)

August 1938. Pat Bowers on leave from the Navy with his mother and Uncle Arthur near Rose Cottage, Bransford. (PAT BOWERS)

Above: *A wartime letter sent by Harry Banner to his wife Dorothy.*
(DOROTHY BANNER)

Cyril and Ray Dyson during the Second World War. Their father, Bill Dyson, ran the garage at Leigh Sinton, and the brothers each owned a garage, one at Leigh Sinton and the other at Bransford.
(CONNIE TOHTZ)

Right: *Wedding of Stan Jones and Muriel 'Bib' Hunt at St Edburga's, Leigh, June 1942. Lawrie and Maisie Jones are standing behind them.*
(MURIEL 'BIB' JONES)

Below: *Leigh, Leigh Sinton, Bransford Home Guard, 1940–44. The Worcestershire (Malvern) Battalion. Taken in the playground at Leigh Hurst School, 1944.* Left to right, back row: W. Davies, H. Bowker, T. Thomas, W. Phillips, J. Pritchard, C. Edwards, P. Bladen, E. Pritchard, W. Hardcastle, S. Passey, L. Alford, R. James, J. Weaver; third row: R. Jauncey, C. Vine, H. Phillips, W. Clarke, H. Brookes, A. Smith, W. James, T. Bosley, F. James, R. Holmes, L. Hill, S. Haggitt, R. Hunt, W. James, J. Phillips; second row: W. Costello, C. Ching, W. Smith, A. James, A. Hunt, J. Barnett, L. Recordon, H. White, E. Lewis, E. Jay, H. Emson, R. Weaver; front row: A. Rowley, O. Edwards, A. Evans, F. Phillips, W. Lewis, A. Ball, W. King, V. Banner, G. Alford, H. Hodges. (ERIC VINE)

The Home Guard

In the Second World War the possibility of being invaded was a very real one. As a consequence, and in order to increase the numbers of men with at least some Army training, the Home Guard was set up. Men who were too old for active service, or were exempt, could enrol in it. They were issued with Lee Enfield rifles, and went to West Malvern for firing practice, where some also learnt on a machine gun.

They had a range of duties. For example, at Great House Farm there was a platform on the roof, accessed by a trap door. In the early years of the war members used to stay there all night, to watch for enemy parachutists. As well as reporting any who did land they were supposed to try to apprehend them. The Home Guard also used to man roadside bunkers and checkpoints, both to monitor passing traffic and simply to keep an eye on what was going on. There were observation points at The Fox, by the school in Leigh Sinton, by Bank Farm and at Smith End Green. They also used to go to Malvern, to guard the railway tunnel.

One of their tasks was connected with guarding the 'decoy station' in the flat fields beside the Teme, at the end of Teme Lane, Brockamin. Mick Wilks – who is an expert on the Home Guard and a member of the Defence of Britain research project – says that these decoy stations were areas which were lighted so as to represent poorly blacked-out industrial complexes. The local lighting layout simulated a factory and marshalling yards in Worcester, the idea being to get the German bombers to waste their bombs on the open countryside. Eye witnesses say that the decoy lights could be seen from the A44 Worcester to Bromyard Road, on the other side of the Teme Valley, and that it looked as if there was an airfield there.

The decoy site had a command post halfway down Teme Lane, which is still there. Brick built, with a reinforced-concrete roof, its walls were banked up with earth to protect its occupants from bomb blast in the event that the decoy worked – which it never did! It was 30 feet long and had two rooms, one for the RAF personnel who ran it, the other housing an electricity generator. These RAF personnel would have been brought in at night. In addition to lights, the decoy site would probably have had baskets of wood and troughs of paraffin which could be ignited remotely, to simulate fires in the event that bombs were dropped. Incidentally, although this decoy site made Brockamin and Leigh a target for bombers, Nora Jay, who was living at Great House Farm, says that nobody was worried about this aspect at the time, in part because it was all so secret.

In some Home Guard units, a handful of selected members with very good local knowledge were formed into special units (GHQ Auxiliary Units, or GHQ Reserve) and received intensive training in guerrilla warfare. The intention was that, if the Germans invaded, these units would undertake a whole range of sabotage activities designed to harass them. Although the local Home Guard did not have one of these units, Alfrick's did, and Roy Dorrell (of Dorrell Brothers agricultural machinery at Bransford) was a member.

Wartime Experiences in the Parishes

Because the Air Force was in its infancy during the First World War, civilians were generally not at risk. As a result, the main outward evidence in the parishes that a war was going on was the fact that so many men were away from home, serving in the Forces, and women were taking a far greater range of jobs. As the war went on, however, prisoners of war were housed locally, in order to work on the farms. Some German soldiers were housed at Bull Ring Farm, Brockamin, in a building which they built themselves, their officers being billeted in the farm itself. The records show that at least one soldier died whilst he was there.

Joseph Hughes, who was born in 1906 and lived at Holywell Cottages, at the l, remembers all these events:

I was eight when the First World War broke out and I lost a brother in France. Many men from the village went off to join the Army, and the women did all the work on the land. Women also came from the towns to help, similar to the Land Girls in the Second World War, and they stayed in a hostel in Leigh. About 20 German prisoners from the camp at Bull Ring Farm, Brockamin, worked at Norbury's. They were marched up and back again to work on the farm, with one guard with a gun. As children we got on well with them. They were nice chaps.

In contrast, the Second World War had a far greater impact on the civilian population. For one thing, BBC radio – which did not start operating until 1922 – made it possible to follow the course of the war more closely. But the biggest difference was, of course, that aircraft were used. Not only were civilians bombed, but it made dropping enemy troops by parachute possible. Furthermore, the German supremacy at the start of the war meant that the threat of invasion was a very real one.

It was the threat of invasion which led to the construction of pillboxes and anti-tank defences. One of these pillboxes was in Leigh Sinton, on the junction of the Malvern and Hereford roads, by the Royal Oak. Another – which is still there – was down Mill Lane, Bransford, beyond Bransford House. Then there was a dug-out by the Methodist Chapel at Smith End Green, which Eric Vine remembers helping his father to dig. Near it were placed two large old Blackstone oil engines, which were to be used as roadblocks.

The threat of being bombed meant that windows had to be 'blacked out', so that no lights showed.

Workers at Norbury's farm, 1944. Left to right, back row (standing): *Vic Banner, B. Powell, E. Coley, Sid Haggett, F. Powell, Don Badham, Frank Smith, ?, B. Dance, F. Symonds, F. Smith, O. Edmonds, ? Powell, ?, ?, G.K. Davies, E. Hughes, ?, ?, ?, ? Watkins;* third row: *Mrs Moore, Mrs Rowley, Mrs Smith, Mrs Lewis, Mrs Hemming, Annie Clarke, Mrs Gregory, Mary Davies, Mrs Powell, ? Banner, Mrs Brigden, Mrs Edmonds, Marjorie Badham;* second row: *Mrs Lewis, Mrs Loman, Mrs Tibbet, Mrs Spencer, Mrs Norbury, Mr Norbury, Reuben Turley, Mrs Hadley, Mr Hayes, Mr Spencer;* front row: *Freda Spencer with five Land Girls.* (PAT AND CECIL DEE)

Right: *First World War prisoner-of-war camp at Bullring Farm, Brockamin, in 1956. It has since been demolished. The date marked out in bricks on the end is 1917.* (WRO/I.W. SPARES)

Left: *Workers and POWs on Norbury's farm during the First World War.* (PETER NORBURY)

Right: *Second World War blockhouse by The Royal Oak, taken in 1955.* (WRO/FREEMAN PAYNE)

Left: *Second World War pillbox on Mill Lane, Bransford, 2002.* (MALCOLM SCOTT)

Because of the wartime petrol shortage Frederick Wenden bought a Brougham. The picture shows John Turner, the landlord of The Fox (on the left) greeting Frederick Wenden, with Fred Pullen holding the reins. (JOHN WENDEN)

Some people used black curtains. Others fitted wooden frames inside their windows, covered with roofing felt or special black paper. A few put wooden shutters outside, to also stop the windows being broken by any bomb blast. In addition, vehicles had to have very dim, and hooded, lights. Horse-drawn vehicles were not exempt. Because petrol was rationed, John Wenden's father bought a horse-drawn Brougham, which had a candle in each lantern. Even then, he was once stopped by a policeman for having too bright a light. As John's father said, he could not have less than one candle!

For children it does not seem to have been too frightening a time. As the Weaver sisters (Ivy Keeling, b.1921, Beryl Hope, b.1927, Dorothy Hughes, b.1931) from Orchard Cottage, Leigh, put it:

We were very lucky in that we were not really affected by the war. We had occasional aircraft come over and perhaps the sirens would go off about once a month. Rationing didn't really affect us – we had plenty of vegetables. We always grew our own, and Mother used to moan if she had to buy any. Uncle George used to send us a box of fruit from Cardiff for Christmas.

Indeed, there were some new experiences for children. Ronald Simcock recalls picking rose-hips to take to the WRVS, who paid 2d. per pound for them: they were used to extract vitamin C. Then there were strips of aluminium foil, dropped by enemy aircraft to confuse British radar, which were eagerly collected. Very occasionally, even pieces of shrapnel were found.

The fear that enemy troops might be dropped in by parachute at night made some people anxious. Eric Vine recalls that, when his father went out on Home Guard duty at night, he and his mother used to

lock the front door and go upstairs. The front-door key was then dangled on a string from the upstairs window, for when his father returned. Coral and Des Clarke both remember seeing German bombers going over at night, particularly if it was a moonlit night. The sky used to be thick with them, on their way to Birmingham or Coventry, but: 'We did not take any precautions, because we knew that we would not be bombed, being in the country. There were no guns nearby, only a searchlight.' However, Coral did see the German bomber which dropped a string of bombs in daylight, starting at Halfkey and finishing up at Malvern Link. It was so low that she could see all the markings clearly. Lilian Morris (b.1910) also remembers this event. She was walking at Sherridge with her fiancé, and they took shelter behind a wall.

In order to escape bombing of the big cities, many children were evacuated to the country. The book on the Worcester to Leominster railway records that 740 people were evacuated by train from Birmingham to Leigh Court in August 1939, where they were handed over to a Local Reception Officer. If they stayed, this large number must have been widely dispersed, because nobody locally has mentioned this influx. 1939 was, however, the period of the 'phoney war', when people were misled into thinking that maybe things would not be too serious after all. Nora Jay, who was then at Great House Farm, knew one evacuee family for whom this lull had tragic consequences:

Through friends of friends we took in a family from Birmingham, a grandmother, mother and daughter. Unfortunately they decided not to stay, because they said it was a 'phoney war'. But when the bombing of Birmingham commenced, they asked if they could return, to which the answer was, or course, 'Yes'. But the night before they were to return to Leigh, they were all killed in an air raid, which was very sad, and we were terribly distressed.

The Leigh Sinton School log-book records on 10 October 1939 that seven children from London, Birmingham and Gosport were admitted who were staying with friends in the district. Another entry reads: 'November 6th 1939. Admitted Reginald and Jean Lawrence, Government Evacuees boarded with Mrs Banner.' They were from Foundry Road Junior School, Birmingham, and one of their school-mistresses is recorded as visiting them.

Coral Clarke (née Ball), who lived with her grand-mother, Mrs Banner, at Shrubbery House, remembers that they filled the house with evacuees from London or Birmingham. After the war, her grandmother received a letter from the Queen, thanking her for opening her doors to strangers. Coral became very friendly with Jean Lawrence, who was happy with them, and they were in touch after the war.

According to Harry Banner, some evacuees took a long time to settle down. But John Swindell settled down quickly, and is still here! He was evacuated from London with his mother and two sisters in about 1941, and went to stay at one of the Top Cottages, Brockamin. Some of his wartime memories are very different from those of local children:

We were living in Bethnal Green when our family home was bombed, and we had to move. Then the new house was bombed, and we went to live in a drill hall for some time. At night I would go down to Victoria Tube Station [which was used as an air-raid shel-ter during the war], spread out our bedding between the lines and then go to fetch my mother and sisters.

The Friends (Quakers) brought me and my mother and two sisters to Top Cottage around 1941. My father, who was injured when he fell off the side of a

fire engine, joined us later. I was about 11 or 12 years old then. We came with just suitcases to Shrub Hill, and then caught a train to Bransford, where we were met by a cattle wagon owned by Bill Bond. We were met at Top Cottage by a couple from the Friends. The cottage was lit by paraffin lamps, had an outside toilet and no running water – things I was not used to. Even after being in the dark in London, and sleeping down in the Underground, I was afraid of the dark.

Although local children did not seem too affected by the war, adults, of course, were. For one thing, with so many men away, women had to take a much wider range of jobs, particularly on the farms. And in this war the Government did not rely simply on patriotism to get vital work done. In 1939 single women between the ages of 19 and 40 (later raised to 45 in 1942, and then to 50 in 1943) had to register and, if they did not have any dependants, could be told where to work. Nora Hadley was one of those affect-ed. She was sent to work at the Royal Worcester Porcelain factory, where she made insulators for tanks and Army vehicles – although she did not find out that this is what they were until after the war! Others were conscripted to work in local factories, including the Ordnance factory at Worcester.

In addition to local women under-taking more farm work, Land Girls were brought in to help, which is how Ivy Coley came to live here. However, like John Swindell, she found that country life here was sometimes very different from what she was used to.

Ivy Coley in her Land Army uniform, around 1943.
(Ivy Coley)

I lived in Netherton, near Dudley, and worked part-time in a factory at night. But when I registered they said that this was not enough, and I joined the

Second World War German POWs at Norbury's Farm. Mr Tebbitt, the farm manager, is on the left. Des Clarke says that the POWs, some of whom were officers, were 'real gentlemen and very kind to children'. One German POW was buried at Bransford Chapel, but later re-interred. (Coral and Des Clarke)

The workers at Norbury's apple-packing shed, c.1940. Left to right, back row: *Vince Badham, Frank Powell, Percy Smith;* middle row: *Arthur Rolph, Conice Dance, Dora Rolph, Dorothy Lewis, Charlie Norman;* front row: *Minnie Rowley, Mary Hemming, Alice Smith, Brenda Rowley, Doreen Lewis.* (DOREEN ROWLEY)

Land Army. My first job in the Land Army was at Rock, near Bewdley. This was a gentleman's residence (Major Goodwin) and the produce was sold from the garden. I had a nice bedroom and there was plenty of hot water.

It was different when I came to work in Leigh Sinton for Mr Harold Yarnold, who owned Elmhurst. At Netherton I lived in a new council-house, with a bath and inside toilet. At Elmhurst there was no running water, only a pump. You had a jug of hot water in the bedroom to wash with. And there was an earth toilet outside. But I had good food. It was a mixed farm, cows for breeding, poultry, fruit, potatoes. Mr Yarnold had a brother, Arch Yarnold, who farmed Pipe Elm Farm which was owned by the Norbury family... When Arch Yarnold wanted extra help potato planting and picking up, also threshing, I was loaned out. Threshing was a dirty job – no showers in those days!

As the war went on, so prisoners of war also worked on the land, both Germans and Italians. The Italians, in particular, seem to have been well received. One person remembers them for their marvellous singing: indeed she received a note from one of the best singers, inviting her to meet him. Nora Hadley thought that they were clever, but lazy, because some of them used to knock off work and go and sit by the River Teme and weave baskets from the willow which grew there.

Commemorating the World Wars

After the First World War there was a determination to commemorate the sacrifices made by those who served in the Forces – both the dead and the survivors

– and to 'build a land fit for heroes'. These activities took several forms. The first was simply to erect war memorials, the local one being in St Edburga's Church.

In order to have a memorial which would benefit and serve the community, it was decided to build a village hall. The Leigh and Bransford Memorial Hall was built on land at Smith End Green donated by the Norbury family, who also donated the land for the adjoining playing-field. Funds for the hall itself (£1,300) were raised by running social events like whist drives and dances, by public subscription and by loans from parishioners. It was opened on 22 January 1920.

The Memorial Hall is, of course, still in use. The fact that it has been continuously enlarged and improved means that the original aim – of having a memorial which served the community – is still being met 80 years later.

Having a wreath-laying ceremony and church service to mark the 11 November Armistice of the First World War – Remembrance Day – is another lasting way by which both it and the Second World War are still remembered. Les Alford and Harry Banner remember that:

In the late 1920s all the First World War soldiers would assemble for Remembrance Sunday and Colonel Farquhar from Leigh Lodge would drill them, and march them up the Leigh Road with their Standard Bearer. There were about 40 of them, all with their shoes shining, on time and in their civvies with their medals.

Nowadays, 57 years after the end of the Second World War, there are very few veterans of it to attend the service.

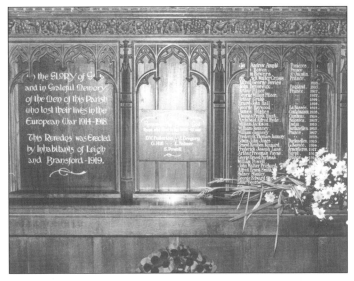

Left: *The war memorial in St Edburga's.*
(MALCOLM SCOTT)

Right: *Memorial to those who served in the First World War, in the Memorial Hall.* (MALCOLM SCOTT)

Left: *The memorial to those who served in the Second World War, in the Memorial Hall.* (MALCOLM SCOTT)

Above: *Remembrance Day Ceremony outside St Edburga's Church, just after the Second World War.* (JOHN FARR)

Left: *At the Remembrance Day Ceremony at St Edburga's, November 2001. Left to right, facing: Des Symonds, Sir John Willison, a visiting Chelsea pensioner, Brian Peters, Ken Jones, John Soley, George Burton; with their backs to the camera: Harry Banner, John Turner.* (MALCOLM SCOTT)

SCHOOLS

Leigh Sinton School, c.1920. (PETER NORBURY)

Introduction

To appreciate why schooling needed to be made compulsory, we have only to look at the records in Bransford Chapel. In 1836, a Government Act made it a legal requirement to register all births, marriages and deaths. The first entry in Bransford Chapel's Government Marriage Registration Book was on 20 February 1838, when William Mann and Sarah Tyler (both of 'Full Age') were married. On the certificate, the bride, groom and two witnesses all signed their names with an X. None of them could read or write. In an age where 30 per cent of the 18-year-olds go on to some form of higher education, it is difficult to believe that less than 200 years ago most of the population were illiterate. Yet this was the norm: it was not until the 1870 Education Act that it became a legal requirement for children aged from five to 13 to go to school – and even then exemptions could be obtained after the age of ten.

There were schools before 1870, established by the Church or by private benefactors. In Leigh, in 1778,

William and Henry Bullock gave lands worth £4.12s. per year to establish a school. We do not know where this school was, but it was held in a partitioned-off room in the house where the master lived. It catered for about 15 boys in 1833, teaching them the 'three Rs' and the Church Catechism. Later, in 1867, there were 77 children, boys and girls, who paid 1d. or 2d. weekly to attend.

Billings' 1855 Directory & Gazetteer for Worcestershire lists a parochial school at Leigh Sinton, with 45 scholars and Thomas Hobro as the master. There is also a girls' school at Bransford listed, supported by the Hon. and Revd Somers Cocks (the rector of Leigh), with Miss Abrahams as the mistress and 40 scholars. Harold Portman's father (who was born in 1896) told him that there used to be a school at Grove Cottage, on the Suckley Road, Bransford, but it is not clear if this was the same one.

We know that the old school at Leigh Sinton was built in 1867, when Thomas Hobro was the master and was living in the adjacent School House. (Interestingly, the school also contained an Anglican

Chapel, saving the inhabitants of Leigh Sinton from having to walk to Leigh for church!) When Leigh Sinton Church of England School became a National School, in 1885, it occupied the same premises, and Thomas Hobro was its first master although he left on 20 October of the same year:

Scholars were detained after 4 o'clock, awaiting arrival of the Rector, Curate and several ladies. Mr Hobro, the late master, was presented with purse of gold and beautifully hand-coloured address.

The first Leigh Hurst School was built in 1865, on the same site as the school which closed in 1990, although the name changed to Bransford School along the way. Whether it was to house the girls' school mentioned in 1855 is a matter for conjecture. Leigh Hurst School later became a National School, and was enlarged in 1891 to take 106 children. Like Leigh Sinton, it had an adjacent schoolhouse. Unlike Leigh Sinton, it was not a Church school.

In the early 1930s the original brick school at Leigh Hurst burnt down and 'temporary' wooden buildings were erected on the same site. Harold Portman remembers watching the remains of the old school being knocked down, the children being given a holiday whilst the new one was being built.

As with many temporary buildings these had a long life, remaining in use until the school closed in 1990!

With the foundation of the National Schools came the requirement for the head teacher to keep a school log-book. Unfortunately, nobody knows where the old log-books for Bransford School are. Certainly Thelma Spencer could not find them when she became the head teacher in 1984, so we only have the last log-book, covering the period from 1980 to 1989. For Leigh Sinton, on the other hand, we have the complete set, from 1885 until 1990.

The two schools were obviously different in some respects – not least because a school's character is set by both the head teacher and the staff, and because Leigh Sinton was a Church school. Nevertheless, the two schools developed in the same national and local environment. Hopefully, therefore, the picture which will emerge from the Leigh Sinton log-book is appropriate for both establishments.

Reading through the school logs, several strands stand out from the host of detail. One is the way in which the health of the children has changed. The second is the way in which the children's involvement in farming affected their schooling. Last, but not least, is the way in which the school was regulated, through inspections. Let us look at each in turn.

Left: *Class at the old Leigh Hurst School around 1890.* (GEOFF WRIGHT)

Below, left: *The front entrance to Leigh Hurst Primary School (the wall is covered in Aubretia).* (JUNE ROBINSON)

Below: *Leigh Hurst Primary School and playground.* (JUNE ROBINSON)

*Leigh Sinton School, c.1890.
Mrs Wareham is pictured on the
left of the second row and her
husband Mr Wareham is on
the right of the third row.
Both were teachers at the school.
Second from right, back row,
(in black dress): Dora Banner;
fourth from right, second row,
(in black dress): Gladys Banner.*
(DOREEN ROWLEY)

Children's Health

Leigh Sinton National School opened on 4 January 1885, and by 4 February had 75 children registered. However, we read almost immediately: 'In consequence of a severe attack of measles on this side of the Parish the School was closed from February 13th to March 10th.' In the following year the school was shut for six weeks on the orders of the Medical Officer of Health, because the master's child had scarlet fever. In HM Inspector's Report for 1887 we read: 'The work has been much hindered by illness: otherwise I think the school would probably have reached the first class.'

The entry for 14 August 1891 lists the children who had been away for extended periods, mainly through illness. Out of 85 on the roll, seven had been away for six weeks or more, with another four away for between two and four weeks. Sometimes a lot of children were away, but due to a range of causes. For example:

December 21st 1894. A great many children away this week, suffering from colds, sore throats, etc. Infants class especially bad, about one half away.

In 1896 we read that:

August 21st. School closed this afternoon. Having been closed so recently for measles we have only given five weeks holiday instead of the usual six weeks. Hop picking is sure to be over in five weeks as the crop is so light.

As we shall see, the school had agriculture as well as illness to contend with in keeping up attendances!

Leigh Hurst School in 1918. Third and fourth from the left, back row: daughters of PC Weaver; first on left, third row: Mr Owen George Davies, the headmaster; fifth from left, third row: Fred Banner, Harry Banner's brother; first on left, second row: Nancy Banner.
(HARRY BANNER)

At the start of 1899, the school was closed because of an outbreak of scarlet fever, but even when it reopened only half the children attended, some not having recovered. At the end of the same year 26 children are listed as having been away for extended periods with whooping cough or influenza. The start of the next year, 1900, was little better – a mumps epidemic combined with colds, etc., led to 40 children being absent on the first day, whilst measles strikes again at the start of 1901, with 21 children away, out of 164 on the roll. Later in 1901 the school was closed for three weeks because of an outbreak of scarlet fever.

Some of the illnesses were not so serious, but led to the children being excluded from school: 'November 15th 1900. Sent Albert and Nellie T* home. Ringworm.' Other causes for individual exclusion included scabies and impetigo and, occasionally, personal hygiene. For example: 'December 18th 1908. The S*s (3) were found by the Doctor to be in a very dirty state – head & body lice. Sent off at once.' And:

*February 16th 1915. The two B*s came to school this morning. They were in such a dirty state that after consulting the Correspondent I sent them home. The smell arising from them was intolerable.*

Fortunately this last example was easily dealt with, because the following day we read: 'February 17th 1915. B*s returned cleaner.'

However, as time goes on, the number of epidemics and school closures drop gradually. Individual cases are noted, but their importance has been apparently downgraded. Thus in 1915 an entry reads:

October 11th. School re-opened this morning. Attendance very bad. During the holidays 11 children have left the village, reducing the number on the books to 88 (68 juniors + 20 infants). Nine boys are away engaged in agriculture. 4 cases of scarlet fever, 1 tonsillitis.

Not surprisingly though, at the end of the First World War the school was caught up in the national flu epidemic, so that on 18 November 1918 the log records: 'Nearly every child has been down with influenza during the last fortnight: some very serious cases', and the school was closed for three weeks.

After this there were isolated outbreaks and school closures – for example in 1925 and again in 1945, both for measles. Over the same period, but particularly after the Second World War, came the rise in preventive health care, involving regular visits to the school by nurses, dentists and doctors. The days when ill health affected the whole school's performance were over.

Leigh Sinton School, 1920. Left to right, back row: *Eva Jones, Bert Fitzer, Bert Rone, Edna Fitzer, ?,
Edna Lewis, Jack Froggatt, Eric Pritchard, Syd Haggitt, Rosie Fitzer*; second row (seated): *Beryl Booton,
? Booton, Eva Banner, Gerald Jones, Dorothy Yelland, Win Rone, Albert Jones, Winnie Pritchard,
Jim Haggitt, Nora Bruton*; front row: *Fred Fitzer, Cyril Dyson, ?.* (DOREEN ROWLEY)

Leigh Hurst School in 1928. Left to right, back row: Frank Symonds, Roy Warner, Harold Hooper, Chris Edwards, Fred Mason, ?, Frank Pass; third row: Jessie Poole, ?, ?, Hazel Morris, ?, ? Bosley, O.G. Davies; second row: Florrie Rowberry, Barbara Oldham, Nancy Cross ?, Marjorie James, ?, Lily Jones, Flossie Phillips, Olive Knapper, Vera Amphlett, Freda Amplett; front row: Harold Alford, ?, Harold Portman, George Rowbery, Alf Jackson, Dick Jones.
(RAY JACKSON)

Farming & School

Up to the nineteenth century, children were routinely involved in agriculture and, because it was so labour-intensive, hop picking was, locally, probably the most important, single activity. Indeed, the school summer holidays used to be held in September, to allow children to take part in the harvest and in hop picking. It was not until 1945, following the 1944 Education Act, that the holidays were moved back to August. Of course, this change was not only because of the diminished role of children in farming. It reflected the widened educational opportunities which the Act offered for all children, raising the leaving age to 15 and allowing them free access, via the 11-plus examinations, to secondary, technical and grammar schools – and even to universities.

It is, of course, not surprising that there were problems in moving from a society where children contributed to the family welfare to one where they were at school five days a week, and hence non-productive. A series of entries for Leigh Sinton School's first year, 1885, paints an immediate picture of the way in which children were involved in rural life.

May 15th 1885. During the week ending this date there has been a better attendance of scholars, but some children have been with their parents gathering cowslips for sale for making of wine...
July 3rd 1885. During the week ending this date there has been a very good attendance of scholars especially in the first standard: but some in the fourth have not been so regular having to take food to their parents who are Clover making.
July 10th 1885. ... some of the parents have taken their children to the fields to assist in picking pease [sic] for sale.

July 24th 1885. During the week ending this date there was not a large attendance of scholars as boys are employed by farmers in getting in the Hay Crop.
August 7th. ... there has not been a large attendance of scholars during the week ending this date as older boys have been still been employed by their parents in taking food to the Hay fields and others employed in nursing while their mothers have been employed in thinning Swedes.
August 14th. During the week ending this date there was not a large attendance of scholars as the boys in the higher standards have been assisting their fathers in tying up wheat.

The school closed for the summer ('Harvest') holidays on 21 August and reopened on 5 October. The hop-picking season cannot have been delayed that year, because there are no entries relating to absences through hop picking! In contrast, in 1895, for example, we read: 'October 2nd. School re-opens. Only 78 present [out of 150]. Hop picking not yet finished.' Again, two years later:

September 28th 1897. School re-opened this morning. Only 90 children present [out of about 120]. Owing to the heavy rains during the holidays the hop picking is not yet finished.

In subsequent years the number of entries relating to absenteeism due to farm work decreased, although they were rarely absent. Thus we have: 'July 19th 1909. Pea picking commenced at Mr Phillips farm this morning – only 54 present out of 72 in standards.' But in the following year, the farm-related school problems were different:

July 7th 1910. Currant picking commenced. The

little children began to arrive at school soon after 7.0 o'clock, being turned out by their mothers who are engaged in picking. The children are simply tired out by mid-day, not having had their proper rest.

During the First World War, when patriotism was at a premium, involvement in agriculture seemed to have been condoned, if not actually encouraged. In addition, by this time the school taught gardening. Thus, a report for 31 October 1915 notes:

With the exception of carrots and beet, all the crops were very good, hardly a weed visible on the plots and they were judiciously arranged in order of rotation – a point overlooked by many persons. There were 12 boys on the register but on the day of inspection 6 boys were away helping farmers, where probably their gardening training would prove to be very serviceable. There are 7 plots, 1 general plot and 1 seed plot.

While a year later we have:

November 17th. Several children away this week, potato sorting, mangold pulling, etc. Ellen D minding baby while mother goes to work on the land.*

And in 1918: 'October 4th 1918. Children desiring to pick blackberries have been allowed to leave school at 3.0 o'clock on Tuesday and Thursday.'

Clearly, in going from a situation when schooling was optional to one where it was compulsory meant that there had to be changes in parental attitudes. Then there was an added complication that, for the first time, children had to go out into a wider society, so things like personal hygiene became more important – at least, to the schoolmasters and mistresses! Finally, children had to pay for their education – although whether in the earlier days it was some or all of the children in the parish is not clear. From the figures given of the 'pence received' it seems as if they paid 1d. or 2d. per week.

The logs record these personal hygiene problems, and the entry for 18 June 1888 records that:

The children are very clean with one exception – a boy in St. II, who is in rags and filthy, a strong aroma from him assailing over a distance of two yards. The boy alluded to is Thomas B.*

The problems of fees and personal hygiene come together later in the year, because on 29 October 1888 we read:

73 children present. Great difficulty to get David B to school: as they come in such a dirty condition and without pence. I cannot allow them to attend after this date unless they come clean and with pence. Sent a note to parent. C H*, G H* and SJ T* not allowed to attend school till they bring pence.*

The B*s were obviously repeated offenders, because the following year we read:

Monday October 20th. Readmitted W, G and D B who have not been at school for some months owing to their dirty conditions and irregularity in paying their fees. Number at school 80.*

If children were dirty, or did not pay their fees, they could be excluded. But what was done if the children simply failed to attend? One thing was simply to punish the child, either by detentions or corporal punishment: 'October 15th 1885. Truant players stay after school each day during the week to make up lost time.' Then: 'July 27th 1900. The two G*s who have been playing truant since Thursday came to school with their father. Gave them both a sound thrashing.'

Another action was to write a note to the parents, though since they were probably illiterate – at least in the early years – this may not have been entirely successful. The last resort was the Attendance Officer, to

Leigh Sinton School, 1930.
Left to right, back row: *Douglas Spencer, Hilda Smith, Doreen Jones, Kathleen Dunnet, Kathleen Best, Dotsey Grubb;* second row: *Charlie Wilcox, Robert Fisher, Lawrence Jones, Peggy Johnson, Barbara James, Freda Spencer, Eileen Bowkett;* front row: *Bernice Rolph, Jean Kimber, Doreen Lewis, Geoff Bartlett, Norman Kimber, Edward Hill, John Gardner and Raymond Smith.*

(Doreen Rowley)

Bob Hunt and Muriel 'Bib' Hunt at the entrance to Leigh Hurst School, 1934. (Muriel 'Bib' Jones)

whom the master could report truants:

Tuesday 15th April 1890. I had a visit from Mr Mann the Attendance Officer and gave him a list of children who attended irregularly. They were George H*, Charles and Florence J*, Clara T* and Sydney P*.

A similar entry six years later notes:

March 9th 1896. Sent list of absentees to Mr Mann. I only reported three boys. Charles R*, who is always having a day off to help father on some such trivial excuse, and Charles and Ernest S*. These two boys were away ill about exam times but they are quite well enough now to race about the fields and play football and therefore told them to come several times but it has been of no use.

If the truancy continued, the Attendance Officer could take the parents to court, as these two entries over a ten-year interval show:

Friday 20th March 1891. This week two summonses were heard against parents of G H* and S P*. H* was fined 5/- and P*'s case adjourned for one month.

Then, in 1901:

November 21st. The parents of G* and M* were brought up before the Malvern bench yesterday for not sending their children (James G* and Edward M*) regularly to school. G* was fined 5s.0d. and M* 7s.6d. This is the second time this year that M* has been fined.

It was possible for children under school age to work legally provided that they got a Labour Certificate. From the logs it appears that there were regular examinations held in Malvern to obtain these. Presumably, if children satisfied the examiners that they had reached a suitable educational standard, they were allowed to be employed legally, and did not have to attend school. Hence the entry on 12 February 1904: 'At the Labour Certificate Exam held at Malvern on January 30th Ernest S* passed and George B* failed.' Though not everybody passing the exam took advantage of it to leave school: '25th May 1894. Gave Labour Certificate to James R*, the only one of those examined who wishes to use it.'

As with health problems, so it was with poor attendance because of agricultural activities, either of the children themselves or of their parents. Agriculture-related absences diminished slowly up to the First World War, and then essentially disappeared.

As an aside, we have seen that corporal punishment was one of the methods used to try and stop truancy. We also know that its use diminished over the twentieth century. Do the school logs give any record of how much it was used, and why? A record

during the school's first year reads:

November 4th 1885. Harry T* gave great trouble during morning attendance. Cut a boys ear during meal time and refused to stand out when called up for enquiry – obliged to punish the boy severely – nose bled while receiving the correction.

In his first year as headmaster, Frederick Wareham – who was to stay for 37 years – noted: 'July 27th 1894. Punished Arthur W* this morning for swearing', but he does not say how. It was on 7 August 1901 that a Code of Practice was set out by the managers, which was as follows:

1. That no corporal punishment be administered except by the head teacher.
2. That corporal punishment be only effected by the cane.
3. That a punishment book be kept, stating the number of strokes and the cause of the punishment and that this book be open for the inspection of the managers.
4. That the head teacher bring the punishment book to the Treasurer's meeting every month for Inspection.

Unfortunately, we do not have the punishment book, so have no record of how frequently corporal punishment was used after 1901. But Frederick Wareham was the headmaster for so long that several of the parishioners we have spoken to in connection with this history were at school under him. Their reminiscences, including those relating to being punished, follow later. We only note here that an HM Inspector's Report for 1922 suggests that his was a benevolent rule:

The Headmaster, who has been here for many years, is kindly in manner and earnest in his efforts for the welfare of the children. He is loyally assisted by his staff. Under easy discipline work of a sound character is, in general, being done...

School Inspections

One of the very surprising things which emerges from the school log-books is the number of school inspections. Being both a Church of England and a National School meant that Leigh Sinton faced inspections from both the Diocesan authorities and the national Government. Leigh Sinton opened as a National School on 4 January 1885 and the first inspection was from Diocesan authorities a month later:

February 4th 1885. The infants have been carefully taught, and if they were more ready in connecting texts with the pictures would do their Teacher more justice. They repeat their prayers distinctly, and join in the hymns with others: having also learnt several by themselves. Division II has much improved in their slate work, which is now very creditable. If Division

Leigh Hurst School when it had become Bransford School, June 1979. Left to right, back row: *Mrs Jones, Mrs Purvis, Alan Speers, Emma Dickinson, Rachael Evans, Tracy Rathmell, Craig Barry, Gary Cowell, Charles Wood, Peter Gardiner, David Hopkins, Willow Jeffries, Paul Nightingale, Edward Seymour;* third row: *Mrs Gorman, Mrs Milledge, Wayne Smith, Jill Page, Robert Costello, Rachael Portman, Darren Oliver, Alan Barnes, Christopher Purvis, Stephen Sheriff, Mark Barry, Marc Powell, Zoe Farrant, Henry Smith, Paula Crofts, Mrs Statham, Mrs Robinson, Mrs Withers (seated); second row: Joanne Pritchard, Alan Gardiner, Debbie Bloomfield, Matthew Wellersley, Ayesha Taylor, Kevin Oliver, Annette Garrett, Terry Nightingale, Gorse Jeffries, Andrew Lyons, Debbie Goble, Martin Brooks, Esme Farrant;* front row: *Mark Quinton, Anne Speers, Becky Mair, Tina Brant, Damian Barry, Kenneth Douds, Stephen Edans, Ian Graske, Mark Dickinson, Sally Costello, Yvonne Bloomfield, Jane Speers, Richard Rathmell.* (Eileen Purvis)

III can make the same advance upon paper the School will probably next year reach the first class.

A further Diocesan inspection came a month later, in March 1885, when already the children's poor health was having an impact:

The order is good. There has been an epidemic of whooping cough, and measles now threatens the school. These hindrances considered, the work is very fair, and much of it good. The infants are very bright and intelligent. The arithmetic is weak in the second standard, especially the notation, and in the fourth standard, and the grammar is weak in the third standard. The rest is good, and much of the reading and geography intelligent. The sewing is good...

As well as telling us how the school was developing, these reports also give us an idea of what the children were taught. By 1886 the topics included tables, arithmetic, dictation, copy books, sewing and scripture. The list of songs which the children sang included 'The Poor Blind Boy', 'The Brave Comrade', 'The Little Busy Bee' and 'Father's Return'. There is also a list of 'Poetical Extracts' for each standard (I to VI) which were mainly the works of Longfellow and Wordsworth.

In addition, the children had 'object lessons' in a list of topics, which were: Post Office, railway, stagecoach, seasons, chief employment of district, fox, otter, cow, mole, cuckoo, clock (tell time of day) and hops. In later entries, the list of topics expanded and became more varied, covering both topics of local interest and more general topics such as wolf, elephant, lion, cotton, pins, a candle, etc.

When the school first opened it had 75 children enrolled. By 1894 the number had increased to over 100, and by 1901 there were 164. Not surprisingly, as the numbers increased, both the accommodation and the teaching staff were stretched to their limits. As HM Inspector comments in 1893:

The standard children are in good order and have passed a creditable examination particularly Recitation and in Singing by note. The weak points are the geography and arithmetic of the upper standards (the 4th, 5th, 6th and 7th). Handwriting and Mental Arithmetic need increased attention throughout the school and finger counting in the first standard should be abolished. The premises have been improved by the provision of a capacious porch to the main building and this porch contains sufficient space for the elder children's hats, caps, etc., but is not available for the Infants on account of its position. There is no playground. The Offices [toilets] do not comply with the rules of the Code (Schedule 7 Rule 13).

A number of the elder children have been retained in the Infants Room and taught as Infants, contrary to the rules of the Education Department. This error is not likely, however, to be repeated.

The Infants' teacher should not be required to teach Needlework to the elder children. She has quite enough work to occupy her time fully in the Infants'

Room. This room needs a gallery, desks suitable for Infants' wants, a cloakroom and a porch. The huge table which encumbers the centre of the floor must be removed in accordance with the frequently expressed directions of HM Inspectors.

At this time there were two staff, Frederick Wareham and Harriet Wareham, and there were over 120 children enrolled. Perhaps not surprisingly, in his 1897 report HM Inspector was critical of the staffing level:

Some of the scholars are too apt to talk during their lessons, but this fault arises mainly from the want of teachers to supervise the classes. If the managers desire to carry on this school any longer they should provide adequate staff. One person cannot fairly be expected to teach 85 children [i.e. the Mixed School] unassisted...
The Managers should at once provide for an increased staff in the Infants' room, as there are now 46 infants' names on the books and the average attendance for the year is perilously near the maximum allowed by the Code (article 73) for a teacher approved under Article 68.

By 1901 five staff are listed – the Warehams and the Misses Ellen Hanley, Maud and Agnes Lloyd – but the accommodation is still attracting criticism:

With reference to the need for inlet and outlet ventilation in the main room, the attention of the managers is hereby directed to the various entries by HM Inspector in the log-book. The defect should be remedied forthwith.

According to an entry in 1943, the school's two rooms had areas of 721 square feet (75 square metres) and 343 square feet (36 square metres). With less than one square yard (or metre) per child it is not surprising that the ventilation needed improving! By 1903, not only had the need to improve the ventilation not been heeded, but it is clear that the children also lacked a proper playground:

HM Inspector's Report January 21st 1903
Mixed School
Some of the desks should be replaced by others of modern form. It is understood that the ventilation of the main room will be improved without further delay.
The playgrounds should be drained and levelled in order that Physical Exercises may be practised regularly under more favourable conditions.

Poor ventilation, making the school very hot in summer, was not the only problem which the children faced. In the winter it was the cold too:

January 16th 1902. The weather has been extremely cold this week, almost impossible to get the school warm (i.e. the large room). The children in standard I and II suffered much from the cold.

In the 1900s things seemed to go from bad to worse as far as accommodation is concerned, for in the 1908 report of HM Inspector we read:

The main room is approached through a low porch which serves as a cloakroom for the boys and girls; it has no ventilation; the roof is falling, square patches of the plaster of the ceiling having given way. The damp from the cloaks can only find its way into main room in wet weather or winter as there is no other outlet. The main room 38 feet by 20 feet has no exhaust ventilator, it gets very stuffy. The west window should be made to open; the other windows should open at the top... A new cloakroom should be provided. The playground on which several loads of large stones have been emptied is unusable.

Despite these censures the Inspector goes on to say:

Considering the extraordinary heat in the unventilated main-room and the very great weakness of the staff, the Head Master deserves great credit for the state of the school...

Interestingly, the school faced other problems about this time too, although why these should have occurred when they did is not clear. As Frederick Wareham put it:

October 27th 1905. Changes are continually going on among the labourers in the parish. They come for a few months to a farm here and then off somewhere else. I get children of 10 years of age who have been to four or five different schools in the county. A few years ago we had nothing of this. The children admitted too are as a rule poorer both mentally and physically than those admitted five or six years ago.

Although there were some building improvements after the damning report of 1908, they were not enough to satisfy HM Inspector in 1910, and most of the recommendations are repeated. In 1912, however, the only recommendation made relating to the buildings is that the outside woodwork be repainted! Subsequently, recommendation relating to the buildings become rarer, although one intriguing one for 1913 says: 'The offices smell badly and more earth and ashes should be provided for them.' 'Offices' is, of course, a euphemism for the toilets.

During the First World War no reports of HM Inspectors are entered in the logs, although the religious knowledge inspections continued, and gardening inspections appeared to assume greater importance. The first Government inspection after the war, in 1920, makes no comments about the buildings, although the war, not surprisingly, seems to have affected the staffing:

Frequent changes of staff have taken place during the past few years and some of the teachers appointed have had no teaching experience. The order is good and much of the work is satisfactory.

It goes on with some critical comments, from which one gets the impression that the teaching was a little backward and that the record keeping not all that it should be. However, perhaps reflecting the wartime preoccupations, gardening gets a glowing report:

Gardening is well taught at this school... The crops are not only of fine quality, but are arranged in a good order of rotation and well spaced without waste ground.

In subsequent years, references to the building become few and far between, although when they do occur they can be quite startling, and one in particular shows how soft we have all grown in recent years!

January 24th 1939. The new system of heating is no use during the severe weather. The temperature ranges from 32°F to 44°F [0°C to 7°C] and is extremely cold for working purposes. It is almost impossible to write properly.

As time went on, Frederick Wareham's entries in the log got shorter and shorter. After he retires, in 1931, it is not until Miss Fream takes over, in 1945, that the Government Inspector's reports are entered. The first of these is good as far as the teaching is concerned, as recorded in HM Inspector's Report of 2 October 1946: 'The children are happy and industrious. Satisfactory general progress is obtained and staff and children enjoy a happy friendly relationship.' The only serious comments about the buildings again refer to the 'offices':

... it is evident that very little care has been shown to the comfort and health of the children relative to the sanitary accommodation. This is a matter for grave concern.

However, it took an organisational change to put right any remaining building defects. This came in 1953, when the school acquired 'Controlled Status' within Worcestershire County Council. The County Council assumed financial responsibility for the school, and undertook the much-needed improvements. After that, the most important building problems relate to the new joint school which was to follow the decision to merge Leigh Sinton and Bransford Schools. We will look at the events leading up to this later, but let us first look at probably the most important aspect of both schools – what their pupils and those working there thought of them!

Memories of School
Leigh Hurst (Bransford) School

Both George Alford and Harry Banner were at school in the late 1920s:

We walked to school, and if you got wet you were wet all day. Even when we went to school at Somers Park in Malvern (at 11 years old) we still had to walk to The Asp at Bransford to catch the bus to Malvern. The bus was either the Chicken Coup, which collected the children from around the Sandlin area, or Mark's, from Rainbow Hill in Worcester.

Mr O.G. Davies was the Headmaster who lived in a house by the school. He was very strict and kept a cane, which was used. There were three classes in the Little School and two in the Big School. A Miss Senter was one of the teachers who lived opposite the Bank House. There was a lady who came from Worcester and a Miss Herbert, who lived opposite the school, in Harley House.

A coke fire heated the school, and before you went home at night the children had to fill the coal buckets ready for the next day. We also used to have to pump the water for the farmer's cows at The Grove behind the school, and the Headmaster used to get the money for that job. We used a slate to write on in class. When we were about nine or ten we used to have an afternoon of gardening. You would have your own plot and were allowed to grow what you liked.

We took sandwiches to school as there were no school dinners. It was usually bread and jam and a bottle of cold tea. You would sit on the iron seat around the oak tree and eat this. A little later on there were the third of pint bottles of milk, which had to be bought. They would put them in buckets of warm water to warm them up. There used to be a hospital week, when you took food in for the hospitals in the days when there was no National Health Service.

We would play football on the ecclesiastical ground, rounders, hopscotch and play with our tops (a stick and piece of string).

Ronald Simcock, who started school in 1939, particularly remembers the punishments:

The Headmaster was Mr Owen George Davies. He was very strict, but a good teacher. If we were to be punished he would make us fetch the cane from where it hung and we could choose hands or backside. He used to cane us in front of the whole class – that was the worst bit.

Des Symonds was a pupil from 1936 until 1944:

We walked there and back every day, 6 miles in all. We had an Infant, Middle and Top Class. Mr Davies could be very strict some days, but on the whole he was good.

In lesson time he would get us lads to go outside and wash his car – a 1935 Standard Eight, registration number AUY 513 – and do his garden and other practical work. At lunchtime we would be delegated to go into the field behind the school and pump the water into the tank for Mr Amphlett's cows. There used to be a big oak tree in the centre of the playground with an iron seat and railings all round, we had some games there.

John Roberts, who started school in 1936, remembers the iron seat too, because he got his foot stuck in it and had to be released!

For Eileen Purvis, who started at four-and-a-half years old in 1936, the walk to school was something she remembers:

I used to walk down to the school from Smith End Green every day come rain or shine. The highlight of a rainy day would be if I was picked up by the school bus (the Chicken Pen) which took the secondary school children over to Malvern.

Eric Vine, who went there from 1942 to 1948, remembers that although there were only three classrooms there were four classes, and that Mr O.G. Davies taught every subject to two classes in one room – English, geography, gardening, etc. He also remembers the school meals:

We had meals in our classrooms. These were prepared in the Memorial Hall by local ladies, who also provided the meals for the Leigh Sinton school. The meals cost 2s.1d. per week, and they were beautiful. There was a main course, with lots of variety, and pudding. The lady in charge of preparing the meals was Mrs Drew, who lived in Post Office Lane, Bransford. My mother, Ethel Vine, helped to cook. We ate at our desks. The sloping tops were propped up to make them level by a peg inside the desk. Two desks were put together and a cloth put over them, and the dinner ladies put out the cutlery.

Glenda Merrell, who started in 1944 when she was four ('to be with my older brother'), remembers that the games they played included skipping, hopscotch, hide and seek and 'running around'. She remembers that when they were walking home to Coles Green from school and met the postman on his afternoon round, he would give them a lift! She liked Leigh Hurst, but did not like Somers Park, the secondary school where children went from 11 to 13. Later she went to The Chase when it opened – 'It was brilliant and new.' Bernard Atkinson also went to school early, at the age of four. According to him 'they took you into school, as parents were glad to be rid of you!'

June Robinson was not a pupil. She came to live opposite the school in 1960, and was later employed there:

The Headmaster was Mr Daniels, who was a law unto himself. He couldn't stand well-meaning parents interfering in any way, and made this quite clear. While the children were at school he was in complete charge.

One of her first memories of the school was watching Mr Daniels climb up a ladder to the bedroom of the then schoolhouse. The resident was a former headmaster's widow, who was well into her eighties and had not been seen that morning. He found her dead in bed.

June Robinson's memories cover a wide range of school activities:

I started work at the school in September 1968 as a dinner lady and playtime supervisor. The playtime supervisors ('Pink Ladies') wore a pink, long-sleeved overall and the dinner ladies wore blue, with a white cap. The toilets were brick built, and stood opposite the school, across the playground. They only had the most essential cover overhead, with most of the standing room open to all weathers. The staff toilet was kept locked and the key had to be asked for – Mr Daniels believed that the toilet should only be used by staff at specific times! Next to the toilets were two wooden sheds – one for the caretaker's cleaning materials and the other was a kitchen. It had an old flat brown sink with a wooden draining board, and a warming oven to warm the plates and pudding dishes in.

The school always celebrated May Day with the children carrying decorated hoops, baskets or hats and, of course, one little girl was May Queen. They all used to parade around the playground, down the road and back up the steps into the school.

Every Christmas there was a party held straight after dinner. The food was prepared by us dinner ladies and bought by Mr Daniels. We had to make jellies and blancmange in big tin trays. There would be four sliced white loaves, half a pound of margarine, a couple of pots of fish paste and two jars of jam, followed by chocolate fingers – one each. I remember that I took some bags of crisps in one year. The children loved them, but I got told off, and had to promise not to do such a thing again.

Mervyn Philpott taught at Bransford School for four years from 1949, and brings another perspective:

Heating arrangements were such as would make the present-day Health and Safety Officers go berserk – there were, in my classroom, three two-bar electric fires on the floor between the rows of desks. Some time before I left they were wall mounted and were much safer and provided better heating.

When I was there the retired head, Mr O.G. Davies, was still hale and hearty, and lived in the adjacent schoolhouse... I don't know how he ruled the school but I think he wielded a very firm hand, because when-

ever he appeared, either in his garden or crossing the playground, a deadly hush fell on the place!

A couple of years after I started at Bransford Mr Clayton moved, and was replaced by Mr Vaughan. He had been there only a few days when a mother came to speak to him to say that one of her boys had either measles or chicken pox. The advice handed out was that she should draw the curtains in the bedroom and keep the patient in the dark. She took the advice calmly and departed. I had overheard the conversation and afterwards told Mr Vaughan that at lunch-time I would show him where the family lived. We walked to the road and in the orchard opposite the school was a framework of poles with a dark green tarpaulin over. 'That is the boy's home' I said. It wasn't until the mother came out that I was believed.

Mr Daniels was clearly quite a commanding person, because Basil Wadley remembers that he used simply to clap his hands to end the school breaks. However, we will let the final word on Bransford School come from Pat Bowers, who was there in the 1930s:

I remember they were very happy days... for the life of me, I cannot remember who the teachers were, other than O.G. Davies the Head, who was a firm but fair and compassionate man.

Leigh Sinton School

Joseph Hughes, who was born in 1906, was one of the oldest people we spoke to, and he started school in 1911:

I and all my brothers and sisters went to Leigh Sinton School at the age of five, and stayed there for all of our school lives. It was two miles to school, and we walked it every day. We took our own food to school, as there were no school dinners. We used to go to Leigh Hurst School for Sports Day but otherwise we didn't mix much.

The Headmaster was Fred Wareham and he lived in the schoolhouse. He was a good teacher – very kind and treated everyone the same. I remember he smoked a pipe in his breaks. There were three classes and three female teachers. The summer holidays were later, so that the children could go with their parents to help with the harvest and hop picking in September.

Gerald Jones was born just 11 years later than Joseph Hughes, in 1917, by which time pupils went to Somers Park at the age of 11 until they left school at 13. Some of his memories of school are not too happy:

I used to be carried shouting and screaming to school at the age of five... I got the cane six times one afternoon because I couldn't answer the history questions.

However, he was in the school choir and he played football. He also remembers the school's alternative use as a chapel:

The bigger room was divided by a curtain to make two classrooms in the week. On Sunday it was all cleared up to make it into a church and that was what the altar was for. It was a Church of England Chapel – like Bransford Chapel. More people attended this than went to Leigh Church, since there was no transport. The Sunday School was at 9a.m. run by Mrs Page, who used to farm at Moat Farm. Miss Gould used to play the organ, and there was a choir of twelve chaps. Mind, there were not so many in the summer time, but there was a good turn-out come Christmas. There was a Communion every other Sunday.

Bernard Atkinson, who was born in 1930, lived at Haywards Cross, just beyond Crowcroft. He recalled that:

By the time I was three years old, I cried to go to school with my brother who was two years and ten months older than me. My mother went to see the headmaster at Leigh Sinton School and he agreed to take me. My mother and father worked for Norburys, and I apparently used to leave home at about 7a.m. and walk to school about two and a half miles away, which is quite a way for a three year old. On the way we used to play hoop-la and look for birds nests. If there were any swedes in the fields we would get the knife out and eat one, and we would scrump apples. My mother would give me a sandwich or something for my lunch, but I had eaten that before I got to Leigh Sinton. Mr Wareham, the headmaster, obviously used to see that I had nothing to eat or drink (there was no school milk or anything like that then). He always had bread and butter and mustard for his lunch, and if he had any left over he used to give it to me. I hated mustard but I always used to eat it, because I was hungry and it was food.

We were all in one classroom up to about six years of age and again from six to 11 years and the headmaster would take us all. There would be a history lesson going on, drawing somewhere else, and writing somewhere else, because there were so many different ages. And if we did something wrong the cane would be used. It was a Church School and I was in the church choir. We had choir practices during the week and church services on a Sunday.

Eileen Kebby started at Leigh Sinton School in the mid 1920s, and remembers that the school was cold, despite it being heated by a round coke stove. There were ink pots and dip pens, but 'there were no exams like now. An Inspector walked from Newland Station.' Like everybody else she had sandwiches for dinner. For her the transition from a village school to Somers Park, at the age of 11, was not easy:

Leigh Sinton School, 1925–26. Left to right, back row: *Frank Goodyear, ?, Fred Sturmey, Gordon Clarke, Tom Smith, Les Piper, Stan Piper, Les Powell, Dennis Rowley, Bert Fitzer, Ernie Coley, Les Taylor, Reg Burston, Pete Smith, ?;* third row: *Alice Smith, Nora Burton, ?, Hilda Bruton, Nancy Taylor, Nora Smith, Violet Burston, Phil Tyler, Rose Phillips, Eva Jones, Syd Haggett, Bill Powell, Roland Taylor, Gerald Jones, Ron Bowkett, Eric Lawrence;* second row: *Eileen Weaver, Vera Kimber, Rene Powell, Doris Coley, Doris Nicklin, Win Smith, Floss Phillips, Doris Curtis, ?, Cyril Dyson, Jack Pritchard, ?, Ben James, Colin Clarke, Albert Rowley, George Oliver, Gordon Clarke;* front row: *Ewart Kimber, Norman Kimber, Doreen Jones, Frank Powell, Eileen Bowkett, Jim Haggitt, ?, Mr Fred Wareham (headmaster), Tom Nicklin, Arthur Burston, Gwen Taylor, Chris Taylor, Stella James, Alfred Haggitt, Bill Hoper, Vic Bartlett, Annie O'Ryan, Fred Powell.* (DOREEN ROWLEY)

Right: *A letter sent by King George VI to all schoolchildren after the Second World War.*
(PAT AND CECIL DEE)

8th June, 1946

I send this personal message to you and all other boys and girls at school. For you have shared in the hardships and dangers of a total war and you have shared no less in the triumph of the Allied Nations.

I know you will always feel proud to belong to a country which was capable of such supreme effort; proud, too, of parents and elder brothers and sisters who by their courage, endurance and enterprise brought victory. May these qualities be yours as you grow up and join in the common effort to establish among the nations of the world unity and peace.

George R.I

Left: *Four schoolboys, c.1931.* Left to right, back row: *Geoffrey Bartlett, Frank Powell;* front row: *Norman Kimber, Douglas Spencer.* (NORMAN KIMBER)

You felt funny 'cos it was such a big school – you felt lost. You stayed in one room and the teacher came to you. When you got used to it, it was alright. We used to have cookery, I liked that. But I think we learnt more after we left.

Finally, Norman Kimber (who was born in 1920) touches on some different points about the way the school was run:

Mr Wareham, the Headmaster, didn't care much for us locals, we were all 'turnip eaters!' It was rather amusing in our class, because the first five places were taken by 'turnip eaters'. When Mr Wareham left [in 1931] we had a lady teacher from Worcester, and she gave us the opportunity of sitting the Scholarship examination, and I was the first boy from the village to go to the Grammar School in Worcester.

As we have already seen, he was fortunate. It was not until after the Second World War, with the passing of the 1944 Education Act, that many others were to be able to go on to good secondary schools.

Postwar Developments & the New School

In an age when parents expect to know about their children's education, and every school has a Parent Teachers Association or something similar, it may be something of a shock to realise that there was no parental involvement in schools until well after the Second World War. Up until then, the only contact between parents and the school was over matters of health, discipline and the progress, or otherwise, of their children. In other words, teaching and the conduct of the school was left to the teachers and the managers, mediated by the requirements of the Education and Diocesan Authorities.

After the Second World War the whole education scene changed dramatically. In particular, the logs for Leigh Sinton show that it became much more outward looking. In the 1950s school visits began to feature prominently – theatres, cinemas, local factories, farms, zoos and beauty spots were amongst the destinations. In addition, visiting speakers – who were sometimes parents – covered a range of topics outside the normal curriculum. There was also an expansion in sporting activities – netball, football, rugby and athletics. In 1971 the school acquired a television set. The school world was opening up, and the 1970s and early 1980s seems to have been a stimulating time for both children and staff.

The log-book for Bransford School for 1980 onwards shows that the same trends had clearly occurred there too. There were swimming lessons at Lower Wick, netball and football matches, a modern-

dance group, and gymnastic equipment was installed. There were visits to theatres, castles and museums, and participation in music festivals and athletics matches. Activities within the community also featured strongly: singing harvest songs to the inhabitants of the sheltered housing at Bensfield, maypole dancing and holding a Summer Fayre. And the parents took part in a host of activities, from decorating the school to organising outings and fund-raising events.

The log also records that they, too, had building problems: in addition to the classrooms being old and 'temporary' there are frequent entries about the outside toilets freezing.

With the election of the Conservative Government under Margaret Thatcher in 1979 there came the start of very big changes in the education system. Words like 'accountable' and 'cost-effective' started to be used for education. 'Cost-effectiveness' meant, in practice, that the cost per pupil took precedence over other, non-quantifiable factors – for example, the social value to the community of having a local school. And being 'accountable' meant that ways had to be found to assess school performance, leading to the establishment of the National Curriculum and of school league tables.

The Bransford school log for 5 May 1982 records the first impact of these trends locally:

Meeting at Alfrick school with Mr Pryce [the County Education Officer] *to discuss school rationalisation – proposals to close Alfrick School and bus these children to Suckley. Leigh Sinton and Bransford to remain unchanged.*

But, with hindsight, this was wishful thinking: Leigh Sinton and Bransford Schools were not to remain unchanged. Both had quite low enrolments – about 50 for Bransford and 70 for Leigh Sinton – and 'magic numbers' like 100 for village schools were being talked of by the Government. (Interestingly, in the Leigh Parish Council minutes for 13 February 1939, Councillor F.P. Norbury objected to taking children to senior schools in Malvern, because of the cost, and suggested building a senior school on the Leigh Hurst site!)

There followed several years of discussions on all the factors involved before the final plan relating to the two schools was agreed. Not surprisingly, these discussions were occasionally difficult. For one thing, both schools were highly valued by their communities, so many people did not want to lose them. If improvements were needed – and we have seen that both schools were housed in outmoded premises – then let them be made to each school!

So, there was some parental opposition to any merger. In addition, the two sets of governors had their views. Understandably, in such an atmosphere, the teachers became anxious about their own job security. But this anxiety was never

Old Time Music Hall at Leigh Sinton School, 1984. Left to right, back row: Claire Knight, Cara Myers, Nicky Bradley, Russell Kirby, Ryan Harris, Chris Horne, Claire Wilks; front row: Catherine Bradley, Zena Edwards, James Farwell. (DAVID STEEL)

Leigh Sinton School Christmas Show, 1986, given at the Memorial Hall. All the pupils in the school had a part – an amazing achievement. The headmaster, David Steel, and his deputy, Judi Creed-Newton, wrote the lyrics and script, Mrs Bush accompanied the singing and dancing on the piano, and Mrs Pat Frost organised the costumes. Left to right, back row: Kathy Horne, Katy Herbert, ?, Suzanne Phillips, Claire Wilks, Zoe Tyler, Michael Quinton; front row: ?, Anjia Harris, Beth Harris, John Goode, ?, Anna Parsons, James Brazier, ?.
(PAULINE PHILLIPS)

Staff and pupils of Leigh Sinton School, summer 1985. Left to right, back row: Christopher Horne, Stephen Goode, Cara Myers, Katy Herbert, Sarah Spilsbury, Matthew Berning, Claire Knight, Richard Merrick, Simon Embley, Jason Lowndes; fourth row: Suzanne Phillips, Zoe Tyler, Joanne Steel, Rachel Edden, Stuart Cane, Caroline Clark, Nicholas Bradley, Neil Roder, Ryan Harris, Louise Smith, Michael Quinton, Claire Wilks; third row: Andrew

Spilsbury, Anjia Harris, Simon Clarke, Zena Edwards, Mrs Judi Creed-Newton, Mr David Steel, Mrs Janet Ashen, Mrs Pat Frost, Russell Wilby, Nicola Embley, Tracey Jay, Cathy Horne; second row: James Tolley, Robert Roder, Donna Smith, Catherine Bradley, Samantha Edwards, Beth Harris, S. (?) Goode, David Lowndes, Emma Tolley, James Brazier, Christopher Lyons, James Farwell, William Chaundy, Jessica Pollard; front row: Charlotte White, Adam Harris, S. Collins, N. Hoggins, A. Dyson, Robert Chaundy, Mark Lowndes, A. Longhurst, Nicola Tink, David Broom, J. Ballantine. (PAULINE PHILLIPS)

Left: *Lunch-time at the Leigh Hurst School. Mrs G. Portman (left) and Mrs Smith (right) in the background. The children include Margaret Chapman, Linda Drew, John Moore, Lennard Tyler, Geoffrey Portman, Barry James, Derek Portman, Mary Jones, Eric Garness, Martin Edwards, Janice Spiers, Elizabeth Bishop and Ivan Bullock.* (HAROLD PORTMAN)

Right: *Bransford School Spring Fayre, 1980. Parents' football team. Left to right: June Seymour, Christine Carmichael, Sue Barry, Angela Pulford, Pam Williams, Betty Douds, Jane Duncan, Maureen Costello, Judy Sherriff, Lyn Parsons, Sandra Rathmell, Terry Eden.* (SCHOOL PHOTO ALBUM)

Left: *Bransford School, winners of the Small School's Rounders trophy, 1981. Left to right, standing: Peter Gardner, Rachael Portman, Dean Crawford, Zoe Farrant, David Hopkins, Annette Garrett, Robert Costello, Jill Page; kneeling: Paula Crofts, Craig Barry, Willow Jeffries.* (SCHOOL PHOTO ALBUM)

Right: *Bransford School, visit to Bensfield, 1983. Left to right: Alan Gardner, Darren Gobie, Gorse Jeffries, Simon Cowell, Elizabeth Seymour, Mrs Fraser, Zena Edwards.* (SCHOOL PHOTO ALBUM)

reflected in the children's education: both schools continued to be lively places, with a full range of extra-curricular activities and involvement in the parishes. Indeed, in 1985 Leigh Sinton School celebrated its 100th anniversary as a National (i.e. State) School, and there were elaborate celebrations, at one of which the then oldest-surviving pupil, Miss Annie Ball, aged 91 – who was at the school around 1900 – cut a celebration cake. Miss Blanche Beaumont, who taught there for 33 years, was also a guest.

At one stage it was suggested that, if the two schools could not agree to merge voluntarily, then both would be closed, and the children sent to out-of-parish schools. In the end, a public meeting was called by the rector, John Herbert, at which a number of vital decisions were made. It was agreed that there should be a new school, which would be sited at Leigh Sinton, and that it should no longer be a Church school.

With these decisions made, the school staff and governors then worked to bring about a smooth amalgamation. For example, there were an increasing number of joint activities for the children. In addition, in November 1985 the two schools agreed to have a split ('federal') school for a period before the new building opened, the infants being taught at Bransford and the juniors at Leigh Sinton. The two heads (David Steel at Leigh Sinton and Thelma Spencer at Bransford) drew up detailed proposals for this, which were accepted and funded by the County Council.

The new school, called simply Leigh and Bransford Primary School, was built on a site purchased from Guinness Farms. It officially came into being in 1989, but still operating as a 'federal unit' on two sites. The new building was completed in 1990, and the physical merger of the two schools took place during the half-term break in the autumn 1990. David Steel was the head teacher and Sylvia Gorman his deputy, the two other teachers appointed being Judi Creed-Newton and Nina Bush.

Initially, the new school had four classrooms, together with a library and reception area. A fifth room, the Father Herbert Room, was built later. Between the classrooms are two activity areas, which house computer suites. There is a large hall, which is used for dinners, school events and as a gymnasium. In addition, there is a library, a reception area, and changing facilities, as well as toilets for disabled children. Outside is a large playing-field. All of this is a far cry from the facilities in either of the two schools which it replaced.

As in the two schools which it replaced, there continued to be a wide range of curricular and extra-curricular activities. There are currently clubs for football, netball, tag rugby, dance, drama, recorders, computing and art. In addition, peripatetic music teachers take groups of children for brass, flute and clarinet lessons, and each child can go on two residential visits whilst at the school, one largely historical and the other involving outdoor activities.

David Steel unfortunately had to retire through ill health in 1997, and Peter Gill is his successor. There are now two full-time teachers and four part-time ones, together with four teaching assistants.

Bransford School, Edwardian Day at Hartlebury Museum, 1986.
Left to right, back row: *Simon Williams, Mrs Gorman, Shelley Jones, Samantha Ching, Louise Randall, Emma Carter, Laura Williams, Gillian Stodart, Alastair Douds;* front row: *Andrew Robinson, Alex Moores, Jonathan Davis, Jamie Gill, Sam Jones, Antony Kordas, Matthew Sherriff.*
(SCHOOL PHOTO ALBUM)

Right: *Leigh and Bransford School, 1990–91. Comic Relief Day. Judi Creed-Newton, Laura Marriott with Andrew Spilsbury sitting.* (DAVID STEEL)

Below: *Working on the foundations of the new Leigh and Bransford School, 1989. At the back: Judi Creed-Newton, David Steel; in front: Kate Gloster, Lauren Saunder, Anthony Kordas, Emma Tolley, Michael Tink, Daniel Chesham.* (DAVID STEEL)

Below, right: *Leigh and Bransford School, Mixed Rugby Team, 1993–94. Left to right, back row: Andrew Tyler, Daniel Chesham, James Bush, Liam Kirlleen, Henry Burnett; front row: Susan Hunter, Beth King, Emma Tolley, Lizzie Dexter.* (DAVID STEEL)

Leigh and Bransford Primary School, Christmas play, 2001. Left to right, back row: Harry Wenden, Cait Duggan, Aaran Lawrence, Harriet Tope, Tom Ridley; in front: Tom Vernalls as the dog. (PETER GILL)

Leigh and Bransford Primary School, 2002. (PETER GILL)

Sports Day, 2002. Left to right: *Richard Burton, Fynn Page, Oliver Harcombe, Nicholas Snowdon.* (PETER GILL)

Chapter Four

CHURCHES & CHAPELS

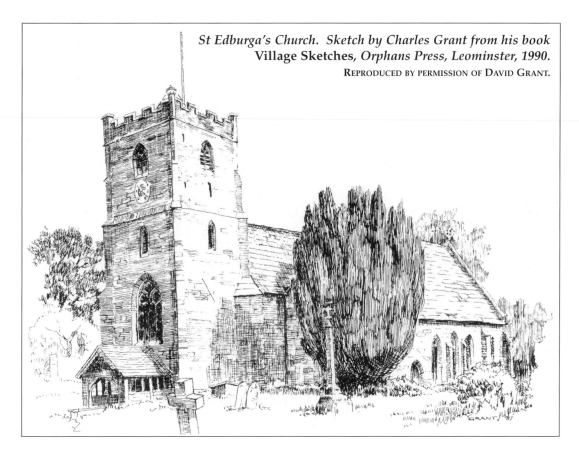

St Edburga's Church. Sketch by Charles Grant from his book
Village Sketches, *Orphans Press, Leominster, 1990.*
REPRODUCED BY PERMISSION OF DAVID GRANT.

Introduction

From the mid 1800s to the 1970s, there were five churches or chapels in the parish. St Edburga's was the Anglican Parish Church, and it had associated chapels at Bransford and Leigh Sinton. Then there were two Nonconformist chapels – a Wesleyan one at Smith End Green, and the Countess of Huntingdon's Connexion, at Leigh Sinton. Today, only St Edburga's and Bransford Chapel are still used for worship.

The Parish Church of St Edburga, Leigh

The Building

Edburga was a Saxon princess, the granddaughter of Alfred the Great, who remained as a nun in Winchester Abbey where she was educated,

renowned for her humility and gentleness. After she died, in AD960, her relics were brought to Pershore Abbey. The manor of Leigh was at that time under the authority of the Abbots of Pershore, so Leigh Parish Church was dedicated to her. Her Feast Day is 15 June.

The church is Grade I listed, which highlights its architectural importance. Started by the Normans, around AD1100, it stands on the same site as an earlier monastery. Initially it had only a nave and chancel. Towards the end of the twelfth century a narrow south aisle was added, and the chancel arch altered. In the thirteenth century the south aisle and transept were enlarged to their present size. In addition, the chancel was enlarged and lancet windows were inserted in the north and south walls. In the fourteenth century the tower was built, buttresses were added to the nave, and new windows installed in the north wall of the nave. A century later a carved wooden screen was installed in the south aisle.

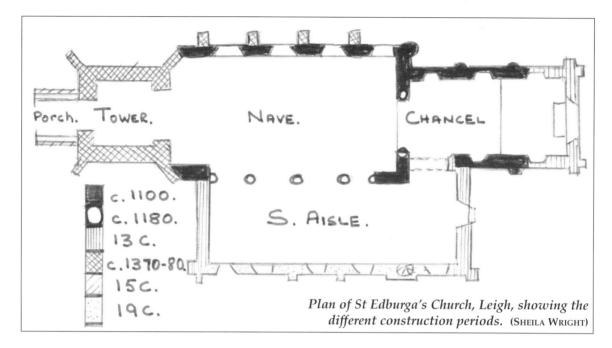

Plan of St Edburga's Church, Leigh, showing the different construction periods. (SHEILA WRIGHT)

Within the plan:
Porch. TOWER. NAVE. CHANCEL
S. AISLE.
c.1100.
c.1180.
13 C.
c.1370-80.
15 C.
19 C.

There were extensive restorations in 1855, when a gallery was removed from the east end of the nave, the south wall of the aisle was rebuilt and plaster was removed from the nave and south aisle walls. A bell-ringing chamber was constructed in the tower, and a new east window and door inserted in the chancel.

These are the bare bones of the church's history. To appreciate it fully we have to visit it. Walking through the front gate and down the path, on the right is a stone preaching cross, only the base of which is original. In country villages a stone cross often preceded the building of the church, and remained in use as an outdoor pulpit for preaching to those infected by plague and cholera. (There was a cholera epidemic at Upton as recently as 1832.) Alms for the poor were also left there.

In front of us are the tower and porch. The porch is believed to have come from Chirkenhill, which, with Leigh, was one of the three chapels which existed in pre-Norman times. Nothing is known about the third, at Kemenhall. Above the porch there is a large stained-glass window, and above that a clock, which strikes the hour. Both were given by parishioners in 1858 in memory of Revd Henry Somers Cocks, the rector of Leigh for 29 years.

Going through the massive doors with their marvellous old lock, supplied by Mr Chubb from Leigh Lodge, we are in a small lobby at the base of the tower. On the right is the entrance to the tower. Inside the tower, a narrow spiral staircase goes right to the top. The chamber where the bells are rung leads off first, then the room housing the clock, and finally the bell chamber. At the top, a door opens on to the roof, with wonderful views over the surrounding countryside – hence its strategic value in the Civil Wars.

An inventory made during the reign of Edward VI (1547–53) said that Leigh church possessed six bells

'five grete bells in the styple, with a Sanctus bell.' None of these exist today. New bells are installed for a number of reasons – for example, because they crack, or are of poor tone. Usually bells have an inscription – often the name of the bell-founder and the names of the people responsible for having it made. Of the present ones, all except the fifth were made by Rudhall of Gloucester. Listed from the lightest (treble) to the heaviest (tenor), the inscriptions are:

1. Richard Harris and James Jones Ch.Wardens T.R.1766
2. God Save Church and Queen A.R. (Abraham Rudhall) 1711
3. 1711 A.R.
4. Prosperity to Leigh. Amen A.R.1711
5. G.B.Essex. W.Trinder Ch.Wardens Cast by John Warner & Sons London 1863
6. Rev.H.B.Domville Rector Benj.Gardner & Benj.Gabb Ch.Wardens 1819 J.Rudhall.

These bells were last refitted and rehung in 1904.

The bells of St Edburga's, Leigh, 'up' and ready to ring. (MALCOLM SCOTT)

Bell-ringing

For many people, bells and country churches go hand in hand. Historically bells were rung much more than they are now, not only to celebrate marriages and funerals, but also to alert people to important events. But, because they are normally rung out of sight, few people know what is involved.

People who ring bells call themselves 'ringers' – the term 'campanologist' is only normally used in crosswords and Scrabble! At rest, the bells hang mouth down. For ringing they have to be mouth up, so at the start and end of ringing sessions they have to be 'raised' or 'lowered'. If not well done, this can be very jangly! Once up, the simplest way they are rung is in order of their musical pitch – highest (treble) to lowest (tenor). This is called 'ringing in rounds' and ringing always starts in this way.

One way of changing the order is through the conductor (the person leading the ringing) calling out a new order. So, instead of ringing 1-2-3-4-5-6, they might ring 1-3-2-5-4-6, this new pattern continuing for a time. Outside the Westcountry, where this change ringing is an art form, ringing call changes is not as widely practised as ringing 'methods'. In 'methods', the order of the bells changes each round. There are hundreds of different methods, although most towers only ring a handful. Each ringer has to know how the order changes each round. Ringing methods is both a challenge and – when it goes well(!) – a pleasure. People have to work well together, and the social aspect of bell-ringing is important. Visiting ringers who drop in unexpectedly always get a warm welcome, and are invited to choose which bell, and even which method, they would like to ring.

Left: *The bell-ringers of St Edburga's, 2000 (and where they come from).* Left to right: *Terry Ellard (Alfrick Pound), Jill Ellard (Alfrick Pound), Chris Phillips (Tower Captain) (Leigh Sinton), John Robinson (Leigh Hurst), Malcolm Scott (Leigh), June Robinson (Leigh Hurst), Derek Bradley (Alfrick Pound), Alan Soper (Alfrick).*
(MALCOLM SCOTT)

Right: *In 1966 the spindle of the fifth bell broke, and it smashed the bell wheel. Gerald Jones, the wheelwright in Leigh Sinton, pieced the 40 fragments together and then made a replacement, whilst John Wilesmith, from Bransford, made a new spindle. The picture shows Ken Jones helping to re-install the bell.*
(GRAHAM JONES)

Standing just inside the entrance, the quietness is striking. All one can hear is the gentle ticking of the clock and, in summer, the sound of swifts calling. Looking back, one sees the memorial window in the tower. Going through into the nave of the church, its size is impressive, as is the contrast between the red sandstone walls and the warm grey of the Cradley stone, used for the massive pillars which separate the nave from the right-hand south aisle.

Immediately on the right is a framed list of the 65 incumbents who served from 1274 to 2001, starting with Ricardus de Mucegross. The list includes Treadway Nash, who wrote a well-known, but somewhat imaginative, history of Worcestershire. He served from 1792 to 1811, although whether he was ever resident in Leigh is open to doubt. Looking down to the right is the font, with a twelfth-century Norman bowl resting on a later stem and base.

Walking down the central aisle, over worn red and black tiles, the elaborately carved wooden war memorial is halfway down on the left. It used to be behind the altar. Further down on the left are two large stained-glass windows. One is dated 1861, and the other, in memory of Henry Richard Norbury of Sherridge, is from 1866. We now go up a small step, onto the tiled dais which was constructed in 2000, to accommodate a nave altar, or for use as a stage for concerts and plays. Soaring above us is the large, twelfth-century transitional arch between the chancel and the nave. Just to the right, the wall is pierced by a hagioscope, or 'squint', a device to allow lay persons – who were not allowed beyond the chancel arch – to observe the blessing of the Sacrament. Beyond this to the right is a second twelfth-century arch, looking into the Lady Chapel in the south aisle.

Walking towards the altar, on the left is the monument to Walter Devereux, and on either side are small Victorian stained-glass windows, three on the left and two on the right. Above the monument is a memorial to Essex Devereux commemorating his death by drowning in 1639. Beyond that is the Jacobean altar rail, and above the altar is an enormous stained-glass window in memory of the Day family, who lived in the parish in the 1800s. This is much softer in colouring than the other Victorian windows, which are in rich reds and blues, and it gives off a gentle, warm light. Standing at the altar rail, on the right is the tomb of Edmund Colles, who died in 1606 at the age of 76 – a good age in those days. On the left, his son William, who died in 1615, lies with his wife Mary, their 12 children arranged along the base.

Walking back a little and going left, we enter the south, or 'Bransford', aisle, which has been extensively rebuilt. At one end is the Lady Chapel, divided from the rest by an elaborate fifteenth-century wooden screen, decorated with Tudor roses and an inscription from the Gospel of St John. It is thought to have connected with a gallery which originally spanned the east end of the nave, and was restored and partially repainted by Revd Edward Bradley, the curate of Leigh 1855–57.

On the back wall of the Lady Chapel – between two narrow windows with representations of Matthew, Mark, Luke and John – stands a figure of Christ with his hand raised in blessing. It was originally in a niche on the outer, north wall of the nave, where it somehow escaped damage in Cromwellian times. Underneath the original niche housing this statue was a 'penitent's door'. Now blocked in, it was used by people who came for penitential sacrament. In 1970 the figure was removed from its outside niche and examined by archaeologists from the Victoria and Albert Museum. They were impressed by its quality, and dated it around 1100. As Sheila Wright observed, 'It is a rare treasure which still radiates an aura of sanctity and peace.'

At the opposite end of the south aisle is a two-manual Nicholson organ, originally from St Nicholas, Worcester. Then, on the long south wall of the aisle, is a pair of small stained-glass windows. One is dedicated to Thomas Norbury, who died in 1866, and who built Sherridge. One of the other two windows has small fragments of medieval glass at the top.

Leigh Church over the Years

Writing in 1848, John Noake describes a service:

There were many latecomers to the church of Leigh on the morning of my visit; some did not arrive till after the lessons had been read; and as the rustics passed to their seats, the rattling of their hobnails against the

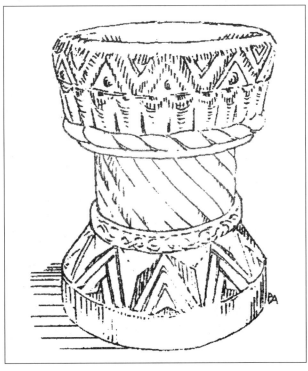

The font in St Edburga's, Leigh. (SHEILA WRIGHT)

Left: *Harold Portman as a choirboy, late 1920s.* (Harold Portman)

Below: *Reception for the wedding of Maude Agnes Pritchard and Hector Walter Banner at Smith End Green. Left to right, back row: Mrs Hill, Mrs Rolph, Doreen Rowley, Gladys Jones, Gerald Jones, Arch Ball, Victor Banner, Fred Phillips, Susan ?, Arthur Rolph, Mrs Maund (Morn?), Bett Morris; centre: Jim Thomas, Eva Thomas, Gwen Ball, Ron Morris, Hector Banner (groom), Maude Pritchard (bride), ? behind the bride, Mrs Anna ?, Myra ?, Granny Phillips, Billy Williams, John Hill, Amy Bowkett (sideways), Elsie Davies; front row: Walter Banner holding Bernice Rolph, Mrs Banner holding baby, Coral Ball, Lil Pritchard, John Wenden, Winnie Pritchard, Mrs Pritchard, Mr Pritchard; sitting: Eileen Hill, Eileen Bowcott, Mary Vine.* (Connie Tohtz)

Above: *The presentation to the rector, A.M. Moreton-Jackson, by Edward Jay, on the occasion of his leaving after 28 years in the parish, May 1975.* (Mike Grundy/Berrows)

pavement was anything but a desirable accompaniment to the congregational act of devotion. The singing was entirely confined to the school children, who were ranged along the aisle, led on by a master and mistress; they were unassisted by any instrument, but I understand that an organ has subsequently been erected here.

Exactly 100 years later, in June 1948, 400 people packed the church for the annual patronal festival, at which Christopher Norbury presented a new polished brass 'electric candelabra' in memory of his father, Frederick Paget Norbury. The ringers marked this occasion by ringing a 'peal' of the method called Grandsire Doubles – 5,040 changes without stopping, taking nearly three hours. The bells were silenced during the war, only to be rung as a warning if enemy paratroopers were sighted, or if there was a full-scale German invasion. This, combined with the fact that the Leigh bells are not the easiest to ring, meant that this was the first peal rung for 25 years.

We will see that attendance at the two Nonconformist chapels fell to a level where they had to close in the 1970s. Falling attendance has also affected the Anglican churches. However, even back in the 1960s it seems that the rector felt that people needed 'persuasion' to attend. June Robinson, who lives opposite Leigh Hurst School, says: 'Back then, the vicar, whose name was Revd Moreton-Jackson, came knocking at the door if you didn't go to church regularly.' The Revd Moreton-Jackson retired in 1975, after 28 years in the parish. But there were 125 people at his farewell party at Leigh Memorial Hall, so he cannot have been too hard on his parishioners!

Many people remember going to church as children. The Weaver sisters recall that:

On Sundays we had to go to church in the morning, and to Sunday School in the afternoon. Then in the evening we went for a walk with our parents along the railway line towards Hayley Dingle, there being no trains on a Sunday.

Gwen Hawkins was a child in the 1930s. She has some vivid memories of that era:

We all went to church on Sundays, dressed in our best clothes, although it was quite a long way to walk from Leigh Hurst to the church at Leigh, and very dark when one had been to Evensong in Winter. We also attended confirmation classes at the Rectory, and I remember how proud all the girls were of their white dresses and veils which we wore to the service of Confirmation.

However, confirmations did not always go smoothly, as Janet Long recalls:

One year when the Bishop came (for confirmation, I think) the church was gradually filled with fumes. The rooks had built a nest in the flue, and more and more people had to go outside. We were all lying in the churchyard, more people outside than in.

In the 1920s and '30s, the headmaster of Leigh Hurst School, O.G. Davies, was also the organist and choirmaster. Then the choir was all male – boys sang the treble parts – and he was able to select his choir members from his pupils. But there did not need to be much coersion. Harold Portman was a choir member from the age of six until 18 – well after he left school: 'It was something to do, and we got paid a halfpenny per service if I remember rightly, so we used to pick up a few shillings every six months.' O.G. Davies used to insist that the choir sang out loudly. He used to put the choir at one end of the church and go and listen at the other: 'If I can't hear you, how can the congregation?' he used to say.

In 2000 the church celebrated the 900th anniversary of its foundation with a range of activities, including a quite spectacular Flower Festival, organised by Sandy Rathmell and attended by over 1,500 people. There were associated activities in the tithe barn, and it was a memorable occasion. The church has, of course, always been an important centre for social activities in the parish, the annual garden fête and the harvest supper being two important events. The church is also used as a venue for concerts, having extremely good acoustics.

St Edburga's choir, late 1920s. Left to right, back row: *Reg Alford, George Pass, George Pass senr, Owen George Davies, Revd A.M. Manley, Fred James, Bill Band (sexton), Frank Pass, Fred Mason, Fred Banner;* front row: *Lionel James (standing), Leslie Hill, Sid Moore, Harry Banner, Harold Portman, Harold Alford, George Rowberry, Ernie Gale, Gilbert Hill, Horace King, Bill Moore.*
(HAROLD PORTMAN AND HARRY BANNER)

Left: *Choir of St Edburga's, Leigh, 2000 (members and where they come from).* Left to right, back row: *Jeremy Morfey (Leigh), John Colley, churchwarden (Sandlin), Michael Westall (rector), David Armstrong, choirmaster and churchwarden (Lulsley), David Chaundy (Sandlin), Tim Watson (Worcester);* centre: *Jean Clift (Lulsley), Sheila Wright (Leigh), Jean Colley (Sandlin), Angela Lloyd (Sandlin);* front row: *Ellen Gwynne (Leigh Sinton), Susan Jones, organist (Bransford), Della Colley (Sandlin), Shirley Tasker (Bransford).* (MALCOLM SCOTT)

Right: *The church fête at the Old Rectory, Bransford, 1961. Mary Gale presenting a bouquet to Mrs Harding (from Alfrick), who opened the show.*
(GILL AND MARY GALE)

Below: *Harvest supper entertainment at the Memorial Hall, 1965.*
(ELSIE PORTMAN/BERROWS)

Below: *Serving maids at Leigh Church Fête, 1930. Third from right: Phyllis Thomas (née Tyler); far right: Vera Raybould (née Kimber).*
(NORMAN KIMBER)

Below, left: *A flower arrangement on the theme of 'Music' at the 900th anniversary Flower Festival, St Edburga's Church, Leigh.*
(MALCOLM SCOTT)

Above: *Harvest Festival at the Somers Arms, mid to late 1950s. Left to right: Frank Symonds, Ernie Clay, ? Goodyear, Revd Moreton-Jackson, Dennis Clewer, Shirley King, ?, Freda Young, ?, Harold Yarnold, Mrs Florence King* (the rest have not been identified). (SUSAN JONES)

Top right: *Auction at the Leigh Church Fête, 2001. The auctioneer is Andrew Grant, the booker is Jean Colley, holding the item being auctioned is Sheila Wright, whilst Peter Norbury is helping in the tent.* (MALCOLM SCOTT)

Right: *Church Fête accounts in the Leigh and Bransford Quarterly Report, 1919.* (PETER NORBURY)

Garden Fete.

This function was, by the kind invitation of **Mr. and Mrs. Norbury,** held at Sherridge on July 10th. Mrs. Hugo Martin, who had been asked to open it was unhappily unable to be present. The weather was perfect and the attendance good, especially in the evening. Altogether the fête was a great success, giving much pleasure and substantial pecuniary results. The proceeds (including a gift of £5 from Capt. and Mrs. Essex, who were unable to be present) amount to £121. 2s. 0d. A short statement of receipts and expenses is given below.

	£	s.	d.
Work Stall (Mrs. H. Busk and others)	18	4	3
Provision Stall (Mrs. Rimell and others)	15	10	6½
China Stall (Mrs. Featherstonhaugh)	2	7	6
Flower Stall (Mrs. Norbury)	3	6	0
Hardware Stall (Miss Foster)	2	13	4½
Teas, Ices, &c. (Mrs. Manley, and Mrs. Phillips and 12 others)	25	18	6
Whist Drive (Mrs. Pope and Mrs. Clift)	7	14	0
Concerts (Mrs. Bomford)	5	11	6
Donations (Mrs. Hugo Martin £2, Capt. and Mrs. Essex £5)	7	0	0
Gate Money (Messrs. Trupp and Yarnold)	5	16	9
Dancing (Messrs. O. Davis and W. Band)	2	1	9
Mystery Tent and Golliwogs (Mrs. Farmer)	4	10	6
Rifle Range (Mr. W. Tomkins)		19	2
Buried Cities (Mr. F. Wareham)		3	6
War Trophies (Sergt. C. Banks)		12	1
Bean Bags and Skittles (Mr. B. Morris)	3	5	9½
Bran Tubs (Master C. and Misses R. and M. Norbury)	1	0	0
Clock Golf (Capt. R. Coventry)		8	0
Croquet Ladder (Rev. T. V. Evans)		17	3
Bowling (Mr. A. Robinson)	4	4	7
Fowl Weight (Miss Davis)		11	9
Cake Making (Miss Veel)	1	4	6
Candle Lighting (Misses Jones)	1	4	2
Advertisements (Miss Gould)		8	7
Fortune Telling (Mrs. Best)	2	0	0
Cheese Weight (Miss Williams)		18	6
Buttonholes (Miss Turley)	2	2	6
Raffles	1	16	6
Total	£122	11	6½

	£	s.	d.
Expenses		1	9	6
Balance (for Assistant Clergy Fund)	121	2	0½

Bransford Chapel

Bransford has always been a chapelry of St Edburga, Leigh, and never a separate Parish Church. In the Domesday Book it says: 'Bradnesford burying its dead at Legh but maintaining its own poor.' This situation has since been reversed – Leigh churchyard was closed for burial in 1910, and a cemetery for both churches was established at Bransford.

Bransford Chapel before restoration, 1956. (WRO/BERROWS)

In contrast to Leigh church, which is large and imposing, Bransford Chapel is petite and unassuming. But both are architectural gems. In its semi-isolated position about a mile off the main road, surrounded by fields and lit only by candles, the chapel is a welcome reminder of a less frenetic age.

Made mostly from grey stone, some of it from Cradley, the chapel was possibly founded in the eleventh century, in Saxon times. The walls show evidence of work from around then through to the thirteenth or fourteenth century. On the south wall there are traces of a mass dial carved on the wall. At the west end is a wooden bell tower housing three bells. One dates from 1300, and bells of this age are rare. The other two are more recent, the older one dating from 1621. This was made locally, for which the Churchwardens 'payd for castinge of one of our bells the xv the day of July £3.0s.4d.' The inscription on it reads 'SANCTA TRINITAS UNUS DEUS MISERERE NOSTRI' (Holy Trinity, one God be merciful to us). The third bell was cast in 1717 by Abraham Rudhall of Gloucester, and is inscribed 'PROSPERITY TO THIS CHURCH AND PLACE.' The bells can only be tolled, not rung in the way they are at Leigh.

Going through the Elizabethan or Jacobean porch into the church, one is struck by its elegance and simplicity. Having no electricity, the candle holders immediately make it very distinctive. There is no ceiling below the rafters, adding to the feeling of age. The roof itself – on which the original carpenter's marks can be seen – is believed to have been sponsored either by Wulstan de Bransford, or by the de Bracy family from Braces Leigh. Wulstan de Bransford, who was the Prior, and later Bishop, of Worcester in the 1300s, built the first bridge over the Teme at Bransford.

Looking down the church, the Jacobean altar rail and altar are illuminated by a large, very simple, plain-glass window. This was installed by a churchwarden, John Winnall of Braces Leigh, in 1812, when the east end was rebuilt, following complaints that the church was too dark. At the other end of the church is a handsome looking, single-manual pipe organ. Made by the Positif Organ Company, London, and dating from about 1910, it is an extremely good example of its kind. Installed in 1993, it uses an electric blower, a portable generator being housed in the churchyard when the organ is used. The wall between the body of the church and the bell tower is wattle and daub, some of which has been exposed inside the tower.

The chapel was extensively renovated in 1957, when John Tooby was the churchwarden, and the bell tower was rebuilt. During the course of the work (which cost £4,400) traces of paintings and decoration were found on all except the restored east wall, dating from post-Restoration back to medieval times. However, the additional cost of restoring these (£1,000) was considered too much at the time. They were therefore covered with a special plaster for later generations to remove if they wished, a small section – though not the best – being left uncovered by the altar.

Above: *Rebuilding the Bransford Chapel bell tower in 1956. The oak timbers for this came from Norbury's estate. The figure on the left of the scaffolding is believed to be Gerald Jones.* (BRANSFORD CHAPEL/BERROWS)

Left: *Bransford Chapel just before a service, spring 2002.* (MALCOLM SCOTT)

Right: *A view of the bell frame at Bransford Chapel, showing the half wheels for the second and third bells, which date from 1717 and 1621 respectively. The half wheel only allows the bells to be tolled, not rung in the traditional manner.* (BRANSFORD CHAPEL)

Children's Christmas party, c.1955, at the Countess of Huntingdon's Connexion. Mr Lance, who ran the Methodist Chapel Sunday School, is on the left of the tree. **Other children and adults include:** *Martin and Andrew Dyson, Phillip Ralph, Maureen Haggitt, Tuddy Parkinson, Dianne Monk, R. and S. Tandy, Jane Bartlett, David Twigg, Linda Haggitt, Carol Lewis, Dorothy Symonds, Alice Dee, Maureen Ralph, Emmie Schmidt, Mrs Roberts, Mrs Rowberry, Vernon Davis, Dorothy Clay, Wendy Webley, Anne Green, Freddie and John Davies, Keith Jones, Martin Cane, Gwen Cane, Gert Tyler.* (GEOFF BARTLETT)

Countess of Huntingdon's Connexion Chapel on Malvern Road, Leigh Sinton, 1956.
(WRO/BERROWS)

Countess of Huntingdon's Connexion Chapel, Leigh Sinton

Built in 1831, the chapel on the Malvern Road, Leigh Sinton, which formed part of the Countess of Huntingdon's Connexion was one of several built locally. There are others at Cradley and Suckley, but the best known, and largest, is in Worcester. The Leigh Sinton chapel is a typical nineteenth-century chapel building, with a gallery. Unusually, it also had a graveyard and, unlike the Wesleyan chapel at Smith End Green, it had a resident pastor, who lived in the adjacent Manse. The chapel was managed by the Malvern Village Chapels Committee. In 1931, its centenary, 55 children attended Sunday School, and there were seven teachers. It also ran a Sisterhood, which had about 50 members in the 1930s.

In the 1920s and '30s church attendance was very important for many families. Children, in particular, often had to attend more than once. Indeed, far from being a day of rest, Sundays seem to have been very busy! For example, on Sunday mornings, Eileen Kebby, Doreen Rowley and Connie Tohtz ('the gang' as Eileen Kebby called them) used to go together to the chapel before breakfast, and then to (Anglican) Sunday School at Leigh Sinton School. In the afternoon they went to chapel again, and then to the evening service at the school.

Much later on, in the early 1950s, Janet Long – who lived at Malvern House, Leigh Sinton – also had to go to Sunday School twice, but by then numbers attending the chapel were very low.

Sunday school was held at Leigh Sinton School in the morning and in the afternoon Mr Ross from the Manse held another class at the chapel. He and his wife had been missionaries, and he showed us slides of Africa. Sometimes I was the only one there and so was invited to stay for tea, usually boiled eggs and soldiers.

As well as holding a Sunday School, there were other activities for both adults and children. Eileen Kebby remembers that:

Mum went to Chapel a lot. On a Wednesday afternoon the women used to meet, calling themselves the Sisterhood. They used to go on little outings to Weston and the Old Hills. We used to have a tea party – a piece of bread, jam and cake. We thought that was great.

Coral and Des Clarke recall that in the 1940s a Mr and Mrs Grimes were resident in the Manse, and organised its activities including outings.

The chapel closed in the 1970s, and is now a private dwelling.

Leigh Sinton School Chapel

Leigh Sinton School was used as an Anglican chapel from the time it was built, in 1867. The chancel and altar were at the far end of the large schoolroom, and were curtained off on school-days. On Friday evenings the caretaker used to open up the curtains and prepare the seats. When Gerald Jones first went to school, in the early 1920s, the school desks were used for seating, but later special chairs were bought, school benches being used around the edge. The chairs were stored in the chancel, with a harmonium and a carved wooden lectern. Heating was provided by the fairly inadequate school stove, and it was often very cold. After the service the children in the choir would put away the chairs, and get the place ready for school.

The rector alternated with a lay preacher (Mr Dark in the 1920s and '30s) in running the evening services, and there was communion every fortnight. Sunday School was held every week, run in the 1920s by Mrs Page, from Moat House Farm, who was also the organist. The choir of 12 or so boys and girls from the school was run by a Miss Gould, and practised weekly. Unlike the children in Leigh choir, they were not paid, but at Christmas a special party was given for them.

It is nearly two miles to Leigh church from Leigh Sinton, even going across the fields, and it 'seemed even further on a cold, dark winter's evening.' So most Anglicans in Leigh Sinton went to the school chapel – about 30–40 going regularly in the 1920s and '30s, summoned by the school bell. The number attending was about as many as used to go regularly to Leigh church at that time. However, for special services – for example at Easter, Harvest Festival and Armistice Day – there was a combined service at Leigh church, special buses being run to take people there.

The school ceased being used as a chapel in 1980, before the school itself closed.

Weslyan Chapel, Smith End Green

This chapel was built on land leased by Earl Somers in 1839 to John Burrow, a wheelwright and carpenter from Leigh. He, in turn, leased it for 99 years 'for erecting and building a chapel... for the use of the Methodists.' A conveyance relating to the chapel dated 1866 has the seal and signature of Earl Somers and Revd Henry Kirkland, the superintendent Methodist preacher from Worcester. Later, an extra 'schoolroom' was added for Sunday-School classes. The title 'Wesleyan' was dropped in 1933, when the Wesleyan and other Methodist groups formed the Methodist Church.

The trustees were both local and from Droitwich and Worcester. The first ones included a builder, tailor, leather cutter, timber dealer and glover. The 1877 list includes John Burrow (now an implement maker) and two other local men; William Harvey, a stationmaster, and John Haywood, a shoemaker, both from Bransford. The trustees from Worcester and Droitwich are listed as being a tailor, a brush manufacturer and a commercial traveller.

Over 40 years later, in 1921, John Haywood is still listed as being a trustee, and all the others (a grocer, printer, draper, railway foreman, laundry proprietor and three farmers) are said to live in Worcester. By 1954 there are fewer trustees, most living in Worcester, but there is one local man, Evan Carol

Altar of the chapel in the old Leigh Sinton School, taken in 1893.
(Peter Norbury)

A Sunday School group at Leigh Sinton School, around 1938.
Left to right, back row: *Cecil Dee, Roy Bartlett, Cynthia Adams, Miriam Grubb;* centre: *George Senter, Eunis Portman, Vera Adams, Coral Clarke;* front row: *Jimmy Dee, David Adams, Eric Bartlett.* (Coral Clarke)

Above: *Smith End Green Wesleyan Chapel, 1914–18. The notice on the wall reads 'WESLEYAN CHAPEL. SPECIAL SERVICES DURING WAR. NEXT SUNDAY AT 6.30p.m. COME.'* (PAT BOWERS)

Above: *The Methodist Chapel at Smith End Green, 2002. A pen-and-wash sketch by Peter Gwinnett.* (PETER GWINNETT)

Right: *Members of an outing of the Smith End Green Chapel to Stratford, 19 July 1930. Left to right, back row: A. Hammond, A. Pepper, C. Bradburn, W. Bradburn; middle row: Miss Shaw, Mrs F. Burrow, Mrs J. Dance, Mrs F. Bowers, Mrs A. Hammond, Mrs A. Pepper; front row: Miss D. Morris, Gordon Dance, Miss E. Phillips.*
(PAT BOWERS)

Some members of the Methodist Chapel, Smith End Green at Evesham, c.1943. Left to right, back row: Carol Vine, Mrs Hammond (from Worcester), Mrs Gertie Bower, Mr Bradburn, Mrs Edith Vine (Eric Vine's grandmother); front row: Two gypsy boys who used to attend and Eric Vine. (ERIC VINE)

An Evangelist used to come and hold services in a big marquee, and later in a large wooden shed. The picture (taken in 1937) is of people attending one of the parties which he held, standing outside the chapel on the Malvern Road. In the picture are Connie Tohtz, Doreen Rowley, Coral Clarke and Mavis Alford. (CONNIE TOHTZ)

Vine, who is listed as being 'a bricklayer of Smithsend Green, Leigh Sinton.' In 1930, the widow of a descendant of John Burrow, Lizzie Annie Burrow, sold the land and the chapel to the trustees.

The services were run both by visiting preachers from Worcester and by local lay preachers. In addition to a regular Sunday service, there was a quarterly Holy Communion. In addition, there was an annual Good Friday rally, attended by members of all the chapels in Worcester. As John Guise said, 'The food was plentiful and the singing, as befits Methodists, was hearty!'

From the 1920s to the '50s a number of non-parishioners were active in the chapel's affairs, including Mr A.J. Pepper, a builder from Worcester, but there were also local people, including Mr and Mrs Carol Vine, Mrs Bowers, and Jim and Eileen Purvis. Eric Vine, whose father was a trustee, used to go to the chapel regularly and gives an idea of the activities there:

There was only one service and a Sunday School. There was no minister. The preachers were organised by Mr Bradburn from Worcester. The chapel combined with St Edburga's for the Remembrance Sunday service. A bus went round to pick up the people, and the church was full to overflowing.

Pat Bowers' mother used to help in the chapel in the 1930s:

Mom was very Chapel, a Wesleyan. On Thursdays after school, I had to go with her to the Chapel at Smith End Green, where I would help to dust and clean, and lay out the hymn and prayer books. On Sundays, we went to Sunday School in the afternoon, had tea at The Firs, just across the road (with my Uncle Bill Tomkins) and then back for the evening service, after which I would put all the books away.

However, there were never many members. In the nineteenth century there were only about 30, and by the 1970s membership had dropped so much that, in 1978, the chapel was sold as a private dwelling.

Epilogue

We have seen that, from five churches and chapels 30 years or so ago, there are now only two, both Anglican. People remember that, in the 1920s and '30s, 30 or 40 people used to attend Leigh Sinton School Chapel regularly, with a similar number at St Edburga's – a total of 60 to 80. Now only around 20 attend regularly at Leigh, and a handful at Bransford. This is, of course, a national trend.

Changes in the Church Commissioner's financial fortunes – for example, the need to fund the pensions of a growing number of retired and long-lived clergy – has meant that parishes have to fund a greater proportion of their activities. These two trends combine to place an enormous responsibility on the local congregation. In addition to maintaining Christianity as an important aspect of parish life, they also have to maintain two buildings which are part of our national and local architectural heritage. It is in all our interests – churchgoers and non-churchgoers alike – that we support the church in remaining a focal point in village life.

Top left: *The licensing of Andrew Bullock as the Priest-in-Charge, by the Bishop of Worcester (the Right Reverend Dr Peter Selby) assisted by the Archdeacon of Worcester (Venerable Dr Joy Tetley), April 2002.* (MALCOLM SCOTT)

Above: *The Reverend Andrew Bullock greeting parishioners after his licensing ceremony, April 2002.* (MALCOLM SCOTT)

Left: *Revd Andrew Bullock and his family, June 2002. Left to right: Andrew (holding Barnaby), Peter, Alexandra (holding Edwin), James.* (MALCOLM SCOTT)

Chapter Five

FARMING

Introduction

Estimating the financial cost of the foot and mouth outbreak in 2001 highlighted the fact that the rural economy now depends more on income from tourism and leisure than from farming. A quick journey down the A4103 from Leigh Sinton towards Worcester illustrates the changes locally. Soon after leaving Leigh Sinton there are horse-riding stables on the left. Further along, on both sides of the road, there is the Bank House golf course. The Bank House itself is no longer a farm but a very large hotel, conference and leisure centre. Finally, when we get to Bransford Bridge, The Fox now has a very large restaurant at the back. To encourage families to eat there, there is a large children's play complex on the site of the cottage which was once a Post Office.

Farming Through the Ages

That farming life in the parishes was very different 200 years ago is shown by this account from R.C. Gaut's book *Agriculture in Worcestershire*:

... poaching and stealing of all sorts of farm produce and livestock were rife. An Act of 1770, whereby a convicted person could be imprisoned and, for a second offence, publicly whipped had little or no effect. In 1772 residents of the parish of Leigh formed an association to bring persons guilty of stealing turnips, potatoes, apples, pears and produce of the farms and felonious trespassers to justice. People were appointed as watchmen, covering both night and day. They used subscriptions to offer rewards for the apprehension and conviction of offenders over and above those approved by statute.

Bull Ring Farm, Brockamin, 1956.
(WRO/S.M. HALL)

69

Life in the parishes was very tough indeed, and the poverty severe. Farming work was all done by hand or horse, and control of pests and diseases was either rudimentary or non-existent. However, the coming of the Industrial Revolution, in the 1790s, started national changes which were to affect country life profoundly. For the first time, there was an alternative to farm work. Then the expanding industrial towns needed supplying with food. It became possible to manufacture farm machinery on a large scale and, starting in the mid 1800s, came the spread of the railways.

The slow rate of change in rural life up to then was reflected in the pattern of farms locally. Looking at the 1841 Tithe Map, many of the farms shown had been in existence for centuries. We have seen that Braces Leigh and Leigh Court go back to pre-Norman times. The origins of the motte and bailey castle at Castle Green Farm are thought to have been in the thirteenth century. Some of the later farmhouses have protective moats, and Moat Farm is one of these. Although possibly on the site of an older house, it was built in the sixteenth century, and part of the moat remains. Gilberts Farm, Bransford, is another medieval moated farm, the moat having been neatly cross-sectioned and inspected by archaeologists when a drainage ditch was dug across it in 1970!

There are a number of half-timbered farmhouses dating from the sixteenth and seventeenth centuries – for example, Bull Ring Farm, Hill Farm and Castle Green. Indeed, farms like the Great House, built in the late-eighteenth century, and Hopton Court Farm and Sherridge House, both dating from the early-nineteenth century, were comparative newcomers in 1841!

Despite the nineteenth- and twentieth-century changes in farming practice, all the large farms which were listed on the 1841 Tithe Map were still working farms until after the Second World War.

What had changed was their ownership. In the nineteenth century, most of them belonged to big landowners, and were tenanted. For example, Lady Henry Somerset owned farms in both Leigh and Bransford. The Beauchamps at Madresfield also owned farms in both parishes. This included Braces Leigh, members of the Gabb family being amongst its tenants, although William Henry Gabb, who lived at Beauchamp Court, was himself a landowner, as were the Norburys.

The auction sale of Lady Henry Somerset's estates in 1898 gives an idea of the wealth of the large landowners. The list of farms sold, together with their acreage, at that time (in brackets), is as follows: Moat Farm (161); Half Key Farm (278); Leigh Sinton Farm (258); Castle Green and Lower House Farms (245); Chirkenhill (171); Great House and Bull Ring Farms (351); Pigeon House Farm (136) and Little Brockamin Farm (163). The total acreage is 1,763! To this list we should add Leigh Court and Bank Farm (totalling over 500 acres), which were both sold by her in the same period to William Henry Gabb.

Associated with most of these farms were 'tied' farm-workers' cottages. Employees lived in them whilst they were employed, but had to move out immediately if they changed their jobs, or were dismissed. Not only did this restrict mobility amongst farm workers, it also, in principle, gave farmers a strong hold over them.

This hold was not restricted to housing. Mowey Davies recalls that when his father worked for James Leeke at the Great House, in the 1920s and '30s, he used to be laid off before each public holiday and then re-employed afterwards, so that James Leeke did not have to pay him for the holiday. As Mowey Davies said, 'They could do anything in those days couldn't they?'

James Leeke was a tough employer, somebody

The Great House around 1970. The two chimneys on the left are for the hop kilns. At the top is Teme Lane, with the old hop-pickers' barracks on the left. To the right of the Great House is the old hop and grain store, now converted into a house and called Hill Top Farmhouse. Five houses have resulted from the conversion of the farm buildings.
(STELLA BRAITHWAITE)

Outside Leigh Court barns around 1900. The name on the cart is J.N. Holmes, the tenant of Leigh Court. The figure on the left is George Palfrey, Elizabeth Portman's grandfather. (ELIZABETH PORTMAN)

Workers at Leigh Court, 1930s. Left to right: Jack Lerigo, George Hill, Chris Smith, Harry Phillips; kneeling: Harry Portman. (HAROLD PORTMAN)

Workers at the Great House in the 1920s, including Ted Banner, Percy Leeke, Arthur Emson and Albert Amphlett. (OLIVE BISHOP)

Four horses pulling a loaded Leigh Court dray. The person beside the last horse at the back is Elizabeth Portman's father, George Palfrey. The wagoner's boy at the front is believed to be either Harold Baldwin or Frank Williams.
(ELIZABETH PORTMAN)

Left: *'Dashing Duke', one of the Bransford Court shire horses in the late 1890s. John Wenden believes that the girl standing beside it is his mother, Julia Davis.* (JOHN WENDEN)

Below: *The Moat Farm, Leigh Sinton, around 1910. It was owned by John Pensam Hewlett Phillips from 1902 to 1913. The woman sitting in the porch could be his wife, Gladys, with one of their sons.* (EILEEN KEBBY)

Centre left: *Ernest Coley receiving his Long Service Award from Prince Charles at the Three Counties Show, 1977, after 46 years' service at Norbury's. He was the first man employed by C.P. Norbury when he took over the estate.* (IVY COLEY/BERROWS NEWSPAPERS)

Above, left: *In 1999 four employees at Bransford Nurseries, New House Farm, had nearly 200 years' service between them. Left to right: Ken Hitchins (50 years), Walter Pritchard (40 years), John Tooby, Dennis Carey (40 years) and Cecil Dee (over 50 years).* (CECIL AND PAT DEE)

Left: *Eddie Clarke being awarded a medal by the Three Counties Agricultural Society President Joe Henson for 50 years' service with the Norbury family, June 2002.* (EDDIE CLARKE)

who was supposed to have said to an official asking about his workers, 'These are not my workers, they are my servants.' He was also extreme, although he did hold a Christmas party for his employees. However, the number of farm workers getting long-service awards in recent years shows that we have had some very good employers in the parish.

With the break up of the large estates came the gradual move towards more family ownership of local farms. But the stock-market collapse in 1929 and the resulting Depression in the 1930s meant that these were grim periods for both farmers and the nation. The Second World War gave farming a much-needed boost, placing a premium on food production, because of the threat to food supplies by German U-boats.

The trend towards mechanised farming was limited by the use of horses. Although there was a decline in the use of horses from the 1920s onwards, as tractors were introduced, it was not until after the Second World War – and particularly the introduction of the 'little grey Fergie' – that horses stopped being used *(see overleaf)*. The post-war increase in mechanisation led, in turn, to another development in farming, the need to have larger and larger acreages to make farms efficient – in particular, to make the increasingly expensive equipment pay. The increasing cost and size of machinery also made contracting out jobs like combine harvesting more attractive.

More mechanisation, combined with the decline of fruit and hop production locally, meant that the number of full-time farm employees dropped dramatically. Farms which used to employ ten workers or more are now sometimes farmed by a single family, using contractors for some work.

The growth of larger farms has meant that many of the old farmhouses have been sold separately from their land, and are now used either as private dwellings – for example, Pigeon House Farm, Bull Ring Farm, Ashcroft and Great House Farm – or are used commercially, for example Moat House Farm is now a nursing home and Bank House Farm is an hotel. (As an aside, the acreage farmed at Moat House Farm actually dropped during the Second World War, because some of it was not being farmed to the standard set by the Government. John Tooby, at New House Farm, took over responsibility for it, and subsequently retained it.)

Farming Produce

Leigh and Bransford has always been an area of mixed farming. Hops have been grown locally since the late 1700s, and they continued to be very important right through to the early 1970s. The other crop which has been important for much of the nineteenth and twentieth centuries is fruit. Both of these crops were often grown in conjunction with sheep, cattle and arable crops, on the same farm.

The forge at Leigh Sinton, 1920s.
(Brian Iles)

Top left: *Gerald Jones cleaning off the sides of a wheel before fitting the steel 'tyre', around 1985.* (Graham Jones)

Left: *The wheelwright's shop, Leigh Sinton, in the early 1900s. The sign outside the shop reads 'Coach builder, wheelwright & coffin maker.'* (Coral and Des Clarke)

Wheelwrights and other farm-related activities

Gerald Jones was the Leigh Sinton wheelwright for over 60 years, and his father Thomas was before him. Their workshop was beside Shrubbery House and the forge, although separate, was opposite. John Roberts learned to be a wheelwright at Busks, in Bransford, which combined a wheelwright's shop, a blacksmith's forge and a fitting shop (selling and servicing Blackstone oil engines amongst other things). Both said that it was the little grey Fergie which killed their trade 'stone cold dead'. Why? Because a wheelwright's stock-in-trade was the large, four-wheeled farm dray. But the little grey Fergie had no weight on its back wheels, so could not pull them. To make things worse, Ferguson then bought out a two-wheeled trailer, putting weight on the tractor's wheels and increasing traction: there was no longer a demand for their product.

With the large numbers of horses in use until after the Second World War, blacksmiths were key people. Over the years, forges and wheelwright shops were established at different places in the parish. Billing's 1855 *County Directory* lists blacksmiths at Brockamin, Leigh Sinton and Sandlin, with wheelwrights at Leigh and Brockamin. As time went on, making farm machinery and supplying the stationary engines which farms used for the early mechanisation became more important. In an 1879 directory, Burrows, at Smith End Green, are listed as making a wide range of farm machinery, including 'combined wheat and threshing machines, cider and winnowing machines, portable steam engines, etc.'

In *Kelly's* 1884 *Directory* Burrows are still engineers, and there are blacksmiths at Smith End Green (Busks) and at Leigh Sinton (Thomas Dyson), with wheelwrights at Brockamin (Richard Emson) and Leigh Sinton (Frederick Miles). By 1937, Tomkins replace Burrows as engineers at Smith End Green, Busks are still at Hole Farm, Bransford, and Dorrell Brothers are at Bransford as agricultural contractors. Dorrells were later to make a range of horticulture equipment.

There are now no agricultural blacksmiths in either parish, nor any companies involved in manufacturing agricultural machinery, although John King at Bransford undertakes repair work.

Thomas Jones putting a tyre on a wheel, July 1962. He gave a talk on being a wheelwright on the BBC. (Connie Tohtz)

Above: *John Roberts using a draw knife to dress the spokes of a wheel which he is making, spring 2002.* (Malcolm Scott)

Aerial view of Lower House Farm, Leigh Sinton, 1959. Lower House Farm itself is in the foreground, with a pair of farm cottages on the left. There are two rows of hop-pickers' barracks in the middle, with the cook-house between them, at the far end. To the right is a cider orchard.
(PAULINE PHILLIPS)

Arable Crops & Animals

Up until the Second World War, many farms kept dairy cattle, providing milk locally either directly – as was the case at Leigh Court Farm at the turn of the nineteenth century – or through local dairies like Cutlers at Leigh Sinton. Milking was done by hand. After the war, farming became more specialised; milking was done by machine and milk production became more controlled. Farms stopped keeping milking herds, and the situation today is that there is none in either parish. In contrast, although beef production has also become more specialised, beef cattle are still widely kept locally. However, there are now farms which have stopped keeping animals and are entirely arable – for example, Castle Green and Lower House Farms.

Growing arable crops has changed beyond recognition since the 1900s. Improvements in seed stock, and in the control of weeds, pests and even plant development by sprays, means that yields have roughly trebled. Jobs which used to require three or four different activities, some of them labour-intensive, are now done by a single machine. With the advent of the combine harvester, no longer was it possible to write, as William Weaver did in his notebook, 'January 9th 1945. Finished thrashing at Mr Farr's on Saturday at one o'clock. Killed nine rats.' Both tractors and the machinery that they pull have got bigger, and hence more efficient, the increased cost of the machinery being offset by the reduced manpower needed.

Albert George (Bill) Palfrey, b.1908, Elizabeth Portman's father, at Cutler's Dairy, Leigh Sinton (opposite Moat Farm), c.1920. (ELIZABETH PORTMAN)

Other changes are in the storage of animal feed-stock. Hay and straw are stored in bales, not in thatched ricks. Initially small, square and light enough to lift by hand, bales are now large, requiring machinery to lift them. Silage – grass which is stored green and ferments during storage – now complements hay, if not replacing it, for feeding sheep and cattle over winter.

To see exactly how things have changed, we let Noel Griffin, who was born in 1906 and worked at Moat Farm in the 1920s and '30s, describe a stockman's day:

I looked after and milked the cows, and tended the young stock. The cows would be milked by hand twice a day, before 8a.m. in the morning and again in the evening. It took three of us to milk. Milk was taken to Cutler's Dairy, at Malvern House opposite, twice a day on a yoke with two four-gallon buckets, and they would cool and strain it. The Dairy also collected milk from Froggatt's, Jones' and Corbett's farms. Cutler's Dairy was run by two brothers from Hampshire and their sister looked after them. They delivered milk by pony and float to Malvern Link and North Malvern, and later had a van. One of the brothers married a Malvern girl and they started Cutler's Dairy in Malvern Link.

Most of my day would be taken up with preparing the feed and using the chaff cutter. There was a big 6½ HP engine with two large flywheels, which ground the corn in the mill and pulped up the roots, swedes – whatever you were using. The chaff cutter was a contraption with a wheel about one metre in

75

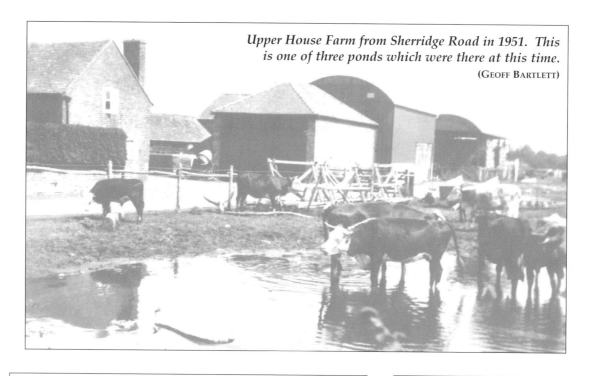

Upper House Farm from Sherridge Road in 1951. This is one of three ponds which were there at this time.
(GEOFF BARTLETT)

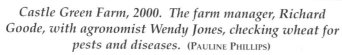

Castle Green Farm, 2000. The farm manager, Richard Goode, with agronomist Wendy Jones, checking wheat for pests and diseases. (PAULINE PHILLIPS)

Castle Green Farm, 2000. Christopher Phillips combining oats. (PAULINE PHILLIPS)

John Harcombe working a field on Bank Farm, autumn 2001. He is pressing, cultivating and drilling oilseed rape. This would have been five operations before the 1970s. In addition to being more efficient, having only one operation helps to protect against the vagaries of the weather. (MALCOLM SCOTT)

diameter with two knives on it. You would feed arm-fuls of hay from the rick into the back and it chopped it up to about one inch [3cm] long, and it all went down into [a] room below where it was mixed up with pulped sweet mangolds, swedes, roots, turnips and molasses. By the time you had put about ten to twelve barrow loads of root vegetables through the pulper and added the chopped hay you would have a pile about 10 feet [3m] high. The animals would be fed twice a day in their stalls. You would use a basket to take the feed to the cows, and all the juices from the pulp would run down your clothes.

In those days cattle and sheep would be walked to market in Worcester, or from wherever they were purchased. Noel Griffin remembers once collecting a dozen or so young cattle from Clifton-on-Teme. As cattle do, they scattered in all directions at every opportunity, 'It was a hell of a walk!'

Fruit

The 1830 Ordnance Survey Map shows orchard development only along the Suckley Road and in Brockamin. It was during Victorian times that fruit production expanded and, along with hops, became a key local crop.

Fortunately, the Ordnance Survey Pathfinder Maps issued after the Second World War were based on 1914 land-use data, so we are able to see the extent of Victorian fruit planting. Both the Suckley Road and Brockamin orchard areas were expanded, and there were also orchards all around Leigh Sinton itself. But the biggest change was beyond Leigh Sinton, between the A4103 and Sandlin, where about half the area is shown as orchard. Much of this was, and is, land farmed by the Norburys (see inset). And the map only shows orchards with 'top fruit' – apples, pears, plums damsons and cherries. There were additional areas planted with soft fruit.

Keeping birds off cherries used to be a major problem. Either there were elaborate arrange-ments of noise-making devices – chains and metal sheets – or somebody would be employed from dawn to dusk armed with a shotgun. Another haz-ard was grazing animals, the grazing under the trees sometimes being rented out. On one occasion this arrangement led to a dispute over damage done to the fruit trees, and one farmer was shot by another, losing the sight in one eye and the use of an arm.

Like hops, fruit required care throughout the year, but it was nowhere near as continuous. However, it created a big demand for casual labour at picking time. Even with less than 30 acres of fruit, Ruth and Pat Beard at Hill Farm, Brockamin employed 30–40 pickers, mainly women. Some of them were local, but many were outsiders. Beards had several outlets for their fruit, but much of the fruit grown around Leigh was handled by the Weaver family. They sent it down to Cardiff by train, selling it through a family company, Sutton & Weaver.

As a railway fireman working on the line in the 1950s, Ronald Hunt remembers that during the fruit season they brought a steady supply of empty wagons to Leigh Court Station, picking up the full ones from the siding. Indeed, it was rumoured that sometimes a fireman used to stay picking at Leigh, the driver working the line to Bromyard and back on his own, and collecting the fireman at the end of the day.

When Britain joined the Common Market in 1973, fruit growing came under threat. Over-production in its member states, combined with the French promo-tion of Golden Delicious apples, meant that European Union grants were given for grubbing up orchards. Many growers decided to quit and diversi-fy, Peter Norbury being one. Within 15 years or so of joining the EU the local orchards, which had been built up over more than a century, were decimated. Some growers went over to 'Pick-Your-Own' in an attempt to maintain business, but today even this has virtually ceased.

Christopher Norbury in a 65-acre pear orchard, early 1960s. (PETER NORBURY)

Ernest Coley adjusting spraying machinery at Norbury's, 1950s. (IVY COLEY)

The Weaver family at the Town House, Leigh, c.1920. Left to right, back row: *Uncle Tom, Uncle George, Maggie Weaver (Dick Weaver's sister), Dick Weaver, Polly Weaver (Dick Weaver's mother), Jack Weaver (Dick Weaver's father), Ivy Louise Weaver (holding Vera), William James Weaver (Dorothy Hughes' father);* front row: *?, ?, Thomas Weaver, Sarah Elizabeth Weaver, ?, ?.* (DOROTHY HUGHES)

Right: *The packing house at Norbury's, around 1960s. Left to right: Mrs Rowley, Mrs Spencer, Mrs Bartlett, Doris Badham, Ivy Coley.* (IVY COLEY)

Below: *Cherry pickers in the Norrest orchards, 1970s. Left to right: Ivy Coley, Dorrie Rowley, Hilda Tandy, Jean Jones.* (IVY COLEY)

Right: *At Norbury's packing station, 1940s. Jean and Bib Jones.* (MURIEL 'BIB' JONES)

The Norbury family

The Norbury family have been prominent locally since the 1800s. In an article in *Berrows Journal* in 1964, Christopher Paget Norbury said that the family, who had lived at Sherridge since 1790, acquired the name Norbury instead of Jones in the 1830s, after Thomas Jones married Mary Anne Norbury. The change of name was a condition of the marriage if Mary Anne's inheritance was to belong to both of them.

Under Frederick Paget Norbury, Christopher Norbury's father, the family expanded their farming base in Leigh Sinton. It was he who first introduced the loganberry into this country from California in 1901. As a measure of their wealth, by the 1930s there were, in addition to nearly 30 farm workers, 12 live-in servants at Sherridge. Frederick Norbury, who died in 1940, was not only a keen fruit grower, but also active in local farming organisations. Christopher Norbury maintained this tradition and served on Government bodies. In the 1960s the total area farmed was over 900 acres. Because the farms were so extensive they were also very self-sufficient, having their own forge and workshops, although they used the wheelwrights in Leigh Sinton.

Christopher Norbury's wife, Lisa, whom he married in 1937, was German and very proud of it, a fact which, perhaps not surprisingly, caused some unease locally during the Second World War. Peter Norbury says that his mother was not affected by this, but other parishioners are slightly ashamed that there should have been any reaction at all.

By 1965, when Peter Norbury started to be involved in the estate, 29 full-time men were employed and 19 women. When Christopher Norbury died in 1975, there were 680 acres of apples, 80 acres of pears and 76 acres of cherries. In addition, there were about 30 acres of soft fruit. Today, Peter Norbury farms about 300 acres and Tom Norbury around 200.

The Norbury family in 1984. **Left to right, standing:** *Kitty Flight, Stephanie Sanders, Julian Norbury, William Norbury, Louise Sanders;* **centre:** *Howard Flight, Christabel Flight (née Norbury) holding Mary Anne Flight, Katrina Norbury, Peter Norbury, Mary Anne Sanders (née Norbury), Andrew Sanders;* **front row:** *Josie Flight, Thomas Flight, Robert Sanders, with Bess the dog.* (PETER NORBURY)

Meeting of Worcestershire farmers at Sherridge, c.1920. (PETER NORBURY)

Hop Production

One of the striking things when looking at old hop yields is their year-by-year fluctuations. Worcester was an important hop market, and records for the number of hop pockets (bags of hops) being handled there in the early 1800s show that they varied from 38,851 in 1803 and 48,274 in 1808, down to just over 4,000 in 1812 and 1816. They went down even further, to 1,530 in 1817, but the following year were up to 19,164!

One reason for these variations is that hops are very vulnerable to aphids and disease, and there was no effective treatment. Longer-term trends were due to changes in the acreage under production. For example, in Bransford there were 61 acres under hops in 1825, but only 20 in 1844. For Leigh the corresponding figures were 230 and 101. Even in those days, hops were imported and were 'dumped' on the UK when there were gluts, depressing demand for the local crop.

Variations in price were also often extreme. From £8–10 per cwt. in 1793, the price dropped to £3–6 in 1797. It then went up to £11–17 in 1799, and to £15–18 the year after. But by 1818 it was down to £3–4. It seems that making an income from farming has never been easy.

The introduction of effective mechanical spraying equipment and sprays in the early 1900s reduced the impact of aphids and fungal infections. Then, in 1932, the Hops Marketing Board was established, which regulated hop production by allocating a quota to each farm. These two factors combined meant that the income from hop production was no longer uncertain. Indeed, hops became one of the most profitable crops, as John Wenden observed, 'When you had the hops, you knew what price you were going to get, and often the price was quite high, so your income was assured.'

During the first half of the 1800s, hops were grown much as we now grow runner beans, up tall, thin poles, groups of poles being tied together to make a 'wigwam'. Then, in the late 1800s, wires were strung in rows on tall poles right across hop yards, the hop vines being grown up strings attached between the wires and the ground. This is the method which is used by the two local farmers still growing hops, Graham Froggatt (at Upper House Farm) and George Price (at Braces Leigh).

Putting up hop-yard wires was a skilled and expensive job, requiring the use of poles which would stand in the ground without rotting for as long as possible. Simply dipping the end of the poles in creosote – as was done with the earlier, thin, hop poles – was not good enough. The hop poles for new, wired yards were about 20 feet (6m) long. How much was treated varied. Sometimes only the part which would be below ground plus a foot (30 cm) or so would be treated, and sometimes the whole pole would be.

John Wenden remembers the process well. The poles were placed in a tall tank filled with a mixture of tar and creosote. The mixture was brought to the boil using a fire underneath the tank, and the poles were left in the boiling liquid for half a day or so. The tank was then allowed to cool, while the poles absorbed more preservative. It was then re-boiled and the poles were lifted out hot, allowing any unabsorbed preservative to drain back into the tank.

Poles treated in this way ('pickled') lasted for decades, as do the hop plants themselves. But the process was not without dangers, aside from those of inhaling tar and creosote fumes. The Wenden's pickling tank, which was by the pond at Smith End Green, once overflowed and caught fire.

Later, more sophisticated and more expensive treatment plants were developed, in which the poles were placed in a pressurised, horizontal cylinder, but still using the tar and creosote mixture. Because of their expense they tended to be used by groups of farmers. Edward Jay was a member of one of these syndicates.

Left: *Hop stringing at Castle Green Farm in the 1960s.* (GEOFF FYNN)

Right: *Judith Smith bracing hops at Castle Green Farm.* (GEOFF FYNN)

Cover of the Hop Year Calendar published by Norman May's Studio in 1947, showing the old Braces Leigh farmhouse and its hop kilns.
(GEOFF FYNN, REPRODUCED WITH PERMISSION FROM NORMAN MAY'S STUDIO)

The Hop Year

Hops were so important locally that the Norman Mays Studio produced a 'Hop Year Calendar' in 1947, a different cultivation activity illustrating each month. As Graham Froggatt commented, what needs to be done has not changed much since then. In January the wire work is repaired and renewed. In February the metal pegs which anchor the hop strings to the ground are checked and renewed if necessary. For Graham Froggatt this means checking about 40,000 pegs! February is also the time when any plants which have died are replaced ('gapped up').

March sees the start of weed control as well as 'stringing' – attaching the strings between the ground pegs and the top wire. In early April, pairs of strings are tied together ('braced'), so as to make a fan shape above the vines. Towards the end of April hop 'tying' starts – persuading the bines (the climbing part of the vine) to go up the strings. May sees the end of the training and the start of growth control – removing unwanted growth. This is necessary to ensure that goodness is not taken away from the main shoots either by leaves or new shoots. The ground between the rows is also cultivated.

June and July are similar to May – cultivation early on, and growth control. In August there is the problem that, particularly in windy weather, a heavy crop might bring the wire work down. So it has to be carefully checked. In September the hops are picked. After that, not much happens until November and December, when the strings and bines are cut down to the ground and burnt, and the ground cleared of weeds.

How have these activities changed over the years? We saw that the use of spraying against parasites was an early development, but it was not easy. Cecil Dee describes how it was in the 1950s:

If you went hop powdering in the morning you had to start about half past three, as soon as ever it was light. You had to powder the hops while the dew was still on them so it would stick. It was nicotine powder! Seven percent nicotine powder. The sulphur used to go on later. It would poison you if you weren't careful. I only ever remember being affected by nicotine once. The powder machines were horse drawn, and you were supposed to ride on them, but they used to send the horse up the hop row and hope that he came out the other end. It saved you going through the powder all the time.

The big change was in the use of chemicals for the control of weeds and plant growth, both things which used to be done by hand and which provided considerable employment for women. The other difference is in the hop picking.

Inspecting the hops at Leigh Court Farm, 1953/54. Kenneth Farr with (Sir) Gerald Nabarro, who was then the local MP.
(JOHN FARR/BERROWS)

Above: *Attaching hops to the conveyor taking them into the picking machine at New House Farm, 1960. In the trailer are Les Page and Cecil Dee.* (CECIL AND PAT DEE)

Left: *Spraying Bordeaux mixture on hops at Moat Farm, Leigh Sinton, early 1930s. Note that the sunhat is the only protection against the spray!* (NOEL GRIFFIN)

*Harold and Elsie Portman hop
picking, with their son Derek
in the pram, 1951.*
(HAROLD PORTMAN)

*Universal Hop
Pickers
Account Book
for Mr W.
Davies,
October 1939,
showing the
bushels picked
and the total
earned.*
(MOWEY DAVIES)

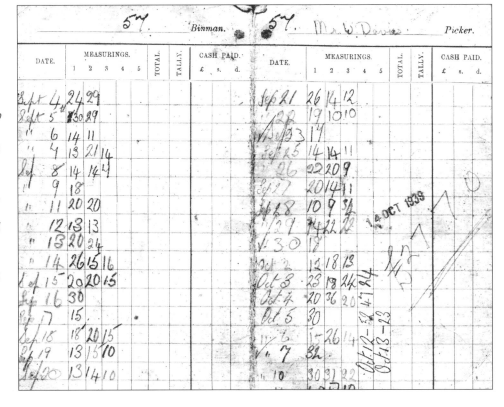

Gathering the hops at Castle Green Farm.
(GEOFF FYNN)

Tractor with hops, 1979. (WRO/BERROWS)

Right: *Josie Froggatt* (facing) *with Kirsty inspecting the hops. Arthur Solway, from Malvern, is loading the sacks, Upper House Farm, September 2001.* (MALCOLM SCOTT)

Left: *Anthony Kordas putting hops into the kiln for drying, Upper House Farm, September 2001.* (MALCOLM SCOTT)

Hop Picking

Until machinery was manufactured after the Second World War – notably by Bruffs of Suckley – all hop picking was done by hand. The hop bines would be pulled or cut down, and the pickers – usually women and their families – picked off the hops into a 'crib'. These were wooden frames about 10 feet (3m) long and three feet (about 1m) high and wide. Hessian sacking formed a long trough-like bag in the middle, into which the hops (the female flowers) were dropped.

The hops were measured using a wicker basket, which held a bushel of hops. This was the job of the busheller. He filled his basket from the crib, levelled it off and emptied it into a sack which was held up by his helpers. As we shall see, the busheller was a key figure as far as the pickers were concerned.

The number of bushells collected from each worker's crib were recorded by a tally man. In the early-nineteenth century, a notched stick was used for tallying, one half of which was given to the worker. Later, tokens were introduced, but in the twentieth century each worker had a tally card, and the tally man (by then called a 'booker') kept a record book.

Nowadays, the hops and strings are first cut about three feet from the ground. The tops are then cut by a man standing on a platform (called a 'crow's nest') towed behind a tractor. The strings of vines are pulled into a trailer under the platform and taken to the picking machine. There they are hung from a moving track and fed into the machine, where the hops and leaves are stripped off. The haulms are chopped up and ejected, then the hops are separated from the leaves and go by conveyer belt to be inspected. Any foreign matter is removed, and they are then either put into sacks to be taken for drying or fed directly into the kiln.

Hops are quite 'fragile' crops, requiring a range of factors to be right to produce them at their best. The picking conditions have to be right, and they have to be carefully handled at all stages to prevent bruising and loss of flavour. Successful hop picking depends on several factors. One is, of course, that the hops are ripe. If picked wet, which has to happen sometimes, they may lose their colour ('bloom') when dried. They may also lose their bloom if the weather is too hot during picking. This is important, because bloom is one of the factors used to assess quality, and poorer quality hops fetch less money.

Drying comes next. In manual kilns, which they have at Upper House Farm, the hops are spread evenly to a depth of about two and a half feet (75cm) on fine netting placed over the slatted floor of the kiln. Hot air is then blown through them for eight to 12 hours. The heat source used to be coal or wood, but oil-fired boilers are used now. This has two advantages. The first is that it does not have to be stoked – which used to require continuous attendance. (Eileen Kebby's father, George, was a hop drier and she remembers that he hardly ever came home for six weeks, except to wash and change his clothes.) The second advantage is that the temperature can be controlled automatically. Even so, the ambient air conditions – especially the humidity – can affect the drying process, so that both skill and experience are needed to get the drying right.

Until it was made illegal, it was customary to burn sulphur underneath the hops, in order to enhance their bloom. Not surprisingly, the kilns had to be evacuated for about 20 minutes whilst this was done.

Finally, the dried hops – smelling sweet and fragrant – are packed either into large, round hessian sacks, called 'hop pockets', or into square hessian-covered bales. In either case, the hops are shovelled into the sack, placed on a hydraulic press and compressed, then the sack or bale is sewn up. The origin of the hops and their date of production are then printed on the outside.

The hop year is finished!

Left: *A lorry load of hops at Chirkenhill, around 1937. Holl and Morgan were one of the Worcester haulage contractors.* (JOHN WENDEN)

Below: *Castle Green Farm, 1978. James (Jamie) F. Phillips with his father, James (Jim) Phillips. Jim took over hop drying after George Bowcott retired.* (PAULINE PHILLIPS)

Below left: *F.P. Norbury with Tom Lane the hop dryer (in bowler hat) at the Norrest, 1912.* (PETER NORBURY)

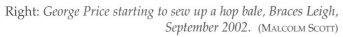

Workers at the Great House Farm with Edward Jay's first hop pocket, 9 September 1939. Left to right: H. Emson, F. Hadley, F. James, C. Mould, J. Barnes, Percy Bladen. (NORA JAY)

Right: *George Price starting to sew up a hop bale, Braces Leigh, September 2002.* (MALCOLM SCOTT)

Above centre: *Julie Price pushing hops into the press for baling, Braces Leigh, September 2001.* (MALCOLM SCOTT)

The Hop Pickers

Up until a decade or so after the Second World War, hop picking was THE big farming event of the year. Sometimes hundreds of temporary workers, mainly women and children, were employed on one farm, and there were several thousand temporary workers employed in both parishes. They used to come by special trains from the Black Country (Blackheath, Stourbridge and Cradley Heath), or from South Wales to Bransford Road or Leigh Court. Because the trains often had more carriages than usual, they had to pull into Leigh Court Station two or three times to let their passengers off.

Incidentally, these trains always used old coaches, with compartments and no facilities. Since the journey took three or four hours, pickers would be bursting for a toilet well before they got here. Ronald Hunt, a railway fireman who worked on the Worcester to Bromyard line in the 1950s, remembers looking back down the train and often seeing men and women hanging out of the doors relieving themselves as the train went along!

When they arrived, they were met by an army of carts and drays (horse-drawn until well after the Second World War) and taken to their 'barracks' – the name given to their accommodation. In the nineteenth and well into the twentieth century, these were simply barns and other farm buildings which were cleaned out and then divided up into family units, often simply by hanging sacking down from the beams. Straw was provided for bedding and food was cooked on open fires outside. Later, on some farms special hop-pickers' barracks were built. At Braces Leigh these were brick-built – a row of small, single rooms to house each family, with a communal kitchen and a washroom at the end of the row.

For the pickers it was the chance of a holiday in the country, albeit one when they had to work hard. On Saturday afternoons and Sundays, when there was no picking, the pickers' families used to come in special trains or coaches to visit them. At all times the villages were heaving with people, and were quite transformed.

For most people, and particularly for the young, it was an exciting time.

Above: *Hop-pickers' barracks at Braces Leigh, 2001.* (MALCOLM SCOTT)

Right: *Hop pickers being collected at Leigh Court Station, around 1940.*
(WRO/BERROWS)

Hop pickers at the Great House, c.1905. To the right of the bushel basket are: *Mrs Elizabeth Johnson (Nora's grandmother), Mrs Emson (Olive Bishop's mother), Ellen Johnson and Tom Johnson.* Standing in front: *Florence Johnson.*
(NORA HADLEY)

Left: *Eileen Purvis aged three, hop picking.* (EILEEN PURVIS)

Hop picking at Ashcroft, 1917–18.
(GLENDA MERRELL)

Above: *Hop picking in the field opposite Vicar's Hill, Leigh (then part of Bank Farm), early 1900s.
In those days hops were trained up poles, like runner beans are today. (Roy Hill, a costume designer
who dated this picture, said that the dress styles ranged over 30 years or more. The most recent belongs to
the woman in the centre, wearing a white blouse and a tall hat with stripes up it. The busheller can
be seen in the centre, just behind her.)* (DOROTHY HUGHES)

Above: *Hop picking at Norbury's, around 1930. Mrs Sarah Bartlett and her sister Ruth Bartlett at the back, with Victor and Geoff Bartlett.* (GEOFF BARTLETT)

Below: *Hop picking in the 1920s. Pictured are: Mrs Tromans (from Old Hill, Black Country), Gwendoline Ball (Coral Clarke's mother), Mrs Phillips.* (CORAL CLARKE)

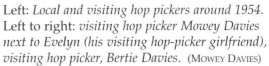

Left: *Local and visiting hop pickers around 1954.
Left to right: visiting hop picker Mowey Davies
next to Evelyn (his visiting hop-picker girlfriend),
visiting hop picker, Bertie Davies.* (MOWEY DAVIES)

Above: *Hop picking at Tooby's, near Bransford
Bridge, 1950.* (WRO/A. WHITE-PANTRY)

Left: *Hop picking at Castle Green Farm in the early
1930s. The busheller is William Phillips (son of
J.H.P. Phillips), and booking the bushels (with the
book in her hand) is Annie Bowkett,
Eileen Kebby's mother.* (EILEEN KEBBY)

Above: *On Bank Holidays, when the factories shut
down, the hop-pickers' families used to visit them.
The picture shows a group of hop-pickers' children
with some locals in a cherry orchard at Pigeon House
Farm, Brockamin, in 1944. Mowey Davies is sitting
fourth from the right, and Harold Cooper is the third.
Dick Cooper is third from the left at the back (to the
right of the woman).* (MOWEY DAVIES)

Left: *Glenda Merrell hop picking at Chirkenhill,
about 1956.* (GLENDA MERRELL)

Reminiscenses of Hop Picking

For teenage children, hop picking was a chance to meet other young people. For boys, in particular, it was a chance to meet new girls. As Mowey Davies said:

When we were 14 or 15 we used to look forward to the girls coming. The lads would sit along the wall outside the Great House waiting for them. I went out with a girl from Tipton for seven years.

He was not alone. Two or three others spoke of long-term relationships with visiting pickers, and two of the people we spoke to could even remember the girls' names and addresses after a lapse of nearly 70 years! Des Symonds remembers being told that his grandfather used to cycle from Leigh to Cradley Heath at weekends to see his hop-picker girlfriend.

For some girls at least, there seem to have been similar opportunities. As Eileen Kebby said, 'We used to have a boyfriend for a month and then that was it. It was good really.' It was also a chance for children to earn some money. Des Symonds got his first bicycle this way. It was a time when there were special activities. Les Alford and Harry Banner remember that:

Hop picking was a fantastic time. There used to be a church service every day at a different farm, with magic lantern shows... The fish and chip van came round and a man with a bike selling ice-cream.

The children used, of course, to pick as well. Pat Bowers went in the 1930s:

I always went with Mom on a Saturday and I had to fill an upturned gent's brolley by 12 o'clock. I always looked forward to hearing the man calling all across the Hopyard, 'Lardy cakes, Eccles cakes and fresh buns.'

The Weaver sisters remember that there was also a kipper van! Children filling an upturned umbrella seem to have been common. But nearly two decades earlier Joseph Hughes (who was born in 1906) recalls:

The adults would pick the hops into a crib and the children would use a box. Sometimes the children would use the crib. They had hop-picking stools in those days, a three-legged stool, and the children would use them.

Not all children went hop picking. Some were even discouraged from mixing with the pickers, though not very successfully, as Gwen Hawkins reports:

In September, the hop picking would be in full swing and nearly all the women and girls in the village would be involved. My sister and I longed to go, but mother always said there were lots of tinkers and gypsies there and she wouldn't be there to look after us, so we were not allowed to go. However, we often sneaked into the hop yard and joined our friends, though we were in trouble when we got home and mother could smell the scent of the hops on us and see our blackened fingers. We were fascinated by the hop-pickers' barracks where the Black Country pickers stayed, and the lovely blazing fires where they cooked their food, whilst their lingo was like a foreign language to us. There was a gypsy lad of about 17 or 18, called Walter, who had a wonderful voice and could be heard singing in the hop yard.

We always kept the outside door of our coal cellar locked at hop-picking time, as we once forgot and all manner of things disappeared in the night, including my Dad's cherished barrel of home-made cider!

We have said that the busheller was a key person, because he used to measure the amounts picked.

Hop picking at Lewis', 1950s. Janet Potter is the child on the right, who lived at Malvern House, Leigh Sinton, until she was eight.
(JANET LONG)

A 'heavy' busheller was one who pushed the hops down to get more into the basket, so that the picker was paid less. As Basil Wadley recalls:

Dick Weaver [who lived at Aubretia Cottage, and was a well-known hop yard wire-work man] did the bushelling for Recordons at the Bank Farm. He was a 'heavy busheller', and used his elbows to push the hops down by resting on them, with the result that his elbows were filthy.

But they did not always get away with it. Joseph Hughes says:

Some of the women were tough, and I remember that when the man came round to bushel the hops, if he was what they called a 'heavy busheller', then they would catch hold of him and chuck him into the crib!

There were other ways to deal with heavy bushelling. John Banner was sometimes Dick Weaver's booker. If he thought that Dick was being too hard, he used to add an extra bushel to the picker's total!

If the hop picking was hard work, the social life seems to have made up for it, particularly at weekends, as Noel Griffin found in the 1920s:

During hop picking the villages would come alive. On a Saturday evening the hop pickers would have all their fires alight on the driveway [of Moat Farm] and they would be singing soulful hymns, 'Nearer My God to Thee' and 'The Rugged Cross', I remember.

The Weaver sisters had similar memories in the 1930s:

Hop picking was the time that Leigh saw life. They would put on extra trains at the weekends to bring the visitors to see the hop pickers and there would be crowds of them. The hop pickers would ask for a sub on their wages and all go to The Bear, or The Fox at Bransford and The Swan at Alfrick for a drink on Saturday nights and they would all come home singing. There was never any trouble... Sometimes on a Saturday night they would all go drinking in Worcester and return on the 9.50 train and walk up the Leigh Road with all their arms linked right across the road swaying and singing.

There was a lot of goodwill between the villagers and the pickers. As Geoff Bartlett put it, 'the Black Country people were very sociable and if they were cooking something they would offer us a sausage or a piece of bacon.' As a child, Eileen Kebby remembers her mother making tea, and serving bread and cheese to the pickers. Later, during the Second World War, her mother used to collect all the pickers' ration books and buy their meat ration from Malvern Link. As Eileen said, 'They were good people, no trouble at all.'

Inevitably, though, there was trouble from time to time. Extra policemen used to be drafted in. But for the employers it could be a tense time. Again, bushelling was one of the key issues, as John Wenden recalls:

On the first day I would arrange a price per bushel, and then I would go out for the day. If they thought the price was too low they would come round the next day and stand around the back door and negotiate a better price – quite threatening really. It was usually about 5d. to 7d. a bushel. Once you had set the price per bushel there wouldn't be a bad word spoken, and they just got on with the job.

Pauline Phillips says that when hop picking was done by machine it added to the employer's problems:

Hop picking was a tense time, worrying if the machine would keep working, worrying if the crop was good enough and would fill your quota. You were concerned with keeping the workers happy, and from not falling out with each other. One year James stopped a man taking a hook to another one: of course he was sacked on the spot. 'Pay them off James' was often heard from Mr Phillips senior if there was trouble with casual workers.

Another worry was if someone's limb got caught in the machine, usually between rollers. The machine was guarded, but of course there were always people prepared to do reckless things. One or two were taken to hospital. And often one or two of the Welsh pickers would go back to Wales. No questions were asked, as they were usually going back for Court appearances.

In addition to having extra policemen, back as far as 1913 the district nurse used to tend the sick who, in those days, included many gypsies. In the 1960s special surgeries were run twice a week by the district nurses, Jill Ellard and Hazel Chambers, who remembered:

There were a few bad accidents. One time a hop-picking lorry pulled up, and they carried in a child of about 3 or 4 who had been found – they thought drowned – in a farm pond. He wasn't dead actually – we managed to pump him out and he was taken to hospital and survived... Jill once delivered a baby at Guinness.

When all the hops had been picked, they had to be sold. In the 1930s the Hops Marketing Board was set up, but as John Wenden recounted:

My father was a rebel and would not join the Hops Marketing Board. He had a contract with Bass but had Bass turned us down we would have been on our own. We grew Goldings, which were of a high quality and used for pale ale. The other varieties grown

Above: *Hop picking at New House Farm, around 1960. Left to right: Frank Symonds, ? Newman, Mrs Newman, Alan Garness, Cecil Dee, Greta and Iris Newman.* (PAT AND CECIL DEE)

Above: *A break during hop picking on Corbett's Farm, 1940s. Left to right: Joseph Kimber, Mrs Tyler and her daughter Phyllis Tyler.*
(NORMAN KIMBER)

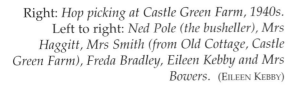

Right: *Hop picking at Castle Green Farm, 1940s. Left to right: Ned Pole (the busheller), Mrs Haggitt, Mrs Smith (from Old Cottage, Castle Green Farm), Freda Bradley, Eileen Kebby and Mrs Bowers.* (EILEEN KEBBY)

Below: *Hop pickers from the Great House (James Leeke) and Pigeon House Farm (William Henry Leeke), Leigh, early 1900s. The woman in black is believed to be Mary and Gill Gale's grandmother, Harriet James.* (GILL AND MARY GALE)

were Fuggles, for mainstream beers, Mathons for better beers and Bramlings for pale ale. My father stayed with Bass until he died and I didn't tell the Hops Marketing Board for five years that he had died, because I didn't have a factor until later.

The factor was the middle man who acted between the grower and the merchant, who operated for the brewer. Our factor was in Southwark, London, and had a showroom with a glass roof – the light was important. I would go up every year and take samples from every fifth pocket wrapped in brown paper. This was how the price was set for every type of hop. They would rub the hops and smell them. The resin was what they wanted, and they would analyse the hops and say what the percentage was. They would pay you by giving you a deposit, and then make another interim payment before Christmas, with a final payment by the end of March.

Although John Wenden installed picking machinery, he stopped growing hops in the late 1960s. The Hops Marketing Board was offering financial incentives to growers to quit, and he decided to go into strawberries instead.

By the 1950s it was starting to get difficult to find pickers, and Geoff Bartlett remembers that they were becoming a little more discriminating:

When a lorry carrying women workers for Lewis' Moat Farm arrived one woman asked, 'Where are we going to sleep?' Jim Lewis pointed to a tin shed with a bit of hessian over the front and a couple of bales of straw in the back and said 'In there Madam'. She looked inside and said 'I can't go in there, that place is full of bloody rats.' He said 'Rats madam, I will give you a pound for every one you can catch.' And I [Geoff Bartlett] said 'They don't half take some catching.' She said 'I am not staying here' and they all jumped on the lorry and the poor bloke had to take them all the way back again.

An article written by Edward Jay, from Great House Farm, reproduced with permission from the Women's Institute book Worcestershire Within Living Memory (Countryside Books, 1995), paints a vivid employer's view of all these activities in the 1940s:

Thank heavens it only took place once a year, one had to spend so many man-hours preparing for this event. Hop-pickers' quarters or barracks had to be whitewashed and partitioned off with hessian to pass the Health Inspectors; hop kilns put in order after having been idle for eleven months; and the cribs all prepared. Then I got in contact with four 'ganger' women representing Great Bridge and Tipton, Blackheath, Newport and Worcester. Some of the latter were resident on the farm, the rest coming daily by bus or lorry.

We had about 400 pickers, some no doubt babies in arms, but they all counted in the gangers' count at a shilling a head. I paid for the rail tickets, they paid the return fare. I always ended up with about a 100 spare return tickets.

Horse or tractor-drawn drays or wagons met the Black Country pickers at Leigh Court Station and the Newport pickers came to Bransford. By the time all the pickers had arrived for the seven farms from Leigh Court to Pigeon House there were up to 2,000 extra people living in Leigh, not counting those in Bransford or Leigh Sinton. Leigh was transformed from a rural village into a small town almost overnight.

One or two extra policemen were resident; one nurse was drafted in, holding a morning and evening surgery at the Great House. Church Army sisters were resident, some staying with Mrs Bough, who, it is said, never served the same pudding twice in a month. They held services and Bible classes.

A man called Jim Clark kept a shop at the Great House and had about 2,000 registered customers; he coped with the ration books. He sold fresh milk daily and gave each picker two pounds of potatoes on a Sunday.

Some farms had to engage extra staff to work in the kilns and measure the hops, and booking staff. Wood and coke were supplied by the farmer for cooking. Wages could be paid on Monday, Wednesday and Friday nights, care being taken that no one was overdrawn.

Nothing was safe, from fire risk to unpicked fruit, so constant patrols were needed. Weekends were the worst time, when bus loads of visitors arrived and apples and potatoes would disappear by the sack load. Most farms would have one meadow set aside for gypsies and their caravans.

Picking on a Saturday was almost a waste of time as so many would go by train to Worcester. Most of the pubs opened special bars for hop pickers. On Saturday and Sunday nights, gangs could be heard singing on their way home. There were just too many people to control though this is, of course, a biased point of view from one grower. My young family loved the excitement of it all and looked out for old friends who came year after year. Nearly all pickers referred to the district as Leigh Court, as that was the station's name.

Normal farm work, like the grain harvest, came to a complete halt, when hop picking and kiln work was one's only thought.

Black Country Hop Pickers' Memories

At Lower Sandlin Farm, the Black Country hop pickers came from around Cradley Heath and Tiverton, and in the 1940s and '50s were organised by Maude Willetts, her mother having done the same before her. Maude's daughter, Emmie Bagley (now 80), used to go picking until she got married at 19, and loved it. She remembers playing with John Wenden – 'He was

Above, left: *Hop-picker's child, aged 18 months, waiting with the pickers' luggage at Cradley Heath Station for the train to Bransford, 1955.*
(MISS EUNICE EMERY)

Above: *Eunice Emery's mother, Polly, who worked in the Wendens' house during hop picking, 1930.*
(MISS EUNICE EMERY)

Left: *The Wendens' farm. Pickers Polly and Agnes Emery preparing to wash their hair, 1949.*
(MISS EUNICE EMERY)

Below: *Eunice Emery's cousin Ruth met a local, Ron Bowkett, whilst hop picking, and married him. They are here with their children, Roderick and Stella, c.1970 at Wendens'.* (MISS EUNICE EMERY)

Right: *Lily Morris, Ada Homer and Eunice Emery picking at Wendens', 1950.*
(MISS EUNICE EMERY)

Left: *Polly and Emmie Emery and Maude Willetts at Wendens', 1950. Maude Willetts, from Cradley Heath, organised the pickers for Wendens' for many years.* (MISS EUNICE EMERY)

a bit of a rascal!' Because of their responsibility, the family was met at the station by the Wendens' car, and they had accommodation with an inside fireplace. She remembers that people rushed to get the same places each year, sometimes sending their children on ahead. A few husbands even used to leave their jobs to pick hops, simply for a change.

Another family member who went was her cousin, Eunice Emery, who has written down her memories for this book.

My Dad didn't like hop picking, but my mother Polly did. Her family had always gone to Wendens' and they all loved it. My Dad never took to it, but he never stopped us going. He stayed at home to work all week, and came out to see us on Saturday. He would take the bus to Stourbridge, then one to Worcester, then one to Leigh Sinton, getting there about lunch-time. That was just the right time, because all the workers in the fields finished about then.

We would all get ready about August. When it got time, we packed our tin boxes with the tinned food which mother had been saving. We also had to put in lots of bed clothes, towels, pots and pans – everything for our stay. So you can see why we needed a tin box. We would mostly go on a Sunday.

At Cradley Heath Station would be lots of people seeing their families on their way. It was a through train to Bransford, and it was the only time we children got to ride on a train. It was great fun.

When we got to Bransford they unloaded the train, and the platform was full of boxes of all shapes and sizes. The wagon and horses were waiting to take the cases to the farm. But there was no room for the pickers. We with good legs walked, and only if you were old did they make a bit of room. We stayed to have a drink at the pub on the way. I always remember that

Eunice Emery's father, Edgar from Cradley Heath, with a maid at Wendens' farm, 1930. (MISS EUNICE EMERY)

the children had ginger ale, which was very hot from the ginger, but we drank it.

After the grown ups had had a drink, we all set out to walk to the farm, which I think was about three miles away, but in the country it was like six miles, it took so long! But we children skipped along. When we got to the farm, all our boxes had been put by our barns, and so we had to make our homes for the next few weeks. Remember that this all had to be done so that we could get a meal and a bed for the night! First we got straw for the bed, and then opened a spread on the top, then the pillow cases were stuffed with straw. That done, we got out the pots and pans, teapot and kettle, to make a meal in the living area.

We always had a good fire in our barn, it was kept going all day and banked up at night so that in the morning it was easy to get alight. By the time it was evening and we children were tired we were put to bed on our new straw beds, and were soon asleep, to be ready for an early rise at 7 o'clock for the start of the picking day.

Monday morning! Mother had been up early, so we had toast and tea, then we put our Wellington boots on. No matter what the weather was, hot or cold, dry or wet, you always wore a good strong pair of boots, because the hop fields could be very wet and there was lots of heavy clay. So, wellies all day!

At Wendens' we always started at the big field first, which was about a mile down the lane. When you got there you got a crib to pick your hops into. That all took about an hour, so by eight o'clock you were ready to start. You picked until about one o'clock, then it was time to get bushelled, which is when they came to get the hops you had picked all morning. You had a book, and they wrote in how many bushells you had picked.

On the first day they decided how much a bushel they

would pay. I have seen sometimes when they did not agree with the price, and everybody stopped work until they got it right. We children loved it, because we could play until they did! Sometimes it went on all day.

So the day started at eight o'clock, and about four o'clock we older children would be allowed to go back to the barns on the farm, to start to get the meal for when everybody had finished in the field, around 5.30. We had a good wash, and could play until bedtime, or go for a walk down the lane – no fear of being stopped by anyone in my days. We could go into the orchard and pick the fruit to eat – but not to waste, just to enjoy. Saturday afternoon was free, and also Sunday. We had a baker who came in a big van, and brought bread and cakes. Mr Wenden gave us all the milk we needed every day. We always saved our hop-picking money until the end of the three weeks, so we would be rich.

Small-scale Animal Husbandry

Possibly because the large landowners dominated the local scene, there were never many farming smallholdings. The situation is no different today. However, until well into the twentieth century, some farmers, and also villagers, kept one or two pigs.

Noel Griffin recalled that, 'They were kept in loose boxes, which had to be cleaned out for the hop pickers.' Joe Dance, the driver of the Chicken Coop, is remembered as somebody who killed the pigs, and Jack Brooke from Alfrick another. Pat Bowers remembers that their pig used to be killed before Christmas. It was cut up into shoulders, sides and hams, and his job was to rub the meat with blocks of salt to preserve it. Most cottages had hooks for hanging the bacon on.

Many families kept chickens, mainly for eggs, but at Leigh Court they also kept pigeons, both for their eggs and to eat. They were housed in a large, square building, on the site of an older, round one. Inside there were 1,380 nest boxes accessed by a revolving ladder. It now forms part of a barn conversion called – not surprisingly – The Dovecote, and it was a condition of the conversion that the dovecote be open to the public by prior appointment.

Few people kept rabbits for food. Most of the rabbits eaten were wild, being poached in one way or another – usually snared, or netted using ferrets. The other small-scale activity that used to supplement some larders was bee keeping. Although not common, it was more widespread than it is now.

Derek Worboys, of Pigeon House Farm, Brockamin, with one of his Dexter cattle, May 1983. Their smallholding was organic and they also had Tamworth pigs and chickens. In the summer they had paying guests, their three children living in a caravan so that their bedrooms could be used.
(Mike Grundy/Berrows)

Moat Farm, 1933. Feeding the chickens is Marion West (Noel Griffin's niece) and the woman in the background is Ethel Page. (Marion West)

Richard Howard and Lillian Somervaille collecting a swarm of bees from the orchard at Aubretia Cottage, Leigh, June 2002. (MALCOLM SCOTT)

Interior of the dovecote in the former Leigh Court farm buildings. The central ladder moves around, to give access to the nest boxes. (WRO/R.A.H. DAVIES)

Farming Today

We have seen that farms have generally got bigger, that hops and fruit are no longer grown on a large scale, and that, in general, farms are more specialised than they used to be. At the same time, there has also been some diversification out of the 'traditional' local farming activities. For example, Beards at Leigh Sinton now have extensive Christmas-tree plantations, and run a retail business. They also have fishing ponds, and there are others at Castle Green Farm and at Brockamin. The Wendens have now gone in for a wide range of crops – broad beans, peas, runner beans, sweetcorn, French beans and sprouts, as well as fruit – which they sell at farmers' markets, together with apple juice and other 'own brand' products. In December 2001 they went to 22 farmers' markets, and they also attend food festivals. Tom Norbury is another farmer who sells his fruit, cider, apple juice, jam and pickled walnuts directly through farmers' markets, attending 125 in 2001.

Another major change affecting farming has been the steady march of regulation, particularly following membership of the European Union. Some of this arose because of changes in the farming support schemes. Guaranteeing prices for certain key commodities by offering price support encouraged over-production, giving rise to the infamous butter and beef 'mountains'. This led to the introduction of quotas;

producing more than your quota could lead to financial penalties, depending on the product. Now there is a trend towards increasing environmental awareness.

Over and above this we have concerns over food safety, so that records have to be kept of each production stage for both crops and animals. And the net result of all these changes? A massive increase in recording, and in paperwork generally. For example, cattle have to have individual 'passports'. Every movement of each animal on and off the farm has to be recorded in it and a card sent to the Ministry. The acreage of each crop has to be recorded, but field areas are not enough. Allowance has to be made for footpaths, trees, pylons and pools, and the area cropped (in hectares) given to two decimal places. And so on. The three guidebooks to the Integrated Administration and Control System (IACS) form, which every farmer has to fill in annually, are 164 pages long!

Finally, the global market in cereals means that prices are no longer dictated by local, or even national, factors. As an example, getting the best price for a cereal crop can involve using the Internet to study prices in the Chicago market, in order to judge the right moment to sell.

There is absolutely no doubt whatsoever that, as John Wenden said looking back over his 60-odd years in farming, 'Farmers are under much more pressure now, and have to work much harder to stay in business.'

Cider Production

Nothing written about local farming would be complete without mentioning cider, which was the staple drink locally until comparatively recently. Indeed, it formed part of the wages for the farm workers, as this record from 1774 shows:

Day labour 1s. per day, with beer, cider or perry: 2 gallons per day the usual allowance, but no restrictions in harvest. Women's labour 8d. per day with drink. Hours of work 6a.m. to 6p.m.: in some parts 5a.m. to 7p.m.: in winter from day break to dark, during harvest no fixed hours.

Nowadays it is produced almost exclusively by specialist producers – of which Tom Norbury is the only one locally – but this was not the case years ago. As Harry Banner and Les Alford said of the 1920s and '30s:

All the farmers made cider, and it would last all year round. Dick Weaver and his family used to keep all their cider in barrels at what was called The Stores, at the side of the Police Station. They used to carry their cider on old-fashioned yokes in buckets. Jack Weaver would sell it for 5d. a gallon. In those days men would cut the hay for free just to get a drink of cider. The policeman wanted to arrest Jack Weaver for selling cider without a liquor licence but of course it was always given in exchange for work done.

The Weaver sisters' memories are similar:

Uncle Tom was well known for his cider and had a mill at the Town House, Leigh. It was a huge Victoria Oil engine, very noisy and difficult to start but our father could do it. It used to scratt the apples which were then put between straw mats called 'hairs' and pressed. All the juice used to run out and the local boys from the farms would come and have a drink of the apple juice before it was put into barrels to ferment. At haymaking time everyone would come and help and my mother used to supply the bread and cheese and my father supplied the cider. They didn't mind how long they stayed, but some of them had forgotten how to walk when it was time to go home!

The Weaver families were all from Leigh, but elsewhere in the parish the picture of cider use is the same. Geoff Bartlett recalls that:

The men used to go to the cider house at the Norrest, where it was made, with two-gallon stone jars hanging round their necks – I think they were allowed a gallon a day each. They drank from a cider horn (a cut-off cow's horn). The cider barrels were gigantic, and we used to have three of them. We used to bring them one at a time upon a cart. We had a lean-to at Haywards Cross, and at night my brother and I would be sent by my mother with a candle to go and draw some cider into a saucepan. My brother and I had to whistle all the time so that my father knew we weren't drinking any neat cider out there! When we got inside my mother would warm a little for us on the fire with some sugar and we were packed off to bed and they wouldn't hear a sound from us! I think my father had most of the cider from the Norrest. Bob from the village, who used to come and cut my Dad's hair, didn't get paid for doing this, but he drank so much cider he would be drunk by the time he finished.

Right: *The cider-mill at Mill House, Leigh, 2002. The mill is used to break down the apples before the juice is crushed out with a press. A pony would be harnessed in the frame on the right, to turn the wheel around. An alternative way to do this is to 'scratt' the apples – to break them down with a coarse 'mincer'.* (MALCOLM SCOTT)

Left: *The cider press at Mill House, Leigh, 2002. This used to extract the juice from the previously crushed, or 'scratted', apples.* (MALCOLM SCOTT)

Above: *Cecil Deakin (the wagoner at Brockamin Farm) and John Swindell (carrying a bottle of cider for the workers), c.1943.* (JOHN SWINDELL)

Left: *Mill House, Leigh. Kit, the pony that used to work the cider press, with her foal. On the left is Mrs Hyde, then Minnie the maid, and on the right Mr Hyde, the miller, 1920s.* (JEAN McGOWAN)

Chapter Six

RIVERS, RAILWAYS & ROADS

Old Bransford Bridge, c.1910. (PETER NORBURY)

What have rivers, roads and railways got in common locally? Well, they are all ways by which goods and people can, or could, move around the parish. Rivers? Well, yes! The earliest large-scale transport of goods – and possibly people – was up the Teme. The Teme was also important in other ways, so this chapter starts with a look at rivers.

Rivers

Transport on the Teme

As the Romans realised when they conquered England and Wales in 43BC, such roads as existed were woefully inadequate for moving large armies and their supplies around. They set about building a magnificent road system, some of their routes remaining in use until the present day. However, rivers afforded a ready-made passageway for people and goods which the Romans exploited. But they were not the first because, as Max Sinclair, a local historian from Lower Broadheath, notes, there is archaeological evidence along the Teme Valley to show that goods were moved up and down the river in Iron-Age times, between 750BC and the Roman occupation.

The Romans used the Teme to bring lead from above Leintwardine, in Shropshire, down to the Severn, although what they did to make the river navigable all the way is a matter of conjecture. Evidence from waterways elsewhere in the country shows that the Romans used to build weirs to raise the water level, but no remnants of any Roman weir has been found yet on the Teme.

As with many things, there is no evidence of activity on the Teme between Roman times and the Norman Conquest. Then a mill was built at Ashford

A young woman crossing the Teme to Broadwas Church on a wire bridge, c.1903. (MAX SINCLAIR)

Left: *Demolition of Bransford Weir, 1955.*
(WRO/SERGEANT)

Carbonel, on the Teme just below Ludlow, using stone quarried at Caen in Normandy. The only feasible route for transporting all this stone was by water, which means that it must have come through the parish. The use of rivers, including the Teme, became more and more important for bulk transport, particularly because roads were still rudimentary, and many became impassable in winter.

It was the construction of 'flash locks' in the sixteenth century which made river navigation possible for larger boats. There were three of these along the Teme locally; at Powick, Bransford and Knightwick. A photograph from 1925 shows a fairly well-preserved flash lock on the Worcester side of the old Bransford Bridge. Unlike the double-gated locks which we have today on canals, these locks only had one gate, set in a weir across the river. This gate was a double-sided open structure, which could be made watertight by inserting flat boards of wood (paddles) between the two sides of the gate.

When the gate was closed, the water level obviously rose upstream until it spilled over the weir. A boat coming downstream would take out the paddles, open the gate and ride down on the flood of water released. Going upstream was much more difficult, because once the water was released the boat had to be hauled upstream against the flow of the water. This was done either by teams of men or using a winch. In both cases the gate had to be closed and the paddles inserted as quickly as possible, to avoid the water level upstream getting too low.

The use of the rivers for the transport of goods started to decline with the coming of the railways,

but it was the building of Lower Wick Power Station in the 1890s which finally stopped boat traffic between the Severn and the Teme. This was because the weir was removed. It was not until the 1950s, however, that the weir at Bransford was demolished.

That the Teme was once an important waterway is difficult to believe now, but there is a host of evidence for it. For example, there is a painting of Ludlow Castle by Samuel Scott (1710–72) showing large, 20-ton boats moored on the river beneath it. Amongst other things, boats like this were used to transport iron ore. And the evidence that this ore was brought down the Teme to the Severn? Well, there was an iron smelter at Powick for several centuries, and at the sites of the various flash locks along the Teme – where boats might have spilled their cargoes if things went wrong – there are iron deposits of various types on the riverbed. Finally, the old bridges along the Teme all had navigation arches, to allow boats through even if the water level rose in winter.

Although the River Teme is not particularly wide, the fact that it was navigable may also explain why there are so few old bridges across it. Bridges needed to be both substantial and high to allow boats underneath. Not surprisingly, therefore, enterprising people wishing to cross the river who faced a long journey to a bridge sometimes built their own, temporary, ones. They consisted of two wires, one above the other: you held on to one wire and walked on the other. One of these, which was last used around 1930, was just outside the parish, crossing the Teme to Broadwas Church.

Other Uses of the Teme

There has been a water-mill at Bransford since at least the fourteenth century. H.W. (Bill) Gwilliam, in his book, *Mills in Worcestershire*, recorded a deed from 1303 in which the Beauchamp family from Madresfield gave the rights to the mill and fishery to Roger Moyne on condition that he provided Dame Alice Beauchamp with 'all the lampreys from the fishery'. He was also to mill her corn and malt, and to keep the mill and its sluices in good order – although she was responsible for the repairs. The lampreys were caught in wicker baskets called 'engines', or 'wheels', and Dame Alice had to provide him with the withies (willow twigs) for making these. Interestingly, behind Grove Cottage, just above Bransford Bridge, there are still the remnants of old withy (or 'osier') beds, the stream which fed them having been diverted when the adjacent railway was built.

The Snuff-Mill in 2002. (MALCOLM SCOTT)

In subsequent years there are numerous records of the different mills and other activities on the Teme at Bransford. In addition to corn-mills, the water power has been used to run a clover-mill, a china-mill, a cloth factory and a snuff-mill. Snuff is made by mixing tobacco with herbs and oils and fermenting it. The mixture is then finely ground and a pinch is inhaled. It was very fashionable in the eighteenth and nineteenth centuries, and the mills at Bransford and Bewdley were the only two in the county. The snuff-mill was quite a small affair, but the last corn-mill was much larger.

Lampreys were not the only fish caught in the Teme. At one time, John Wenden remembers that it was a fine salmon river. Eels used to be caught commercially. Harold Portman remembers when there was a water bailiff at Bransford Mill who would put out eel traps and then send his catch on the train to Billingsgate Fish Market, London. Later on, when Alan Garness was a young boy in the late 1940s, there also used to be a big eel trap at Bransford. Made of steel mesh, it was about eight feet (2.6m) cubed, and the water on one side of the weir flowed through it. He and his friend Martin Horton used to watch when, once a week, a man came from Birmingham with a big open-topped barrel into which he put the eels.

Today there are still some salmon in the Teme, for which there are restocking programmes. According to the Department of the Environment, one problem on the Teme, common to many rivers, is that levels of phosphates and nitrates from both farming and sewage plants have risen. Improving sewage plants upstream will help and this is being undertaken, but the problem of changing farming practice is a longer term one to tackle. Nevertheless, there are still migratory fish like eels and sea lampreys, as well as coarse fish, and it is still a popular fishing river.

Not only anglers enjoy the Teme. There are several walks along its banks, one being given in the Parish Council booklet, *Walks Around Leigh & Bransford*. It was even a holiday destination for some, as the following piece from the Women's Institute book, *Worcestershire Within Living Memory*, shows:

When I was a child in the 1920s our annual holiday was a day by the River Teme. My family would be up early assembling all the picnic gear and fishing tackle, and we would then walk the four miles to Worcester from Kempsey, to catch the eight o'clock train from Foregate Street to Leigh, where we spent the day fishing. My Mum and I would light a fire and thread bacon and sausages onto a stick, which we would hold over the fire with bread underneath to catch the fat. Then, with the kettle boiling, we had a lovely meal and finding some apples and plums in the hedgerow made it a perfect day. Later, we would journey home again by train, hoping to catch a ride on a horse-drawn dray back to Kempsey.

(REPRODUCED WITH PERMISSION FROM COUNTRYSIDE BOOKS, NEWBURY, BERKSHIRE)

The old mill at Bransford, 1902. (WRO/E.A. NEWMAN)

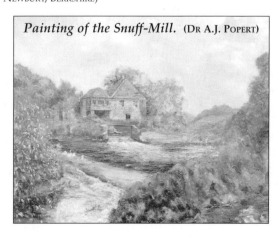

Painting of the Snuff-Mill. (DR A.J. POPERT)

Floods in the hop yards at Leigh, 18 August 1912. (STELLA BRAITHWAITE)

Right: *The Teme in flood, 1920s, showing the old bridge.*
(PAT AND CECIL DEE)

Below: *Wading through the floods on the A4103, 1970–1. Left to right: Tony Symonds, Mrs Salter holding Marcia Salter, Celia Dee, Brian Synmonds, Michael Dee.* (PAT AND CECIL DEE)

*Floods at
The Fox Inn, 1974.*
(WRO/BERROWS)

*Abandoned lorry in floods at
The Fox, 1968.* (WRO/BERROWS)

The Teme in Flood

There is one aspect of the Teme which has not changed – the fact that it still floods the valley and Bransford Bridge at regular intervals, closing both the main road from Worcester to Hereford (the A4103) and the adjacent Fox Inn. There have been some dramatic floods, but none more vividly described than the one recorded in *Berrows Journal* on 9 September 1852. The article starts with a description of the gathering storm, and then goes on to say this about Bransford:

The Teme rose considerably in this locality about 12 o'clock, and the roads were to a large extent inundated. Great fears were entertained for the safety of the Bridge (a wooden structure) but we are glad to state it has been ascertained to have escaped uninjured. The Fox Inn, situated in its close proximity, was deluged with water, which filled the cellars, kitchen, bar and parlour, covering the floors to a depth of nearly five feet. In the retreat of the unwelcome visitor the floor of the parlour was found to be covered with a layer of mud some six inches in depth... We must mention that some poor Irish people, consisting of two women and six or seven children, were sleeping in a stable adjoining The Fox Inn, when the flood reached them, about one o'clock. The poor creatures alarmed for their lives rushed through the rapidly rising water and craved admission to the inn in piteous accents. Their request was at once granted, although the interior, from its flooded state, was scarcely more comfortable than the exterior, and they huddled together in the vicinity of the fireplace until morning. It affords us much satisfaction to state that no loss of life, either of man or beast, took place here. The lightning and thunder were described as having been most terrific.

Soon after this, in 1860, a

brick bridge was built across the Teme to take the Worcester to Bromyard railway line. In his book, *Worcestershire's Historic Bridges*, H.W. Gwilliam records that the floods of 1890 undermined its foundations and it collapsed just after a goods train had passed over. The train driver was oblivious of the collapse, and it was only because a plate layer managed to scramble across the remaining parts of the bridge and raise the alarm that the following passenger train did not plunge into the river.

William Weaver, who lived at Orchard Cottage, Leigh, used to keep a notebook in which he recorded local happenings. His entry for 9 February 1941 was:

River [Teme] overflows its banks, a surprise because we hadn't had enough rain here to make it overflow. So we came to the conclusion that it was the thick snow in Wales melting quickly that made it overflow. There was only a little drop of water in the [Leigh] brook, then the river of course stanked it up.

Ronald Simcock, who lived in the now-demolished Old Post Office just beside The Fox, has memories of the 1947 flood:

We were woken by the Police shouting through a megaphone that the flood was rising rapidly. We all went upstairs and soon after a two-foot wall of water swept through the house. It took the front and back doors with it. We were rescued through the bedroom windows by the Army in a DUKW (an amphibious vehicle).

We stayed in Mr Tooby's barracks for a bit, and then were sent to Bromsgrove for a month. When we came back we had five cwt of coal and a new broom from the WVS as compensation.

Flooding at The Fox, 1946. Ronald Simcock is on the left, pushing his brother Albert in a pram. His cousin Alan Garness is watching. The flood of 1947 was far worse. (RONALD SIMCOCK)

Leigh Brook

Leigh Brook has a surprisingly large catchment area. Starting on the west side of the Malvern Hills the brook runs along through Mathon and Cradley, collecting water from the whole valley. Consequently, in really wet weather Leigh Brook can rise very rapidly indeed, and well before either the Teme or the Severn. Extracts from the report of the 1852 floods show just how destructive these floods can be:

Owing to the sudden overflowing of the Leigh Brook the roads became impassable, and several wayfarers found a hospitable reception and entertainment for the night at Leigh Lodge, the residence of Mr Chubb, one of the firm of Chubb and Son, the eminent lock-makers. The houses in the village were inundated, particularly those occupied by Mr Bradford [the Town House, Leigh] and Mr Hyde [the Old Rectory, Leigh], the water in the latter case being nearly up to the first floor. The fields and gardens were strewn with dead sheep, and all bore evidence of severe calamity...
The turnpike road from the Church was rendered impassable, and everybody living west of it had to get into carts and carriages to enable them to attend divine worship on Sunday morning. In consequence of the flood the postman could not reach Leigh that morning... The mill and stables belonging to Mr Hadley (the Old Mill, Leigh),

Mill House and mill, Leigh.
(JEAN McGOWAN)

which are at some little distance from the bridge, were completely flooded, so much so that great difficulty was experienced in getting the horses out in safety. The water rose to the height of five or six feet.

The Old Rectory is reported to have remained unoccupied for ten years after this deluge.

The most serious flood in recent years was one evening in April 1998, when heavy, continuous rains affected all of Herefordshire and West Worcestershire. Neighbouring farmers used tractors to bring people through the floods by the bridge, when the brook rose about 14 feet (4.3m) above normal. Both the Town House and the Old Rectory were flooded, though nothing like as badly as in 1852, and by the morning the floods had subsided.

Leigh Brook's large catchment area means that there is a steady flow throughout the year, and it was a valuable source of power until the early 1900s. There used to be seven mills along its entire length, of which one was in Leigh. At Leigh, to get a good head of water and a steady supply, a weir was built upstream. Water for the mill was taken from there, and went along a fairly level channel (a 'leat') to the mill. After passing through the mill-wheel, the water then went back into the main stream. Although the mill building is still there, the weir has gone, and the leat has been filled in.

View towards Leigh Brook from Brook House of the floods in April 1998. Note the cars parked on top of the bridge, hoping to be safe. The water level is 14 feet (4.25m) above normal. (GEOFF AND SHEILA WRIGHT)

Wildlife in Leigh Brook

There are still trout in Leigh Brook today, but before the Second World War it had many more. One reason was that it was kept stocked, particularly by Colonel Farquhar at Leigh Lodge. Indeed, according to 'Stroller', writing in the *Worcester Herald* in the 1920s, Leigh Brook shared with another tributary of the Teme, the Rea, the description of being 'most beautiful', and it was 'full of fish, and affording capital sport for those who can fish under bushes.'

Both the Teme and Leigh Brook also had otters, which otter hounds used to hunt, going up Leigh Brook as far as Hopton Court. Indeed, to emphasise the richness of the brook in those days, Ken Wadley, who lived at the Old Rectory, Leigh, for nearly 30 years, remembers seeing an otter take a salmon out of the brook in 1947.

After becoming a rarity, otters are slowly re-establishing themselves locally. A less-welcome change over the last few decades has been the growth of the mink population. Mink are not native to this country, but are descendants of escaped captive mink, kept for their fur. They are voracious in their appetite for fish, birds and eggs, and their spread into the wild has become a national problem. Today, mink hounds are used locally in an attempt to try to control the numbers.

Railways

As W.H. Smith says in the introduction to his book on the Worcester to Leominster railway:

> It took 36 years of planning, financial problems and frustrations before it was possible for a passenger to catch the train to travel between Leominster and Worcester. Many of those who had dreamt of achieving a cherished place in railway history did not live to see its completion.

He goes on to describe the complexity of the whole construction process, and his book details the interactions of the companies and individuals involved, together with the problems they encountered. We will not even attempt to summarise this, but will concentrate on the impact the railway had locally.

After consideration of several alternative routes, the one approved was to run from the Worcester to Hereford line between Rushwick and Bransford through Leigh to Knightwick and Suckley, before going on to Bromyard and Leominster. Work on the line started in the summer of 1864, the first ceremonial cut being made at Bransford by Lady Hastings, using a silver spade. (The men used a stouter spade for their ceremonial dig!) In 1872, Leigh Court Station was being built, but the 70-foot-high, six-arch viaduct necessary to cross Hayley Dingle,

Brockamin, had not been started. By 1873, however, a train could go all the way from Bransford to Yearsett (between Knightwick and Bromyard), although the link-up to the main line at Bransford was not complete.

Once the main-line connection had been made, the line from Worcester was opened on 2 May 1874 up as far as Yearsett. The timetable shows that there were four trains per day each way, linking up in Worcester with trains to London and Birmingham. The journey from Leigh Court to London took four and a half hours, which included a 30-minute wait at Shrub Hill. From Leigh Court to Birmingham took two hours and 20 minutes, again including a half-hour wait.

So, it was possible to get to Worcester by train, but it was not until 1877 that it was possible to get to Bromyard. It then took another 20 years, until 1897, for the line to be completed all the way to Leominster. Once this link was complete, the number of trains per day increased to five, and later to six.

Sadly, the railway closure was much more rapid than the building. Having taken the longest to build, the Bromyard to Leominster section was closed first, in 1952. The rest of the line then closed in 1964, following the Beeching report.

Whatever its financial aspects, the railway proved to be a boon locally. In addition to its value for passenger traffic, it made transporting farm products far easier. It was also extremely 'passenger friendly'. Les Alford and Harry Banner give us two examples:

> If you were late for the train and the Stationmaster saw you coming he would hold the train up and have your ticket ready for you. Mrs Park, who lived alongside the railway at Lulsley, used to drop her shopping off at her house as the train went by. She would pass it to her husband as the train slowed, and then she would get off at Knightwick Station and walk home.

Ronald Hunt, who was a fireman on the line in the 1950s, said that Leigh Court Station was a 'lively, friendly, place'. In those days the signalbox, stationmaster's office and the waiting rooms all had coal fires, for which the station received a coal ration. They inevitably ran out, and then they used to cadge some from the engine driver!

The trains were also very punctual, so that people used them to tell the time. As the Weaver sisters from Orchard Cottage, Leigh, recall:

> All the children walked to Leigh Hurst School, Bransford, together. There would be the 8a.m. train to Worcester and then the one coming back to Leigh Court Station, and if we hadn't reached a certain point in our journey by then we knew that we would be late for school.

If people used the train to go shopping they had to carry their shopping back from the station, or get children to do it. Gwen Hawkins was one such child:

*Leigh Court
Station in 1934.*
(DES SYMONDS)

*Leigh Court Station around 1910. On the left is
James Lane, the stationmaster, who lived at
Vicars Hill, Leigh, in a house where chickens
roamed freely. His son was also a stationmaster
there later.* (DES SYMONDS)

*Bransford
Road Station
in 1911, after it
was rebuilt.*
(DES SYMONDS)

Bransford Road Station in the 1950s.
(DES SYMONDS)

Bransford Road Station. (BRIAN ILES)

On Friday evenings, Gwennie Jackson [who lived near her on the Suckley Road], my sister and I had a duty to perform. Gwennie's mother went to Worcester by train to do her shopping, and we had to take the old pushchair (made out of a sort of carpet material and collapsing flat like an old-style deckchair) to meet the train. We would then load the bags of shopping onto it, and take turns in pushing it home. En route, we were always rewarded with a dripping cake. These were heavily layered with fruit and dripping and were absolutely delicious. The modern 'lardy cakes' don't taste at all the same.

Des Symonds started work at Leigh Court Station as junior porter in December 1944, just before he was 14. At that time two Italian prisoners of war also worked there. His description of his work shows the use made of the railway:

On my second day at work after the Boxing Day, my job was to prepare 17 coal wagons which had been sent from Worcester to be loaded with hops the next day. The hops were from Ted Jay's which he used to store for the Hops Marketing Board at the old Prisoner of War Camp. I spent the day clearing about a foot of slack from each wagon and I had this great pile of slack at the finish and then had to prepare 51 sheets, making sure they had all their ties to cover the hops the next day. That was a day's work, I went home shattered. The next day I worked 12 hours loading the hops and in order to keep them free from damp and wet we would put a sheet in the bottom of the wagon, then straw, then the hops and covered them with more straw and finally two sheets on top. Ted Jay's men would bring all the hops down to the station for loading using horses or tractors and trailers.

After the hops it would be the fruit season. All the empty boxes would come from Cardiff, Birmingham and Manchester and they would be stored in the yard. The apple boxes would hold 40lb and the plum boxes 56lbs. They would be stacked in threes, one flat, one inside, one on the top. Norbury's were our biggest customer, and then Walter Pope [Little Brockamin Farm] and Hodges [Pigeon House Farm]. Tom Weaver sent all his fruit to a relation in Cardiff. There would be special trains at hop picking and during the fruit season to cope with the people.

Des later moved to become stationmaster at Bransford Road, a position later held by his wife, May. It was at Bransford Road that Ronald Simcock started work as a junior porter in 1949, getting 37s.0d. (£1.85) for a 49-hour week. Here he describes his duties:

I had to clean the station and be on the platform when trains came in, make a fire in each Waiting Room and pump water for the header tank for the WC in the Ladies Waiting Room. Monday was lamp-cleaning day, when I had to clean the lamps, trim the wicks and fill them with paraffin. Every afternoon I took the train to Henwick and then walked back along the line checking and lighting the lamps at the Halts at Boughton and Rushwick and Bransford Road Station.

He recalls that, in addition to dispatching farm produce – hops, fruit and sugar beet – they also carried machinery from Busks, the agricultural engineers in Bransford, and timber.

The time when there was most passenger activity was, of course, during hop picking. Special trains were run, bringing thousands of workers from the Black Country to Bransford Road and Leigh Court, where

107

they were met by the farmers with a mixture of carts and wagons. These trains were much longer than usual and had to pull into Leigh Court Station two or three times to let the passengers off. It was also only during hop picking that trains ran on Sunday, bringing down the husbands and any remaining family of the hop pickers for a day together.

An event which is widely remembered is when the Royal Train carrying Queen Elizabeth II stayed overnight near Leigh Court, armed troops being stationed in the adjoining woods. Royal Train journeys were meticulously planned, the booklet produced for the railway staff for the three-day journey from Windsor to Leominster being 29 pages long. Such is the detail that the train's length was given to the nearest half an inch (1cm), apparently so that it was certain that the red carpet would be put out at exactly the right place!

But all did not go smoothly. Des Symonds was on duty at Bransford Junction signalbox on the evening of Tuesday 23 April 1957:

Security was tight, and there was someone stationed at every level-crossing. However, when the train was due down from Worcester – it was very distinctive, having four headlights instead of two – I heard three bangs, which I assumed were detonators. These are put on the line and explode when a train goes over them, warning it to stop. I was right: they were detonators, and the Royal Train stopped.

I later found out that Tom Salisbury, who was at one of the level-crossings, saw a horse jump over the fence onto the line, so he quickly put the detonators down. The horse ran up towards Worcester, past the Royal Train... Everybody teased Tom, saying that he would get into trouble for stopping the Royal Train, but he actually got a commendation certificate and £15.

Incidentally, parts of the track from Bransford to Leigh Court were re-laid before the royal visit, in order to take the weight of the engine, which was much more than that of the engines normally used – we called it 'above routine maintenance'.

To ensure that no trains used the line whilst the Royal Train was 'stabled' there (as the instruction leaflet put it), the chief inspector locked the points at Bransford and walked to the train, carrying the key. What he did not know was that there were several duplicates, so it was all a bit pointless!

Railways are, of course, much safer than roads, and the local line was no exception. There are no records of passengers being killed on the line, although cattle straying onto the line were killed. There was, however, the occasional runaway train. William Weaver, from Orchard Cottage, Leigh, recorded one such incident in his notebook, the entry also giving us an insight into the pace of life at that time:

December 20th 1941
It was thick fog and we were up in the pony orchard digging round trees there when we heard a train coming down the line. Then I said 'What train's this coming down?' Then we listened and he went straight through the station without stopping and we heard him go round the corner in some form. Then all of a sudden the noise stopped. Then about 5 or 6 minutes after we heard the engine coming slowly down, and that sort of confirmed it, that he had run away. So we went down to the station and the engine was in there. And we heard that it had run away from Knightwick. So we were right. It was stopped at the junction by the Bransford plate layers. The train contained about ten trucks including the guard's van. Next to the guard's van was a truck of black cattle, so they had a free ride for nothing.

Poster on Leigh Court Station advertising the last excursion on the Worcester to Bromyard line, held the day after the line was closed to regular train services. (HARRY BANNER)

As we noted, the infamous Beeching report, which recommended wholesale line closures throughout the UK, also resulted in the closure of the Worcester to Bromyard line. To mark the occasion, Bill Morris, who ran the coach company at Bromyard, organised a day trip from Bromyard to Blackpool via Worcester on Sunday 6 September 1964. Despite the imminent closure of the line it seems to have been a riotous affair – although the train was delayed for half an hour on the way back, because a key was missing at Bransford.

With the demise of the railway, a vital transport link from the parishes was lost, and the start of dependency on roads began.

Roads

Although there was a Roman road from Droitwich through Worcester and down into South Wales (Rycknield Street), there are virtually no traces of it south-west of Worcester until Stretton Grandison. The Worcestershire County Archaeological Services' index mentions the possible traces of a Roman road at Sherridge, but it appears never to have been fully investigated.

During and after the Middle Ages, drovers used to bring cattle and sheep very large distances to market, and the drovers' roads came into being. They would bring several hundred cattle, and even more sheep, at a time. Because of the inconvenience which these slow-moving, large flocks and herds caused – and also to avoid tolls – the drovers' roads tended to be separate from the normal ones. Worcester was both one of the destinations for Welsh drovers and a staging post on the way to London. The drovers' road from Carmarthen to Worcester is believed to have followed the route of the Roman Ryknield Street.

There are records of the numbers of sheep and cattle being brought into Worcester market by the drovers, and we know that those coming from the south must have crossed Bransford Bridge but, frustratingly, we have not been able to find any evidence of the road locally. Well, there may have been one piece. The cattle and sheep obviously had to be rested and

The old bridge at Bransford in 1911.
(WRO/COUNTY SURVEYOR)

watered overnight, and the drovers had to know where they would be welcome. It is believed that farmers willing to allow them to stay planted small stands of Scots pines, these being both very tall and very distinctive. Max Sinclair has researched drovers' roads and believes that one such stand was at Bank House Farm, Bransford. Unfortunately they were felled to make way for a car park after the farm became a hotel.

Up until the late 1600s, road maintenance was not undertaken systematically, and they were generally in very bad condition. This started to change in the late 1600s, when the first turnpike trusts were established. In return for maintaining the roads, the trusts were allowed to charge tolls for road use. This led to the establishment of a network of roads along which coaches could travel at speed.

Not surprisingly, there were objections to turnpike roads, because every vehicle and animal using them had to pay. In Worcester in 1726, the charges for entering were 1s.0d. for a coach drawn by four or more horses, 1d. for every unladen horse, mule or ass and 10d. per score (20) of calves, pigs, sheep or lambs. No wonder the drovers avoided the main roads!

A turnpike trust running out to Leigh and Bransford was set up in 1726, and by 1885 there were several turnpike roads running through the parishes from Worcester. One ran along the present A4103 to

Bransford Bridge looking towards Worcester, 1910s. (BRIAN ILES)

Cradley, another through Leigh and on to Alfrick, and a third went along the Suckley Road. There is a Turnpike Cottage at Storridge as evidence of the old turnpike road.

Incidentally, the Suckley Road was known to the older inhabitants as 'Gallows (or Gallas) Lane', because there used to be a gibbet opposite Broadfields, at the start of the footpath which leads directly to Leigh church. This path, known as 'the Coffin Route', is still there. When Patrick Mills was having The March renovated in 1982, the workmen found the remains of the gallows underneath the floor. Unfortunately these remains were not kept, but were carted away with the rest of the spoil. We have not found any record of when the gallows were used, or for what offence, but according to H.W. Gwilliam's book, *Coach Travel and Turnpike Roads in Worcestershire*, roadside gibbets were a common sight in the eighteenth and early-nineteenth centuries.

In 1794, the Worcester to Hereford stagecoach (the 'Hereford Mail') used to go through Leigh Sinton, leaving The Star and Garter in Worcester every Tuesday, Thursday and Saturday at 1p.m., returning on Monday, Wednesday and Friday. It cost 10s.0d. to travel inside and 5s.0d. on the outside, so only the rich could travel in this way.

Of course, the growth in horse-drawn travel meant that there had to be stabling for horses and accommodation for passengers along the routes, and The Somers Arms in Leigh Sinton had both of these.

But although stagecoaches capture the imagination, the improved roads also allowed a local public transport network to be established. In 1794, there were hackney carriages operating from Angel Street, Worcester, out to Leigh and Leigh Sinton. There was also a growth in local carriers, whose horse-drawn carts would take either people or goods to the outlying villages. For example, the *Worcester Calendar* for 1865 lists a carrier going from The Golden Lion, High Street, Worcester, to Bransford, Leigh and Leigh Sinton on Wednesdays and Saturdays.

Despite the coming of the railway from Worcester to Bransford and Leigh, horse-drawn vehicles went on operating into the twentieth century, until eventually petrol-driven lorries and coaches took over. A carriers' list from 1908 shows that on Wednesdays and Saturdays there were half a dozen or so operators offering afternoon services to Bransford, Leigh, Leigh Sinton and Sandlin from the several different Worcester public houses – The Reindeer, The Old Greyhound, The Plough, The Swan-with-two-Necks and The Golden Lion. Of these destinations the Sandlin entry stands out, because it served so few people. Then we see that it was run by a Mrs Turley. She lived at Sandlin and was later to run the first local bus, the Chicken Coop (sometimes called the 'Chicken Pen').

Rather than collect the tolls themselves, the turnpike trusts very often let the toll-gates by tender,

usually annually. The toll rights were sometimes bought by individuals, but often by cartels, who rigged the tendering market in their favour. The difference between the cost of the tender and the tolls collected was the income for the toll-collector – or his employer. In 1801 and 1804 the Bransford toll-gate realised £910 and £1,035 respectively for the Worcester Turnpike Trust, but we do not know what profits the toll-gate lessees made.

Interestingly, with the growth of turnpike roads came the need to keep trees and hedges on the adjoining land from interfering with the traffic. An Act of Parliament of 1734 required the owners of land adjacent to 'common highways' to keep hedges low. A later Act in the 1820s casts a curious light on what went on near, or on, public roads:

If any person shall make or assist in making any fire or fires commonly called bonfires, or shall set fire to, or wantonly let off or throw any squib, rocket or serpent, or other firework whatsoever, within 80 feet of the centre of the road... or play football, tennis, fives, cricket or any other game upon the road, or on the side or sides thereof... they shall for every offense forfeit and pay any sum not exceeding 40s.

It was the growth of the railways that brought about the demise of the stagecoaches and, with them, the turnpike system. The Worcester Turnpike Trusts were abolished by Parliament in 1869 and in 1894 responsibility for road maintenance passed to the County Councils (for the main roads) and to the District Councils. The toll-houses were either pulled down or sold. According to the contemporary records, the toll-house at Dragons Cross was pulled down and the land sold to a J. Shapland for £38.

As motor traffic built up slowly in the twentieth century, so the A4103 Worcester to Hereford road became increasingly inadequate. Bransford Bridge in particular – initially a wooden structure only 12 feet or so wide – was the scene of many accidents. One of the most serious of these was in 1916, when a lorry laden with fuel cans went through the wooden railings. The driver and his mate, a boy, were drowned,

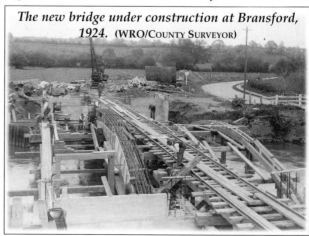

The new bridge under construction at Bransford, 1924. (WRO/COUNTY SURVEYOR)

Diver going into the River Teme off the old Bransford Bridge, to look for a petrol lorry which went into the river in 1916. The bodies of the driver and his mate were later recovered at Tewkesbury.
(SALLY STEWART)

Accident on the Hereford Road outside the Nutshell, Leigh Sinton, in 1998. The Air Ambulance landed in Froggatt's field opposite. The driver of the car was killed.
(CONNIE TOHTZ)

The collapsed roof at The Barn, Leigh Sinton, on the A4103 after a car crashed into it in September 1978.
(MIKE GRUNDY/
BERROWS)

The 'Chicken Coop' or 'Chicken Pen', a coach which operated in the parish from the late 1920s until after the Second World War. It seated about 14, and passengers got in from the back. In addition to taking children to school and collecting WI members, it also took goods to market – hence the nickname. Painted yellow and green, it was owned by Mrs Elizabeth Turley, and driven by her son-in-law Joe Dance, from Sandlin. (ERIC VINE)

their bodies being recovered much later on at Tewkesbury. After being pulled from the river the lorry was simply left by The Fox, and Alan Garness remembers playing on it in the 1940s.

In 1925 the road at this point was re-aligned, a new bridge was built 50 yards upstream and the old one was later demolished. Nevertheless, the main road through the parishes continued to be dangerous, and has been the subject of road-improvement schemes ever since. Some parts have been straightened and others widened. A roundabout has been built at the Bank House, speed limits have been introduced and, most recently, traffic-calming measures have been implemented in Leigh Sinton, to try to cut down vehicle speeds. Despite all these measures, and because traffic continues to build up, the congestion in Leigh Sinton can be serious at times, making it difficult, and dangerous, for both the inhabitants and local businesses.

Public Transport

We have said that Mrs Turley ran the first local bus, starting in the late 1920s. The 'Chicken Coop', or 'Chicken Pen', is still remembered by many local people with very great affection. Painted green and yellow, it was locally made and, according to Geoff Bartlett, built on a Bedford lorry chassis. Only seating 14 or so people, and with an entrance door at the back, it used to go regularly to Bromyard and Worcester Markets. Driven by Joe Dance, Mrs

Turley's son-in-law, it used to take Mrs Turley's own butter, eggs and dressed poultry to market. It also picked up other local produce, which would simply be left at people's front gates for collection. Its nickname derived from the fact that taking live chickens to market was one of its functions, and their feathers were often in the bus when it picked up passengers.

In addition to picking up children to go to the local school, it also used to take them to the Malvern schools. As Gwen Hawkins (née Herbert), who lived at Harley House on the Suckley Road, in the 1930s, recalls:

We travelled each day in a funny old bus with a half-door at the back. One or two of the lads would lean out over the door and shout at all the girls we passed along the road, and if they (the lads) got too noisy or started fighting, the driver (Mr Joe Dance) would stop the bus, walk round to the back and threaten to knock their heads together. We all knew he never would, as he was a very gentle, mild-mannered man, but the threat of punishment seemed to work!

In addition to carrying schoolchildren, the Chicken Coop was widely used locally by other groups – for example, by the WI to collect members for meetings. It even used to make an annual trip to Weston-super-Mare, although it seems that the passengers were always anxious about whether it would get back! According to Mrs Turley's niece, Kathleen Jauncey, it ran for years without a Public Service Vehicle Licence, and the Turleys were eventually prosecuted for this.

Another bus ran in the late 1920s and '30s, and belonged to 'Bunner' Taylor, from Acton Beauchamp. According to Harold Portman, it was larger than the Chicken Coop, seating about 35. Gwen Hawkins remembers this well too:

On Saturdays, Mother sometimes went into Worcester to do her weekly shopping. Bunner's bus would stop outside our house and pick Mother up. The return fare was, I think, about 4d., and children could travel free. If Mother only wanted a couple of things from the shops, Bunner would bring them for her without her having to go herself to Worcester! He always stopped and shouted through our open window, so he didn't have to leave the bus, and Mother would go out to him pay him if he'd done any shopping for her.

As time went on, there were other local coach services, particularly running through Leigh Sinton. Geoff Bartlett remembers that Alec Wood and his brother from Mathon used to run a coach from there to Worcester in the late 1920s and early '30s. Like the Chicken Coop it had a roof rack, and it also used to pick up produce for market, which was left out along the main road, including Crowcroft, where he lived. On the return trip, the money for the produce would be wrapped in newspaper and put under a milk crate at the end of the lane.

In the 1930s regular bus services were established, but they were always few and far between except on Saturdays, when there was about one every hour from Leigh Sinton to Worcester. Cars were still very rare, although a little more common than in the 1920s. Then, Eileen Kebby said that the only car she saw was once a week, when a visitor came, whilst Geoff Bartlett could walk to school from Crowcroft every day for three weeks and not see a car! So until car ownership became widespread, for most people the only options were to walk or use a bicycle to go to Worcester or Malvern. Those in Leigh and in Bransford had the option of a train if they could afford it, in which case they often cycled to the station and left their bikes there, knowing that they would be safe. This was Pat Bowers' experience:

I remember, especially on a Friday, Mom would take me on the back of her bike, whatever the weather, to Bransford to catch the 9.40a.m. train to Worcester Foregate Street, to do the shopping. Then she would catch the 12 o'clock train back to Bransford, and cycle home with me and the shopping. For my seventh birthday [in 1931] I was given a bicycle of my own.

When the local railway closed in 1964 the bus services did not improve significantly. As time went on, more and more people owned cars, but many still had to rely on inadequate public transport. At the same time, both cycling and walking became more

dangerous. Today the situation for people without cars is even worse, although, being on the main road, Bransford and Leigh Sinton are better served than Leigh, having five buses a day – although none of these allow people to have an evening out.

Road Flooding

Although both Leigh Brook and the Teme are responsible for flooded roads from time to time, other roads in the parish also suffer from flooding. In the log-books for Leigh Sinton School there were many times when the children were unable to come to school, or had to leave early, because the roads to Sherridge or Smith End Green were under water. Geoff Bartlett, who worked at Dyson's garage in Leigh Sinton, remembers one such incident:

We had a very nasty flood down Stocks Lane in October 1951. I had a call-out to say that there was someone with a baby in distress on the top of a vehicle. I went down and there was four feet of water swirling across the road, and Mrs Lisa Norbury, Christopher Norbury's wife, was there with her daughter Christabel in an Austin Big-Seven.

She had slid the sunshine roof back and they were sitting there with their legs dangling down. She was quite terrified, and the little girl was screaming. The water was quite strong. I had got all my overalls on, and it was not too easy to wade in it. I put Christabel on my shoulders and Mrs Norbury said, 'What about me?' I said, 'You will have to slide down into the water.' She was quite a big woman, and she tucked her clothes into her old-fashioned bloomers and slid down into the water. By this time Christopher Norbury was down there waiting for us, and when she got out of the water she pulled the elastic on her bloomers and about five gallons of water fell out!

Dyson's Garages

The rise of the motor vehicle brought a need for local garage facilities. The first came in 1913, when William Dyson opened a garage in Leigh Sinton, by Shrubbery House. This not only sold petrol and undertook repairs, but also sold cars. In those days, of course, no driving licence was needed, and William Dyson used to give customers their driving lessons. Having had her brief introduction to her new car driving down the Hereford Road, one woman then set off to Malvern on her own. Some hours later, she phoned to ask if somebody could come out and help her, as she had forgotten how to reverse!

Before the Second World War, William Dyson built a second garage, at Bransford, opposite Bank House Farm. However, both Cyril and Ray Dyson, his sons, were called up during the war, and the Bransford garage had to be closed for lack of staff. It reopened after the war, with Ray as manager, Cyril

Left: *Leigh Sinton Post Office and garage (the franking on the postcard is dated 1927).*
(DOROTHY DYSON)

Below: *John Bartlett, aged about one year in 1948, in front of Geoff Bartlett's first car, a Morris Minor Tourer.*
(GEOFF BARTLETT)

being at Leigh Sinton. In 1962 a new garage was built in Leigh Sinton, on the opposite side of the road. Not only was more space needed, but new regulations meant that the petrol pumps could not be at the curbside, as they were at the old garage, but had to be set back off the road.

After Ray's sudden death in 1980, his wife Dorothy carried on at Bransford for a few years before selling up and retiring. Later, the Leigh Sinton garage was also sold, and so, after nearly 70 years, there were no Dysons running garages in either parish. In 2001 the Leigh Sinton garage was demolished, to make way for nine starter homes. The Bransford garage is still open.

Chapter Seven

PARISH LIFE

Meeting of the Worcestershire Archery Society at Sherridge Court, 8 August 1855. A sketch by Cuthbert Bede accompanying an article in the Illustrated London News *of the same date.*

Introduction

The Industrial Revolution initially brought fewer social changes to the countryside than it did to towns. As a result, the changes which have taken place in rural areas in the last 100 years or so have been all the more dramatic. At the end of the 1800s, the land was still mostly in the hands of the large landowners. The farms they owned provided much of the housing for their workers, whose lives they controlled in a way we find difficult to imagine today.

There was a strongly enforced class system. The majority of the population was working class: the rise of the middle class was yet to come. Within the upper classes there was a strict social hierarchy, so that one could entertain those beneath one, but not those above. This was a period when all the land-owning families would have servants, and entering domestic service was one of the few opportunities for women to get non-agricultural work.

The Social Scene

The break-up of Lady Henry Somerset's estates in 1898 started a major shift in land ownership leading, eventually, to the family ownership of farms which we know today. However, the family whose influence was strongest in the parish at the start of the twentieth century were the Norburys. They do not conform to a picture of an aristocratic landowning class, since their wealth was derived originally from a Droitwich salt business. In that sense, they were in the forefront of the change in land ownership away from the landed gentry.

By the mid 1800s the Norburys were very well established socially in the parish, as this extract from an *Illustrated London News* account of an archery tournament at Sherridge in 1855 shows:

Hopkins's Quadrille Band played at intervals throughout the day. At three o'clock the shooting was agreeably broken in upon by an adjournment to the dinner tent, where an excellent repast was provided by Mr Hambler, of Worcester. Mr Norbury presided; and, after the usual loyal toasts had been duly honoured, Sir E. Blount proposed the 'Health of the Lady Paramount'. Sir J.S. Pakington returned thanks, and gave the 'Health of the Host and Hostess', whose courteous attentions to their guests had contributed to make the first meeting of the season most agreeable, as well as successful. Mr Norbury having duly responded to the toast, the tent was shortly deserted, and the shooting resumed. It did not terminate until after seven o'clock, when... the prizes were awarded by the Lady Paramount.

Leigh Ladies' Hockey Team, 1909–10. (BRIAN ILES)

on the pond and skating was possible, all and sundry seem to have been invited to skate and to join in impromptu games of hockey.

At Christmas they helped to organise parties and entertainments at the local schools, including magic lantern shows and conjuring parties. Early in the New Year there was always the Hunt Ball at Worcester, followed by the County Ball at Malvern. Sometimes there were seasonal entertainments and theatricals at Sherridge. Throughout the winter the ladies of the family ran a weekly series of Mothers' Meetings for the parish, often addressed by the Curate and including the reading aloud of a worthy book. And the Norbury ladies were keen members of a Shakespeare Reading Group, taking turns to meet in the homes of the local gentry and reading through a play at each meeting.

Kevin Allen, who has used the diaries of Gertrude Norbury (1831–1916) and her daughter Winifred (1861–1938) in preparing his forthcoming book, *Gracious Ladies: the Norbury family and Edward Elgar*, has this to say about the Norburys' social life:

The Norburys' social activities were very much related to their sporting and educational interests. The hunt used to meet at Sherridge, as did the local beagle packs. Various friends were invited to shoot on the estate, and the family sons were invited away to stay with various friends to join their shooting parties. When the ice bore

Winifred Norbury, who never married, was Elgar's inspiration for the eighth of his 14 Enigma Variations. But, in addition to moving in musical circles, her social life gives us an insight into the role played by the family locally. Kevin Allen's researches reveal an extremely religious woman, who went to church three times on Sundays:

She used even to help clean the brasses in Leigh Church, she cycled round the parish delivering the

Meeting of a beagle pack at Sherridge, c.1900. (PETER NORBURY)

Leigh Women's Union, 1930, which met at Sherridge. Left to right: Mrs Bullock, ?, Mrs Newman, Miss Violet Allen, Olive Turley, Miss Veal, Mrs Page.
(Doreen Rowley)

Thomas Coningsby and Gertrude Norbury at Sherridge, 1896. In the front row, Winifred Norbury is second from the right, and Frederick Paget Norbury third from the right. On the left of the back row is William Philips, the cowman.
(Peter Norbury)

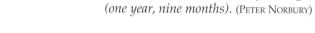

Right: *July 1910. F.P. Norbury's wife, Rosamond, holding Rosamond (nine months) with Christopher Paget (one year, nine months).* (Peter Norbury)

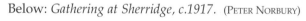

Below: *Gathering at Sherridge, c.1917.* (Peter Norbury)

Above: *Leigh Farmers' dinner at the Somers Arms, mid to late 1950s. Left to right, facing: Zoe Dorrell, ? Dorrell, Jack Froggett, Lucy Froggett, John Tooby, Cyril Dyson;* foreground: *Mick Lynch.* (SUSAN JONES)

Right: *After the Second World War, when petrol was still rationed, Jack Wilesmith, Ted Jay* (standing) *and Ken Farr solved their holiday transport problem by using a gypsy caravan. They got to Leominster in the first day!*
(STELLA BRAITHWAITE/BERROWS)

parish magazine, and visited the sick and the elderly. The salaries of the curate and of the teachers at the two schools were paid by her, by organising rummage sales and concerts.

The Norburys were a leading 'County' family, so she had obligations there, having what she called 'ordeal by afternoon tea'. But people at all ends of the social scale were of interest to her, and she noted the alarmingly frequent comings and goings of those 'below stairs' at Sherridge. One unfortunate new kitchen maid ran away on her first day, only to be promptly returned by her dutiful mother. If for any reason another maid servant was needed at short notice, Winifred would simply cycle around the village until she found a youngster apparently at a loose end, or perhaps helping in the fields. She would negotiate with the parents, and engage the child on the spot.

Des Clarke used to drive for the Norburys in the 1950s, and collected three or four servants daily. Whenever there was a big party, seven or eight chauffeurs would congregate in the kitchen, waiting to pick up their charges. As we shall see, the social life of the Norburys was a world apart from that of both other local farmers and the parishioners.

Although the Norburys were the wealthiest farmers in the parishes, until after the Second World War the farmers were still a distinct social set. Most of them sent their children to public schools and they moved in their own social circles. As Ruth Beard, who was at Hill Farm, Brockamin, from the 1940s to 1980 explained:

In those days we used to have visiting cards with your name, one for yourself and one for your husband, and you would leave these if you went visiting. The first

person to visit me was Mrs Farquhar from Leigh Lodge, then Mrs Farr (Leigh Court), Mrs Recordon (Bank Farm), Mrs Jay (the Great House) and Mrs Secker (Brockamin Farm). These visits were very formal – hats and gloves – and we would have tea together. Then, when the wives had met, you would be invited to supper and things with your husband.

Our social life used to revolve around the Church, the Conservative Association (who held a Wine and Cheese party every year), Whist Drives and the Leigh Farmers Dances, which were revived after the war by Mrs Jay and Mrs Secker. The dance was by invitation only and was held at the Talbot at Knightwick. It was a great social evening and the wives used to make the puddings. Other farmers from the district were also invited.

Pauline Phillips remembers that when she moved here after marrying James in 1969:

... a local farmer's wife apologised that 'she hadn't called on me'. She explained that calling on neighbouring farmers' wives was expected. You left your calling card if the lady wasn't at home.

Indeed, marrying into the farming community meant a commitment to the farm, and the fact that Pauline continued to work as a teacher raised lots of eyebrows.

Not surprisingly, farmers' children also moved in their own circle, and their lives were different from those of the other village children. School is, of course, a great common bond. They did not go to the local schools and Nora Jay told us that:

Our four children would mix with other farmers' children who went to the same schools, i.e. attending birthday parties at other houses, picnics, bike rides, and they only occasionally mixed with the children of farm workers.

The non-mixing was not out of 'snobbery' – it was simply because the farmers' children were not in the parish during term times. During the holidays, many of them played with both local children and with the children of the hop and fruit pickers.

Nowadays farmers no longer form a closely knit and separate social group, but are integrated into the general community.

Childhood Memories of Growing Up in the Parishes

Children are often astute and uninhibited observers. Hence, rather than try to provide a coherent picture of general parish life, we will let people's experiences as children paint the picture for us.

After school the boys would go home and probably have to catch a rabbit for tea or there would be no tea, there wasn't much time to play. The women would be working on the land and would not get home until about 4 o'clock and the girls would have to go home and get the tea ready. [Les Alford, b.1925 and Harry Banner, b.1920.]

The policeman was PC Parry, a very big man who was stationed in Leigh Sinton. He used to confiscate our catapults if he caught us. We used to steal moorhens' eggs from the ponds at Mr Secker's (Brockamin Farm). If we could not reach the nests we used a spoon attached to a stick to reach. Secker was a cripple so, although the ponds were in full view of his house, he could never catch us. We used to go rabbiting with ferrets and snares – Ken Farr agreed to this. [Basil Wadley, b.1933.]

Incidentally, one way in which rabbits were caught by the boys sounds worse than it probably was. A length of barbed wire was pushed down the burrow until they felt a rabbit. The wire was then twirled round to catch onto the rabbit's fur, and the rabbit pulled out.

We now have a girl's perspective:

Childhood was spent making your own enjoyment. We played marbles in the gutters and played with our hoops in the road. We paddled in Leigh Brook and used to catch minnows and take them home in jars and they would jump out. We used to make our own fun. In the holidays we would make tents with sacks in the hedgerow between Yarnolds and Phillips. Daisy Yarnold would give us skimmed milk and we would take potatoes, make a fire and have chips and custard. In our late-teens we would go to the dances at the Memorial Hall or get on our bikes and go to the pictures in Malvern. In the 1920s you could go to the Gaumont in Worcester, you could get the tea-time bus in and catch the last one home at 11p.m.

Dad was a wheelwright, carpenter and undertaker. He used to repair the gypsy caravans on the side of the road if they had a shaft go, or a broken wheel, as they went through on their way to Bosbury for the hop picking. There used to be a gypsy lady who came every Monday with her pram, Mum used to call her Maggie. She sold pegs, wool, cotton, etc.

Christmas was spent with the family, there was

Picture taken in 1904 at Mill House, Leigh. Left to right: Eva Hyde, Frank (in pram), Allie and Peggie.
(JEAN McGOWAN)

Miss Green's School of Country Dancing, c.1930. The school used to give performances at garden fêtes and at British Legion concerts held in the Memorial Hall. Left to right, back row, standing: Reg Powell *and* Norman Kimber, Douglas Spencer *and* Raymond Dyson, Doreen Jones *and* Eileen Bowkett, Barbara James; *front row, kneeling:* Jean Powell, Eileen Hill, Freda Spencer, Doreen Lewis, Hilda Smith, Brenda Barnes, Bernice Rolph. (DOREEN ROWLEY)

Above: *Harold Portman (left, without cap) and his friends playing cards, around 1930. Left to right:* Harold Portman, Les Hill, George Rowberry, Gilbert Hill. (HAROLD PORTMAN)

Above: *Harvey Hunt, the postmaster at Leigh, as a child.* (SALLY STEWART)

Right: *John Hall, a sergeant in the Worcester Constabulary, who served in Leigh Sinton in the early 1900s.* (MURIEL 'BIB' JONES)

always plenty of food, music on the radio (the batteries would have to be charged at Dyson's garage) and we played games like Snakes and Ladders. We did not go on holiday as children, but a Mr Monk from the village used to arrange day trips to the seaside. Doreen was 21 before she saw the sea. We had a happy childhood with placid parents. [Connie Tohtz, b.1927 and Doreen Rowley, b.1921.]

Eileen Kebby spent a lot of her childhood down in the Castle Green farmhouse with her mother. When there were dinner parties she was allowed to sit on the stairs and watch the dancing:

One year I was given a moneybox in the shape of the Queen's house. I had to go round the guests and I collected seven shillings and sixpence. I thought I was that rich.

Now a boy's experience:

When I was a child my father was quite strict and he used a strap if my brother and I didn't obey. He used to blow a whistle at 7 o'clock at night. My brother and I and the two girls and the boy next door to us would probably be playing down in the fields somewhere, and when the whistle went it meant we had about 50 seconds to get back home and he would be waiting there with a strap for us if we didn't do so. Maybe he didn't hit us too often, but we had to obey the rules. I can't remember having any birthday presents and I never had any pocket money of course. Occasionally my mother would give me a halfpenny and I would call at Miss Hayman's (which is the Post Office now) and I would buy a halfpenny worth of broken biscuits on the way to school which I would, of course, have eaten by the time I got to school.

As we lived out in the countryside, my father had plenty of chickens and he always had a pig with his friends. When the pig was killed, they would hand out little bits and pieces. We used to go and dig potatoes out of the fields, and we also had quite a long garden. So we were fed alright, though nothing exotic. There used to be a lady that lived at Dragons Cross. Her husband was a carpenter and wheelwright at Busks at Bransford and they had a little bit more money. A man used to come round selling cakes and they could always afford to have four or five fancy cakes. My mother couldn't afford any. My dad's wages were 25 shillings a week and I think the rent was one shilling and sixpence.

When I was ten I was asked if I wanted a job and I went to work at the bakery at Crowcroft. George Griffiths the old man had just retired, and his son Fred had taken over and of course he couldn't manage on his own. I got four pence (2p) a week, or something like that, and I used to go every night from school, grease the tins, chop wood, get the coke in, clean the ovens out, and help him to mix the dough for the next

day. That was put in the big bin, and the next morning it would all be ready with a lovely smell.

The main event of the year was when the fair came to the common at Malvern and we could walk there. Once a year they used to have a fête in aid of the Church in front of Sherridge House. We would have orange shies, and people would make cakes. My father would take flowers from the garden and my mother would stuff a couple of chickens and take those. [Geoff Bartlett, b.1921.]

There was a Mrs Walker living at Bank House Farm, who would never let any of the local children near. You could not see the house then, as it was surrounded by horse chestnut trees. They were an attraction for the children. She used to chase them with a gun and of course got called a witch for her efforts. [Harold Portman, b.1920.]

There was a hop field at the bottom of the gardens at Winsgrave, oh the lovely smell, and fun in the cribs. Herrings being cooked on a stick over the small fires. The Co-op baker delivered, you chose your bread from the lovely BIG basket held by the baker. For the children this was exciting because if you were lucky enough you would get a Chelsea bun that you would share between two. My older brother David had a little peddle [sic] car and he vanished one day – he had got as far as Alfrick Post Office. Sometimes the organ grinder would come with his monkey and the man with a dancing bear on a chain. [Janet Griffiths, b.1927.]

But when David Chaundy talked to the Jaunceys opposite he got a different picture:

As children they would walk to Alfrick School, but only when they had shoes: if not, they stayed at home. Life was hard, and they never yearned for the 'good old days'.

Now back to Leigh.

A group of boys met on the corner of Dingle Road every day to go to school. Only boys: there were not many girls around. The boys all had catapults, and used to try and shoot birds and rabbits, usually without success. Most of the boys had a dog, and we used to go rabbiting with ferrets. We used to go swimming in the Teme by Leigh Court Station, where there was a shallow gravel beach. The lads formed the Hell's Corner Gang. We had boxing in the triangle, and played football in the road there.

When we got older we used to go down to Alfrick to look for girls. At Alfrick there was a Youth Club run by Mr and Mrs Reid. It was well organised, and they had table tennis, billiards and darts. At the end of the evening, from 9.30 to 10.00, they had dancing. Also a Captain Shepherd used to take us for boxing, and we

Left: *Garden Party at Norburys',
c.1938. Left to right: Ray Dyson,
David Hodges, one of the
Norburys' maids, Janet Hodges,
Joan Clark.* (JANET GRIFFITHS)

Left: *Leaf from the family
record of one branch of the
Jauncey family, giving the
birth dates of the children of
Henry and Elizabeth
Jauncy. Richard Jauncey
is Glenda Merrell's father.*
(GLENDA MERRELL)

Right: *1935. Pat Bowers
aged 14 years in his first
long trousers outside Rose
Cottage, Bransford.*
(PAT BOWERS)

*Coronation
celebrations
for King
George V in
Leigh, 1911.*
(DOROTHY
HUGHES)

used to beat hell out of one another. [John Roberts, b.1931.]

We had a big garden at Holy Well and grew all our own vegetables. We kept a pig or two. We enjoyed a good rabbit stew and killed a pig every year. We would have a joint at weekends. We never went on school trips or had holidays. [Joseph Hughes, b.1906.]

Ben Rowley, Gerald Jones and I used to play football or cricket every night of the week. Sometimes there would be 20 or 30 of us, and occasionally we would chase the girls round. [Norman Kimber, b.1920.]

My teenage years were very happy and memorable ones. We had a lot of friends throughout the village. Lots of memories come flooding back, just like the brook flooding the road, when we had to paddle to get to the station or the village shop and Post Office – right by Brook House [Leigh] – kept by a Mr and Mrs Hainsworth. [Bib Jones, b.1924.]

I never received pocket money, except sometimes Dad would give me a penny, which I would promptly spend the following day at 'Old Ma Dutson's' shop just below the school, usually on 'gobstoppers'. I do remember getting the cane a lot at school, although sometimes I was the innocent party. The event was known as 'Singing to the Nails'; I did a lot of it. At The Firs, there were three huge Walnut trees, alongside the blacksmith's shop. Every September, when I was old enough, I used to shin up the trees and shake all the walnuts off, and Granny Hales from Colwall would spend a couple of weeks' holiday at The Firs, shelling the green husks off the walnuts. Her hands used to be black. [Pat Bowers, b.1924.]

In our day at Harley House, Suckley Road (1930s), we had to draw the water from a deep well. It was at least 30 feet down to the water, and if you lost your grip on the handle of the winding gear on the bucket's way up, it would furiously and noisily unwind the rope right to the end, and you would have to start all over again. Often there would be slugs in the bucket, so you'd have to empty the whole lot and try again. A lot of wells in the village ran dry, but ours never did – it was so deep.

All the youngsters in the village used to gather just below our house, on the low wall of the Rectory. Sometimes we'd play games – top and whip, hopscotch, roller skates or bowl-a-hoop. The older boys would cycle round in the road, showing off and chatting up the girls.

On Friday nights the fish and chip van would come round. Most of the children would have a 'ha'porth of scratchings' (the bits of batter left from the frying). One penny would buy a big bag of chips. Fried fish cost 3d. but we never aspired to that! The travelling hardware shop came round one evening a week, owned by a very jovial fellow called Ernie Cordle, who

I believe had a shop in Worcester. He had a good line in patter and usually accepted a cup of tea at our house. Then, on Wednesday evenings it was the turn of the greengrocer, Mr Roberson, who had a smallholding at Bransford, near the railway bridge. He had a horse and open dray, so the village boys would race up the street and hang on to the back of the dray to get a free ride.

The there was Mrs Dutson, a remarkable old lady who had lots of interesting stories to tell about her childhood. Often my sister Gwennie and I would sit with her absolutely enthralled, and sometimes she would recite the old-fashioned poetry of her day. Always the poems were rather melancholy, and we children would sit with tears streaming down our cheeks. [Gwen Hawkins, b.1923.]

We use to play hopscotch at school, but we used to get into trouble for drawing on the playground. We played marbles, and skipping – everyone had a skipping rope. We played conkers and the first children to the conker trees by Leigh church got the best ones. We used to make chairs out of conkers, if you got the ones with flat tops and used pins and some cotton thread. The boys used to have hoops and the girls would have spinning tops. We were able to play with these in the road, because there were no cars. The only people with a vehicle would be the farmers.

We all used to help Dad with delivering the milk, and Beryl remembers going to Mrs Beechey's at the Mill House every Friday for 6d. [3p] which was the money for two deliveries of milk a day for a week. The milk was measured with a ladle in pints and half-pints. She used to have a black tin on the dresser and she would give me a chocolate biscuit, it was lovely. We always had good food; butter, cheese and meat but never fancy food. Mother was a good cook and made cakes. I remember Dad used to cycle to The Shambles in Worcester on a Saturday and buy steak for 6d. [3p] a pound just before the war.

Dad's bike was the only bike we had and we would ride it in the Orchard, three at a time sometimes. When we first learnt to ride a bike it would be a race home from school to see who could get to it first. Mother had a gypsy caravan which she used to keep chickens in but before that, when it was cleared out, we used to play house in it.

We never went on holiday, Father was tight with money. We would go to Weston with the school for a day trip and also visit our Mother's mother, Granny Bailey in Gloucester. The Policeman was always going up and down the road and you were afraid of him even if you hadn't done anything wrong. Electricity came to the village in 1933 and water later. We used to wash outside under the pump with cold water and then, when it was bath day, we would bring it in and heat it up for a bath in front of the fire; everyone went in the same water. The toilet was outside at the end of the garden. [The Weaver sisters]

When it was icy my grandfather used to open the bedroom window and lean out to break the ice on the water butt, from which he then scooped out his water to wash in. No hot water for him! [Eric Vine, b.1937.]

I was born in Great House Cottages (now 'The Sett'), the youngest of 11 children – eight boys and three girls. Next door lived the Turners. We children slept two or three to a bed, with the girls in one room and the boys in the other. There was no hot water, and the water pump was outside. We had catapults which the local policemen used to take off us if he caught us. He used to flick us on the ear for punishment, but never beat us. [Mowey Davies, b.1937.]

The Police Station, Leigh Sinton, 1956. (WRO/R.J. COLLINS)

Organisations and Facilities

There is no simple way to order the remainder of this chapter. There are a whole range of organisations in the parish, and we will simply give details about them in alphabetical order.

Alfrick and Leigh Pedaler's Society (ALPS)

This little-known society was formed by Pam Williams in 1979, after her husband gave her a bicycle as a present for Mothering Sunday. She mentioned to her friends, Ann Wilks, Pat Milnes, Carol Davies, Chris Spencer-Bamford and Alma Stoddard, that she was going to go for rides and they said that they would join her.

Twelve months later, two more ladies joined, Marjorie Jones and Margo Lyons. Margo encouraged Jill Ellard across the road to join, who in turn persuaded Ingrid Dalgleish, and so it grew, until now there are 24 members. The society meets every Monday from the second week in May to the second week in September at various venues along the lanes, and rides as a group to local pubs. In 2000 a group went to France and cycled from St Malo to Huisnes sur Mere. They also have various social activities throughout the year.

Amenities

The childhood memories which we have quoted are sprinkled with references to various shops in the parish where children spent their precious pennies. Now there is only one, Leigh Sinton Post Office Stores.

Worcester and St John's cycling club, 1890. They used to ride to Bransford. (WRO/H. PERRY)

Above: *View of Leigh Post Office (now the Old Post Office), c.1905.* (Geoff Wright)

George Kimber's shop on the Malvern Road, c.1925, with Norman Kimber in the foreground. The sign reads 'GEORGE KIMBER, PROVISION DEALER, Licensed to sell Tobacco.' (Norman Kimber)

Above: *Newsagent's shop on the Malvern Road, Leigh Sinton, run by the Gorses, 1940s.* (Pat and Cecil Dee)

Above: *The shop on the Malvern Road which was kept by Jim and Jessie Hodges in the 1930s. They moved there from Winsgrave, where they lived in the 1920s.* (Janet Griffiths)

*Leigh Sinton Post Office,
around 1910.*
(PETER NORBURY)

Below:
*Shop in
Leigh
Sinton,
1956.*
(WRO/
FREEMAN
PAYNE)

*General Stores on the Suckley
Road, 1956.* (WRO/A.R. COATS)

Above: *The Old
Police Station,
Leigh Sinton, in
1912. The notice
above the door reads
'County Police
Station', and the
notice-board is
headed
'GR Territorial
Force Training
1912 Worcestershire
Yeomanry.'*
(CORAL AND DES
CLARKE)

The last shop to close was Leigh Post Office Stores in 1997, when Elizabeth Portman retired after 33 years as postmistress. Under the auspices of the Parish Council, a group of Leigh inhabitants looked into the possibility of starting another one – perhaps as a cooperative – but there was not enough support.

Looking at old almanacs gives an idea of the way in which the local amenities have changed. Back in 1855, for the present parish (i.e., excluding Lower and Upper Howsell) *Billing's Directory* lists five shop-keepers, two butchers and no less than five shoemakers, together with a tailor, a farrier, and a saddler and harness maker. Jumping to 1937, *Kelly's Directory* lists five shops, a newsagent, tobacconist and baker, coal and firewood merchants, and a beer retailer. There were no shoemakers, but there was a surgical-boot maker, two agricultural engineers and a petrol filling station.

Today there is still one filling station, at Bransford, which sells groceries, sweets and tobacco, and next door is a workshop, doing both car and agricultural implement repairs. In Leigh Sinton there is a Chinese takeaway and a printing works. Finally, there is a garden centre outside Leigh Sinton which, in addition to plants and nursery products, has a 'farm shop', selling a range of fruit, vegetables, meat and dairy products, some of it locally produced. There used to be police stations in Leigh and Leigh Sinton, but both have closed.

Cotswold Youth Motor Cross Club

Although not based in the parish, this club has held meetings at Brockamin for the last 13 years, on Chris Tolley's land. It was started over 20 years ago by Keith and Ruth Luce, to provide activities for local children living on their Droitwich council estate, including their own. They say that the racing is a 'real family thing', which helps to keep children out of trouble. If the children misbehave they are not allowed to race.

The ages of those taking part range from six up to 'as old as you feel', but the majority are under 25. The course is just over one mile, although the youngest age groups ride on a shortened course, avoiding the steepest section. The races are arranged in age groups and engine size, the youngest (6–8 years old) riding automatic 65cc bikes.

Between 150–200 people take part. Although they have the odd broken leg or arm, it is basically safe. The only fatality was in 1998, when a young rider on his own crashed and hit his head. Nobody else was involved. He was taken to hospital by Air Ambulance, but died the following day. They wanted to stop the racing after this, but the pressure from the parents persuaded them otherwise. They get a very good attendance at the Leigh meeting, because the people like the course and its setting.

For anybody who has not seen these events, the racing is spectacular!

Riders at a Cotswold Youth motor cycle meeting, 2001. (MALCOLM SCOTT)

127

Cricket and Football

There have been football clubs in the parishes for over a century but, like other activities, they have not been continuous. In the early 1900s Leigh Rovers were playing, and in the 1920s Joseph Hughes (b.1906) used to play for them or their successor. Amazingly, he still remembers all the players' names and their positions, which were: Tom Grubb or Joseph Hughes, Watty Bridges, Bert Cole, Arch Ball and Will Lewis (forwards), Jack Grubb, Ned Powell and Jimmy Grubb (half backs), Swagger Hill and Sid Haggitt (full backs), with Bert Rowley in goal.

By the 1930s Leigh United had been formed, and the team was restarted after the Second World War. There was also a Leigh St Edburga team, but it met an undignified end. Opinions vary as to exactly what happened, but when the team was playing in Worcester there was either a fight, or they abused the referee in some way. Anyway, they were banned!

Leigh United was the team which, with Stan Jones as captain, brought the greatest football glory to the parishes by winning the Malvern Hospital Senior Cup in 1948. Ten coach loads of supporters went to the final where, in front of a crowd of 3,000, they beat the much fancied – and almost professional – Royal Engineers team 4–3, the goals being scored by Les Alford, Edgar Green and Tommy Edwards. They played in both the Malvern and Worcester Leagues,

and there was also a junior team. Not to be outdone, there was also a women's team at this time which, according to a newspaper report in 1995, played a really hard game and often gave the men's team a run for their money. John Banner ran Leigh United from 1962 to 1982. Later there was a Leigh United 84 team, run by Dave Collins, which played in Division II of the Malvern Gazette and Ledbury Reporter Football League.

There is no adult team based in the parish at the time of writing, but the Leigh and Bransford Badgers were started in July 2001 by Bosko Medakovic and Neil Coleman for boys and girls from four to 11. Their inaugural match was against Suckley Wanderers on 9 October 2001, the infants (4–7) playing the first half and the juniors (7–11) the second. Starting with 12 members, there are now 53. They train every Saturday morning at Leigh and Bransford Primary School, and the club is affiliated to the Worcester Football Association.

There seems to have been much less involvement in cricket than in football in the parishes, although different teams have played over the years. Norman Kimber remembers playing at the Memorial Hall in 1932, when he was 12. For many years after the Second World War there was also a team based at The Fox, who played on a ground the other side of the bridge, and there was another one in Leigh Sinton. None of these teams played in leagues as far as we can find out.

Perhaps the most idiosyncratic team was 'Fred's

Leigh Sinton Football Club, 1920–21.
Left to right, back row: *?, Jack Bridges, Walter Banner, Alfred Haggett, ?, Sid Haggett, Bert Rowley, ?, Ernie Hill, Hector Banner, Fred Edwards, Maurice Lewis, Ernie Hill senr;*
centre (seated): *Sid Knapper, Edwin Powell, Jack Grubb;*
front row (cross-legged): *Wilf Lewis, Arch Ball, Bert Cole, ?, Tom Grubb.*
(CORAL & DES CLARKE, DOREEN ROWLEY)

Leigh Rovers 1921–2 outside the Memorial Hall. Pictured on the right of the second row is Tom Hunt. back row includes: *Jack Weaver, Dick Weaver, Arthur Emson.* (OLIVE BISHOP, MURIEL 'BIB' JONES)

Alfred (Fred) Symonds in his Leigh Rovers football uniform, c.1910.
(DES SYMONDS)

Above: *Leigh and Bransford Football Club, 1939, in front of Sherridge, where there were two pitches which they played on. At half-time one of the maids, Beth Phillips, used to bring out an urn of tea. Left to right, back row: ?, Reg Bowkett, Bill Oliver, Les Powell, Wilf Barlow, Bob Rowley; centre: Mr Spiers, Harry Powell, Sid Edwards, George Kinnard, Jack Newell, Ben Rowley, Peter Cook, Wilf Lewis; front row (kneeling): Bill Hooper, Doug Spencer, Carol Vine, Ernie Coley, Reg Burston. (Sid Edwards was killed after being kicked by a horse at Moat Farm, where he worked.)* (CONNIE TOHTZ)

Members of the 1948 Leigh United Football Club who won the 1948 Malvern Hospital Senior Cup, together with some of the 1933 team. Left to right, back row: Ernie Coley (33), Howard Clarke (33), Doug Spencer, Norman Kimber, Edgar Green, Billy Norman (33), Tommy Edwards, Norman Symonds (secretary of the Malvern League); front row: Les Alford, Sonny Williams, Stan Jones (captain), Aldie Davies, George Alford.
(LES ALFORD)

Peripatetics'. This scratch team, formed by Fred Covins in the 1980s, played annually against a team of medical students from the University of Birmingham, of which his son Christopher was one. Although cricket was undoubtedly played, eating and drinking seemed to be its most memorable activity. For example, in order not to be separated from his drink, the wicket keeper used to put his pint behind the stumps. Others who were fortunate enough not to be on the field helped themselves to drink from barrels of cider and beer at the boundary, and ate vast quantities of food provided by Maggie Covins.

For members of the parish in Brockamin, The Swan at Alfrick was their local, and was the home of the Swan Alfrick Cricket Club. Formed in 1985, it is still running in 2002, although, with the closure of The Swan in the late 1990s, its base is now at The Fox and Hounds, Lulsley. Richard Lewis from Brockamin has been its captain all this time. They play other pub and non-league teams, with over 20 games each season, and for the last ten years they have also had a short tour. Their other activities include a summer ball and a harvest auction in aid of charity. The Swan also ran a tug-of-war team for many years.

Leigh and Bransford Women's football team, 1950s. Left to right, back row: Wendy Lane, ?, ?; centre: Bib Jones, Winnie Newell, Mari Parkinson, ?, ?, Hilda Smith, Freda Symonds; front row: Janet ?, Pat Atkinson, Betty Shelham, ?, Betty Hooper, Beryl Lewis. (MURIEL 'BIB' JONES)

Leigh and Bransford Badgers football team before their first match against Suckley Wanderers, October 2001. Left to right, back row: Sue Hawthorne (secretary), Mick Hawthorne (coach), Bosko Medakovic (senior coach), John Dubey (coach), Andy Lewin (coach), Neil Coleman (coach and promoter); centre: Jack Hawthorn, Nick Medakovic, Robert Lewin, Oliver Green, Chris James, Matthew Lyons, Angus Singleton, Adam Woronieci, Cameron Snowdon; front row: Jack Coleman, Oliver Harcombe, Christopher King, Eliot Caldwell, Callum Ross, Chris Lewin, Harriet Dubey, Nicholas Snowdon. (MALCOLM SCOTT)

Leigh and Bransford cricket team, 1961. Left to right, back row: Mac McGowan, Roy Cole, Eddie Clarke, Joey Clarke, Mick Cole, Barry Jones, Robin Tandy; front row: John Edmonds, Albert Smith, Peter Spencer, John Banner, Vernon Banner. (CONNIE TOHTZ AND PETER SPENCER)

Fred's Peripatetics cricket team. Left to right, back row: Guy Covin, Geoffrey Cardinal, Anthony Elleray, Gordon Scott, Neal French, Fred Covins, Geoffrey Vos; kneeling: Tom French, Carl Fieldhouse, Tony Elsby, Nicholas Benson. The team ran for three to four years around 1980 and played a team of students from the Birmingham University Medical School, of which Christopher Covins was one. The wicket keeper used to keep his beer behind the stumps, for safety. (FRED COVINS)

The tug-of-war team from The Swan, Alfrick, c.1980. Left to right, back row: Tedda Brooks, ?, Phillip Attwood, Nobby Clark, Ron Jones, Brin Morgan (the coach and Alfrick's police sergeant); centre: Mick Sweeney, Albert Lindsay, Willie Peat, Colin Emmins, John Swindell, Dave Roberts; front row: Bob Oliver, Richard Emmins, Dave Morris, ? Addley. (JOHN SWINDELL/BERROWS)

Members of The Swan Alfrick Cricket Club who won the Six-a-Side Tournament in 2000. Left to right, back row: Gareth Oliver, Sam Orgee, Andy Sanders; front row: Jonathon Pearson, Tim Betts, Richard Lewis. (RICHARD LEWIS)

Evergreen Club

This club, which was formed in the 1950s, succeeded the Darby and Joan Club, and started under the guidance of the WRVS. It used to meet in The Somer's Arms, with active encouragement from the landlord, Dennis Clewer, and his family, and Peggy Dyson was its secretary for many years.

When Dennis and Sybil Clewer retired in 1973 the club met in the Memorial Hall. However, in those days it was a cold place and, helped by Ruth Beard,

they moved to the community room at Bensfield. More recently, when Bensfield closed, they were offered the free use of a room in the Scout hut.

Mary Fynn ran the club for a number of years, followed by Joan Teague assisted by her husband Tom. Now Edna Davies has taken over and organises their two meetings per month. Although there are currently only 15 members, they have a wide range of activities, including talks, demonstrations and concerts. They also have outings to the seaside, for meals, and to other Evergreen clubs.

A Derby and Joan Club outing, outside The Somers Arms. Left to right, back row: ?, Mollie Burston, ?, Mina Hemmings; front row: Mr Clewer (landlord of The Somers Arms, who drove the coach), Mr and Mrs Dick Jones, Mrs Morgan, ?, Mrs Johnson, Mrs Beatty Powell, Mr (Papa) Pritchard, Mrs Haggett, Mrs E. Langford, Nurse Pritchard, Mrs Cyril Dyson. (EVA SMITH)

The Evergreen meeting outside Bensfield for a supper outing to the Old Post Office, Weobley, June 1982. Left to right: Peggy Bufton, Connie Jones, Marge Montgomery, Edith Freeman, May Jones, Joan Ralph (behind), Janet Openshaw, Myna Hemming, Mary Hemming (John Hemming's mother), Jack Gale, Nellie Gale, Mrs Hicks, Albert Handy, Vi Handy, ?, Mrs Dee (Cecil Dee's mother, known as 'Granny Bumble'). (GILL AND MARY GALE)

Left: *Presentation to Tom and Joan Teague when they retired as Evergreen Club leader and secretary respectively after 11 years, October 1997.* (TOM TEAGUE)

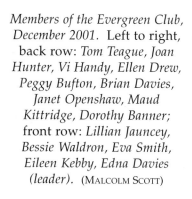

Members of the Evergreen Club, December 2001. Left to right, back row: Tom Teague, Joan Hunter, Vi Handy, Ellen Drew, Peggy Bufton, Brian Davies, Janet Openshaw, Maud Kittridge, Dorothy Banner; front row: Lillian Jauncey, Bessie Waldron, Eva Smith, Eileen Kebby, Edna Davies (leader). (MALCOLM SCOTT)

Left: *Harry Banner with Dr and Mrs Hardy at the opening of the Leigh and Bransford Flower Show at the Memorial Hall, late 1960s.* (HARRY BANNER/BERROWS)

Below: *Jack Weaver's winner's ticket from the 1947 show at The Fox, Bransford.* (MALCOLM SCOTT)

FOX INN, BRANSFORD

1947 FRUIT, FLOWER AND VEGETABLE SHOW

1st PRIZE

Class 23 Name

Horticultural Shows

Horticultural shows, like many activities, tend to be driven by the enthusiasm of an individual or group. When this enthusiasm declines, or people move, the activity ceases, only to be picked up by others later. For example, there was a Leigh and Bransford Horticultural Show which ran from 1851 until 1873 and then again from 1889 to 1898.

After the Second World War, there was a horticultural show held at The Fox, in the building which also served as the hop-pickers' bar (the 'Oddfellows' room'). In the 1960s, Harry Banner and Des Symonds – both members of the British Legion – started a horticultural show, in order to raise money for a new Memorial Hall kitchen, to replace the tin-roofed lean-to which had served up until then. Sally Stewart was the secretary. After the 1968 show Des Symonds wrote in the parish magazine, 'A great success! I think this is the verdict of the six to seven hundred people who were present at this great event.' It grew until they had to hire a marquee to house the exhibits, the hall being too small. After a time, Tom Teague and Gill Gale took over the organisation. Contestants used to come from the surrounding districts to compete against the local experts, who included Olive Emson (lettuces), Nora Hadley (cakes), Don Davies (vegetables), Bill Collins (vegetables and pot plants), Doug Holloway (begonias and dahlias), Joe Dance, Les Alford and Harold Portman (vegetables), Tom Teague (vegetables and flowers), and Harry Banner (vegetables and dahlias).

In addition to the horticultural side, these shows at the Memorial Hall also had a wide range of other activities including, for instance, a tug-of-war competition and six-a-side football. At its height there used to be as many as 18 teams competing for the tug-of-war, including the police and the English champions, with up to 16 teams playing football. Pat Dee remembers that before the show there used to be a parade of decorated floats around the parish. Sadly, interest in the show dwindled, and 1986 was its last year.

Harry Banner went on to achieve importance nationally for his dahlias, being awarded a silver medal by the National Dahlia Society in 1998 for services to dahlia growing. His garden remains a marvellous sight in late summer, with its immaculate rows of dahlias of every conceivable kind and colour.

Another local person to receive national, and also international, recognition – this time for camellias – was John Tooby. Although part of his horticultural activities at New House Farm, growing camellias was also a private passion. A prominent member of the International Camellia Society, he was elected president in 1986. In this connection, he used to travel all over the world with his wife Nancy, as well as promoting camellia cultivation in this country, through trials and shows. It is a tribute to his efforts that in 2002 a new camellia is being introduced from one of his seedlings, and named by his son Will as 'Camellia John Tooby'.

Another show which was held for a number of years, starting in 1979, was the Leigh and Bransford Folk Fayre, dreamed up in The Royal Oak by Will Tooby, Paul Cartridge, Terry Fuller and Steve Seymore. In addition to the horticultural show it also had craft exhibitions, a steel band, a clay-pigeon shoot and a heavy-horse display. It proved to be a huge success, raising over £1,000 in its first year.

There is currently no successor to any of these shows.

Left: *Leigh and Bransford Horticultural Show, mid 1960s. There had been a show organised by the old British Legion but it ceased to run and a new one was started around 1963. The picture shows Des Symonds, Harry Banner and Mr Davies (the judge).* (DES SYMONDS)

Above: *Leigh and Bransford Folk Fayre, 1980. Will Tooby on a reaper and binder, with Charlie Williams leading his shire horses.* (WRO/BERROWS)

Left: *Programme cover for the Leigh and Bransford Villagers' Folk Fayre, held in 1986.* (WILL TOOBY)

Top right: *Winner's ticket at the 1894 Leigh and Bransford Flower Show.* (PETER NORBURY)

Hunting, Shooting and Fishing

We have seen that the Teme is still an important fishing river and that there is now also fishing in the various lakes which have resulted from small-scale farm diversification. Although not conducted on the scale shooting used to be, there are still a number of pheasant shoots in the parishes, whilst rabbit shooting provides both a sport and helps to control an agricultural pest.

A rabbit shoot at Bank Farm, around 1922. (SALLY STEWART)

Members of a shooting party by the Teme with Duncan Stewart, 1994.
(BARCLAY STEWART)

*Meeting of a hunt at
Leigh, c.1905.* (PETER NORBURY)

There are two hunts which operate here; the Croome and the North Ledbury. The Croome is a very old hunt, based the other side of the Severn. Started in 1600, the present one has been running continuously since 1874. The North Ledbury was started in 1905, as an offshoot of the Ledbury Hunt, but in 1948 it became a private hunt with Lady Waechter, from The White House, Suckley, as the Master. Since she died, in 1989, it has (like the Croome) been run by a committee, with several Masters serving concurrently. It does not, however, have its own territory, but hunts over land which is on 'loan' from the adjacent hunts, including the Croome.

Farmers are told in advance when the hunt is proposing to meet nearby, so that they may register their objection to hunting on their land. It is not common for them to do so.

Medical Services

We can find no record of there ever having been a doctor's surgery in the parish, and people go to Cradley, Knightwick, Malvern Link or St Johns, Worcester. There were, however, nurses (or ex-nurses) who were often the first medical port of call. Mrs Ethel Page was one of these. In 1913 she married William Page, one of the patients she met whilst matron at Malvern Cottage Hospital, and she used her professional skills locally when she lived at Moat Farm.

In the early 1930s, Susan Joyce Pritchard (known as Joyce) became the village nurse and had a surgery attached to Malvern House, Leigh Sinton. Aubrey Pritchard remembers that in the summer many of his mother's patients were hop pickers. On one occasion she helped a hop picker working for Kenneth Farr at Leigh Court Farm, to give birth to a baby under a hedge.

In the post-war period, Mary Stevens was the local nurse for many years. Then, from 1960 until she retired in 1985, Jill Ellard (then Curnow) had the triple role of district nurse, midwife and health visitor. Her colleague was Hazel Chambers, who had the same roles in Suckley. Although they were responsible for different parishes, they worked together and covered for each other.

They worked six days a week and were on call 24 hours each day. In the mornings they did insulin injections followed by any midwifery and general nursing duties. Afternoons were taken up health visiting, whilst in the evenings they saw people who were terminally ill, but were being nursed at home. They were bound up in the lives of their patients, nursing families from the cradle to the grave. Asked if they minded the extremely hard work involved in serving the community in this way, Hazel Chambers said simply, 'It was a great privilege.'

Having delivered them, they saw all new babies at least once a week for the first six weeks, then monthly until their first birthday. Three-monthly visits followed for the next year, with six-monthly ones until the child was five. In addition to the everyday activities, they ran monthly child welfare clinics, mobile ambulances picking up the mothers and their children to take them to the Memorial Hall.

Not surprisingly, they have their store of stories. Once Jill was called out to deliver a baby by candle-light in a caravan. The doctor did not come and it was only after the baby had been delivered safely that she learned that the woman had had a heart valve operation – 'A piece of information you were glad not to have had before you started!'

She was, however, enormously impressed with the standards of cleanliness of the travellers. Despite having to fetch water in buckets and heat it up, the children started each day thoroughly washed and with clean clothes, and the caravans were immaculate,

Marriage of William Page, from Moat Farm, to Ethel Harrison at Cookley, June 1913. Left to right, back row: *Revd R. Rowley-Moir* (mainly obscured), *Mrs Rowley-Moir, Mr and Mrs Jackson, ?, ?, Annie Page, James Griffin, Minnie Page, Mr and Mrs Goldspink;* front row, sitting: *Marion Griffin, Alfred Harrison, Jane Harrison, William Page, Ethel Page, Hester Harrison, Margaret Grimes, Walter Grimes;* squatting: *Donald Griffin, Newton Griffin.* (JOHN GRIFFIN)

Left: *Joyce Pritchard as a midwife trainee, early 1930s. The baby she is holding was born at Callow End, and was pronounced 'stillborn' by the doctor. Joyce Pritchard noticed that the child's hand moved and whispered so to the Sister. Overhearing this the Doctor shook the baby, and in a few seconds it cried lustily.* (AUBREY PRITCHARD)

Hazel Chambers, one of the district nurses, preparing to go to work in her Morris Minor. (HAZEL CHAMBERS)

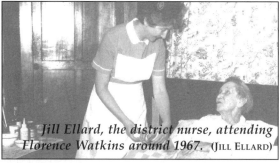

Jill Ellard, the district nurse, attending Florence Watkins around 1967. (JILL ELLARD)

Below left: *Joyce Pritchard (née Potter) (left), the Village Nurse from 1933/4, and nurse friend Myfanwy Tolley (née Davies) with their transport. Village Nurses were overseen by a Nursing Committee, that paid their salaries. It continued functioning after the start of the NHS, in 1947, but only had a marginal role.* (AUBREY PRITCHARD)

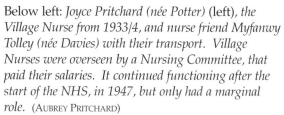

Hazel Chambers, one of the district nurses, treating Ken Portman's thigh in his back garden. (HAZEL CHAMBERS)

inside and out. Not surprisingly, the travellers valued the nurse's visits. The family matriarch – usually the mother-in-law – would have the appropriate things laid out for the nurse, even though the nurses knew that the condensed milk would come out for the children once they left!

With Jill Ellard's retirement, the triple-worker post was dropped and all these services are now administered through doctor's surgeries.

Memorial Hall

When it was opened in 1920, the Memorial Hall conveyance stated that it was to be used 'as a Workingmen's Club and Technical Institute.' Later, in 1968, its purpose became 'a Village Hall for the use of the inhabitants of the area of benefit'. In practice it has always served the whole community, being run by a small committee made up of members from the various local organisations and user groups, together with co-opted members and a representative of the Parish Council.

In 1957 an account of its history by H.A. Yarnold suggested that, certainly in his view, the hall was not fulfilling its purpose ('something of a White Elephant'). In subsequent years there was a programme of improvements, including a new entrance hall, a small committee room and a kitchen. Nevertheless, by the 1980s it was too small for many functions, the population having grown in the intervening period. In 1987, Albert Jones, a local farmer, left £11,500 to the hall, and the committee, under Norman Kimber, used this as a stimulus to consider major improvements.

They proposed to build a new hall adjacent to the old one at a cost of £117,000. This plan was considered too ambitious by some people, so a referendum was held, in which a large majority voted for a new hall.

The new Albert Jones Memorial Hall was opened in 1994. The Hall Committee raised £30,000, some through a 'Rent-a-Brick' scheme, which had over 400 sub-

Albert Pritchard with his banjo in the 1920s. With his daughters Lilian and Maud on piano, and Laurie Bowers on drums, they used to play at the Memorial Hall. (LILIAN MORRIS)

scribers. The rest came through grants from the Parish Council, the Malvern Hills District Council and Hereford and Worcester County Council. It has been a resounding success, and the hall complex can now accommodate a wide range of functions. In subsequent years, the committee under Des Symonds has maintained the hall and grounds to a very high standard. It has also made a number of improvements, the most recent being to install drainage in the playing-field.

Sale-of-work stall at the Memorial Hall, July 1961. Behind the stall are (left to right) *Mrs Jackson, Mrs Allen, Mrs Duncan, Mrs Jolly, Mrs Taylor and Mrs Handy.* (RUTH BEARD)

Memorial Hall, 1956. (WRO/J.R. Pickerell)

Left: *Vi Handy laying the foundation of the Memorial Hall extension, the Albert Jones Hall. (Vi Handy was vice-chairman of the Village Hall Committee and Norman Kimber was the chairman).* (Vi Handy/Berrows)

Below: *At the opening of the Memorial Hall extension, 17 September 1994. Left to right: District Councillor John Young, the Chief Planning Officer of the Malvern Hills District Council, Norman Kimber (Chairman of the Memorial Hall Committee), Chairman of the Worcestershire County Council.* (Norman Kimber)

Bottom left: *First garden ride-about in 1989. Nellie and Mary Gale at 25 Orchard Way, Bransford.* (Gill and Mary Gale)

Although the hall now has a good income from letting, there are fund-raising events organised by Cath Hall throughout the year. The May Fair is an annual event, held in collaboration with the Scouts, but others include gardeners' question time, a garden 'ride-about', bingo evenings and fashion shows.

Over the years the hall has been used for a wide range of functions. Joseph Hughes remembers the whist drives soon after it opened, when there were as many as 42 tables! At different periods there were bridge evenings, concerts, plays, bingo evenings, regular children's film shows and dances. There was also a youth club, established by Revd Moreton-Jackson and run by Des Symonds for nearly ten years in the 1950s and early '60s. This had two groups of children, the 8–12 year olds coming until 8.00p.m., and the older ones for the rest of the evening. They enjoyed a range of activities, including snooker, darts, table tennis and football, and at one stage there were 130 boys and girls attending.

Above: *A play which formed part of a Christmas party at the Memorial Hall, 1960.*
Left to right: *Mrs Mills, Elsie Portman, Mrs Duncan, ?, Mary Edmonds, Pat Dee.*
(Pat and Cecil Dee/Berrows)

An old people's party in 1962–63. **Left to right:** *Edith Monk, Mrs Dee and Bob Rowley.* (Des Symonds)

Meeting of the Village Hall Committee, spring 2002.
Left to right: *Emrys Davies, Barclay Stewart, Sally Stewart, Ron Hall, Paul Etheridge, Alan Lewis, Des Symonds (chairman), Pauline Harcombe, Cath Hall, Joyce Jeynes, Ruth Christie (secretary).* (Malcolm Scott)

The Parish Council

In response to the Local Government Act of 1894, the two civil parishes, Bransford and Leigh, each took a different path. The Act required that an Annual Parish Meeting be held, which both did, in December 1894. However, the Act also gave them the option of electing a Parish Council. Leigh chose to do so, whilst Bransford did not. As a result, both subsequently held the annual Parish Meetings at which local issues were discussed, but Leigh also had Parish Council meetings in between. Following a public meeting of members of

Members of the Leigh and Bransford Parish Council, May 2002. Left to right: Maureen Croall (clerk), Caroline Orgee (chairman), John Young, Chris Walker, Graham Jones, Will Tooby, John Harcombe, Sheila Cridland, Martin Gloster, Brenda Guise (just visible), Barclay Stewart, John Guise (District Councillor), Malcolm Scott (vice chairman). (MALCOLM SCOTT)

both parishes in 1971, it was decided that there should be a joint Parish Council, to be called Leigh and Bransford Parish Council, although each parish retained its own annual meeting.

The Parish Council, a statutory group of 11 people, is the first rung of local government and is intended to provide an elected forum for views on any local issue. It has a small annual budget, currently £7,000, which it gets from the rates. It receives details of all planning applications in the parish and, through its planning sub-committee, sends back comments to the Malvern Hills District Council. In doing so it will discuss issues with parishioners affected if necessary or, in contentious cases, call a public meeting. However, its comments are not binding to the District Council.

There is a Footpaths Committee, responsible for maintaining footpaths, which recently produced the booklet on local walks. Other committees are set up when necessary – for example, one under Will Tooby was responsible for establishing the children's playing-field at Bransford. In the first chapter, the Parish Council's role in getting affordable housing on the Bensfield site in 2001 was mentioned, whilst another recent activity has been to sponsor this book!

Its members attend local and regional meetings relating to parish affairs, and the council sends views on issues like transport and road safety. It also forwards complaints about local services to the appropriate bodies and tries to ensure a satisfactory outcome. Members receive no payment, although there is a professional clerk. Meetings are bi-monthly, at which members of the public are welcome and may ask questions. Inasmuch as central Government says that it wishes to give Parish Councils more powers, it is important that we maintain a strong one.

Poster advertising the new houses at Bensfield.

142

Pub-related Activities

For many people, pubs and village life go hand in hand, and the local ones have certainly been the centre of many activities over the years. Perhaps because they made so much cider, Leigh has not had a pub in living memory, although Nora Jay heard that there was once one called 'The Half Moon' down Dingle Road. Harry Banner had heard that a pub called 'The Bluebell' used to be in Top Cottages, on the Alfrick Road, but no records of either of these have been found. Another, which Harry said was called 'The Bridge Inn', would be the beerhouse mentioned in documents relating to the Old Rectory in the early and mid 1800s.

Of the three pubs which were in the parish in 1900, The Fox at Bransford and The Royal Oak at Leigh Sinton are still open, whilst The Somers Arms at Leigh Sinton has closed. Of those on the parish boundaries, The Swan, Alfrick, has closed, but The Ragged Bear and Staff, Bransford, and The New Inn, Storridge, are still open at the time of writing.

Children's outing to the pantomime at Malvern in January 1964. These outings were organised by the landlord of The Somers Arms, Arch Maund, and his wife, Hilda for their customers and their families, and were annual events in the late 1950s and early 1960s. Pat Dee (wearing a hat) is in front of the driver. Other people in the group are Dorothy Banner, Janet Openshaw, Christine Walker, Joyce Symonds, Keith Portman, June Symonds, Celia Dee, Sue Merrick, Michael Dee, Brian Symonds, Tony Symonds, Derek Symonds, Gladys Walker, Elsie Portman, Derek Portman, Hilda Maund. (HAROLD PORTMAN)

Above: *The tug-of-war team from the Swan, Alfrick, pulling against the Welsh champions, whom they beat in a competition at The Oak Inn, Malvern Link, around 1980. From the front: Albert Lindsay, John Swindell, Bobby Oliver, (a make-weight), Colin Emmins, Ron Jones, Willie Peat (anchorman).* (JOHN SWINDELL)

Above: *Arch Maund, the landlord of The Ragged Bear and Staff, bought a steamroller, but never restored it. The group which did do so gave him the inaugural ride in February 1967 to The Fox – about two miles. Arch Maund is the fifth from the left, with June Symonds on his right. Bill Banner is second from the left and Arthur Salisbury is fourth from the left. Standing on the left in the steamroller cab is Ivan Steel.* (DES SYMONDS)

The Fox

Set back from the road, until ten years ago The Fox was a typical country pub. Quite small, it has a long west-facing verandah along the front, on which people sat and watched the sun go down. Like all pubs, it had a succession of publicans, and with each the character changed somewhat. For example, John Turner never gave free drinks at Christmas, but at New Year used to line up bowls of punch for everybody to help themselves. There were ladies' and men's darts teams, both members of the Hallow and District Leagues.

It was popular not only with locals but with people from Rushwick. Elsewhere we have noted that there was a horticultural show held there after the Second World War, and it also ran a cricket team. It has now changed radically. A large restaurant extension was added to the back and a children's playground built at the side with an enclosed play barn, to attract family groups. There are currently no sports teams, or teams playing 'pub games', based there.

The Royal Oak

The Royal Oak (usually called simply 'The Oak') is much smaller than The Somers Arms. When Bernard Atkinson took it over in 1974 it was fairly run down, and there were still two cottages attached to it. He managed to build up the trade, the brewery made improvements, and it became very popular. Two men's darts teams met there on Mondays, and two women's darts teams on Tuesdays. On Wednesdays there was darts and cribbage, whilst on Fridays the Savings Club met. In this, members saved the whole year for Christmas. But it got too successful! Bernard Atkinson said that they paid out £30,000 one year, and he used to sleep with a gun under his bed at pay-out time! So he stopped it.

Arch Collins was a keen cribbage and darts player and when he died members at The Oak competed for the Arch Collins Memorial Cups. Running from 1982 to 1986, the cups are still on display in the bar. The Royal Oak Clay-Pigeon Shooting Club was another activity started during this time and it is still running. Started by Walter Beard, Rex Dobbs, Ken Jones, Bernard Atkinson and others, it used to shoot on Wendens' ground, but now meets on Chris Tolley's land at Leigh. When Bernard Atkinson's successor, Brian Lynch, left and the public bar was turned into a restaurant, the club – captained by Jim Stubbs and with nearly 30 members – moved its base to The Whitehall at Rushwick.

At the back of The Oak there used to be a skittle alley. It was in this building that Bill Costello, a former landlord, built an early hop-picking machine in collaboration with Frank Portman. Hop-picking machines are big and the old skittle alley was not very big, so Charlie Lewis invited him to work on it at Moat Farm. He produced a portable machine, which could be taken to the hop yards. How many of his ideas were used by Bruffs, at Suckley, in their hop-picking machines, is not clear.

Above: *Bransford Oddfellows' Fête, 1909. They met in a building at the back of The Fox, which doubled as the hop-pickers' bar.* (Brian Iles)

Left: *A match at The Fox Cricket Club ground, early 1950s.* (John Wenden)

Left: *The Cricket Club at The Fox ran from 1946 into the 1970s. It was founded by the landlord, Mr Turner, and Edward Jay. They had matches with a team in Guernsey, with reciprocal visits. Edward Jay was captain from 1946 until 1962, followed by John Wenden. The picture shows players from different periods. Left to right: Edward Jay, John Wenden, Ivor Hale, Roy Booth (who was the Worcestershire County wicket keeper), Bob Wilesmith, Hector James, Stan Watkins, Mick Weaver.* (STELLA BRAITHWAITE)

Right: *The Royal Oak Inn, 1956.* (WRO/R.J. COLLINS)

Below: *Clay-Pigeon Club meeting at The Royal Oak, June 1985. Left to right (men): Bernard Atkinson (Royal Oak landlord), Peter Spencer, John Hundabun, Ivor Lloyd, Peter Spencer, David Wenden, Gerald Crump, Jim Stubbs, James Phillips, Dan Maitland, Mel Newton, Rex Dobbs; front (boys): Chris Phillips, Stuart McKane, Bruce McKane (holding cup), Marcus Stubbs, Jamie Atkinson (in front).* (PAULINE PHILLIPS)

Somers Arms, Leigh Sinton, 1895. The notice on the wall says, 'SOMERS ARMS GOOD STABLING' and the illuminated sign says, 'Salt & Co Ltd, Burton Ale and Stout.' (SUSAN JONES)

Playing cards at The Somers Arms around 1950. Left to right: Mr Jakeway (back of head), Jack Pudge (facing), Bill Lane and Thomas Jones (sideways). (CONNIE TOHTZ)

The Somers Arms

Once an inn with stabling, this was the biggest of the three pubs. Susan Jones remembers that when her parents, Dennis and Sybil Clewer, took it over in 1952, the bedrooms had jugs of washing water and a slop basin, with chamber pots under the beds and an outside toilet. It had large club rooms, which were used by several local organisations – the Darby and Joan Club, and Leigh United Football Club met there, and it was the base for crib, quoits, men's and women's darts teams, table tennis and skittles teams. When it started catering, the Leigh Farmers used to have dinners there.

At hop-picking times the pub was stripped to basics, not least because so many people used to go there. In addition to the pickers from Wales and the Black Country, their relatives used to come at weekends, and Bernard Atkinson remembers seeing as many as a dozen coaches parked in Leigh Sinton.

So The Somers Arms would be packed, with children on the lawn that ran from the road right down to the back of the building.

Under the Clewers there were numerous fundraising activities, for which committees of regulars used to be formed. For example, one children's party was attended by 160 children, and there was a Country and Western evening which raised £650 for Worcester Royal Infirmary in 1984. In addition to providing drink and recreation, The Somers Arms also served as a place to go for help. Susan Jones remembers one frail old lady from Sandlin, Emily Haywood, who dragged herself there and then collapsed, knowing that she would be taken care of once she got there.

The Somers Arms closed around 1995 and now houses a Chinese takeaway and a printing works, with a commercial pre-school organisation ('Bumbles Barn') in part of the old bottle store at the rear.

The Somers Arms, Leigh Sinton, and its surroundings from the air, May 1965.
(JULIAN BURTON)

The Somers Arms women's darts team after winning the Malvern League Championship, May 1961. Left to right: *Mrs Dunn, Sybil Clewer, Connie Jones, Carrie Bartlett, Lesley Dunn (from the Archers, who presented the awards), Freda Symonds, Anne Jones, Dorrie Rowley, Florrie Goodyear, Marjorie Powell, Dorothy Clay, Mollie Burston.* (SUSAN JONES)

Somers Arms darts team, 1953. Left to right, back row: *Frank Symonds, Cecil Busby, Fred Phillips, Frank Johnson, Ben Rowley, Dennis Clewer (the landlord);* front row: *Herbert Ball, Fred Ball, Tony Hooper, Bob Rowley, Bill Lane, Ernie Clay.* (CONNIE TOHTZ)

Somers Arms Darts Club dinner, early 1950s. Left to right, back row: *Tom Hopkins, Arch Ball, Joe Kimber, Vic Young, Frank Goodyear, Bill King, Arthur Shouk, Austin Cole, ? Parker, ?, Freda Symonds, Mrs Emily Newell, ?, Sybil Clewer, Ethel Burnham, ?;* seated, left-hand side: *Eric Pritchard, (PC) Watkin Hopkins, Bert Ball, ?, ?, Fred Symonds, Bob Rowley, ? Woodward, Dennis Clewer;* seated right-hand side: *Bert Clewer, Bert Sturmey, Chris Busby, Ben Rowley, Fred Ball, ?, ?, Frank Johnson.* (SUSAN JONES)

A meeting of the Croome Hunt outside The Somers Arms, early to mid 1950s. The man on the left, taking the cap collection, is Mr Taylor, whilst the huntsman on horseback is Ralph Gwynn. (SUSAN JONES)

Right: *Spectators at a meet of the Croome Hunt at The Somers Arms, 1950s.* (SUSAN JONES)

Below: *Meet of the Croome Hunt at The Somers Arms, 1950s. Sybil and Dennis Clewer serving stirrup cups.* (SUSAN JONES)

Leigh and Bransford British Legion Royal Review, 1937. Left to right, back row: *Dick Holmes, Tom Jones, ? Lawrence, Dick James, Bob Rowley;* centre: *Jack Cooper, ?, Reuben Portman, Charlie Banks, Harvey Hunt;* front row: *Harry Portman, ?, George Hill, Bert Sturmey.*
(HAROLD PORTMAN)

Royal British Legion

The Leigh, Bransford and Alfrick branch of the British Legion (later to become the Leigh and District Royal British Legion) was founded in 1937 by the headmaster of Leigh Hurst School, O.G. Davies, with Ben Jackson as secretary. As well as providing a social base, its aim was to help veterans of the First World War in any way possible. The early meetings were held in the local pubs, to which members were taken in the Chicken Coop. One of its early actions was to put a First World War roll of honour in the Memorial Hall. During the war it ran whist drives, dances and auctions to raise money for active service men and women on their return.

After the Second World War there was an influx of members. We saw above that they organised a series of very successful horticultural shows at the Memorial Hall. They also put up a second plaque in the Memorial Hall, to those who had just served. Sadly, however, there was a conflict between the ideas of the new members and of the First World War

veterans, and membership dwindled gradually until, on 19 December 1970, the branch was closed. Despite the closure, the poppy appeals activities were kept going by Ruth Beard and Rita Hall, and John Hemming looked after former members.

The Remembrance Day ceremonies were also kept alive by former members including Harry Banner, Stan Jones and John Hemming. In 1991 these three, together with Des Symonds, held a meeting to see if there was enough interest to start a new branch. A total of 30 people attended and the Leigh and Bransford branch was formed a year later. It now has 160 members and is the largest organisation in the parish, as well as the largest British Legion branch in the district. At the dedication of the new standard in Leigh Church, carried by Stan Jones, 42 standards attended – 'It was a proud and wonderful day.' Stan Jones won the County Standard Bearers' Competition three years in a row from 1997, whilst in 1999 John Hemming, the branch secretary, was awarded the Royal British Legion gold badge, its most coveted award.

Presentation to the Poppy Day collectors at a meeting of the Leigh and District Royal British Legion at the Bank House Hotel, November 2001. Left to right, back row: *Graham Jones, Des Symonds, Sir John Willison (president), Dennis Cottrell;* front row: *Valda Cane, Coral Clarke, Peggy Emson, Ruth Beard, Jean Hughes, Rita Hall, Alma Stoddart.*
(MALCOLM SCOTT)

Scouts and Guides

The wedding of Gordon Portman to Dora Massey, 1951, with the Scouts forming a guard of honour. (COLIN PORTMAN)

Scouting was started in the parish in 1934 by Maurice Jones, a local architect, who was the first Scoutmaster, Horace Fitzer being his assistant. It met first in Maurice Jones' house next to The Asp, Bransford, then moved to the Memorial Hall, and finally to a carriage and stable block in the former Rectory at Leigh Hurst (which has now been demolished). They had a number of camps, including one at the World Jamboree, held at Eastnor Park, Ledbury. They also held a weekend camp for all the Malvern Scout groups, when there was a 'Silver Bugle' competition for the most efficient camp, which Leigh won.

The troop lapsed during the war and was restarted afterwards by Revd Moreton-Jackson, with Gordon Portman as the Scoutmaster. Although it had 18 members initially, numbers dwindled and it stopped after three years. Then in 1970 a Cub pack was started by Christine Taylor, helped by Ken Allcock and June Symonds (now Etheridge), then a young Guide. June Etheridge has been involved with the Cubs ever since, and is now its leader, her husband Paul being the Group Scout Leader.

Starting from 12 members, the Cubs grew, and then a Scout Troop was formed. In the mid 1970s a headquarters was erected in the Memorial Hall grounds (on the old tennis courts) and they have been there ever since. 'Scouting' is the term used to cover all related activities and there have been many developments since 1970 – for example, the formation of a Beaver colony for the 6–8-year-olds and the establishment of a Venture Unit (for both sexes) for those between $15^1/_2$ and 20.

Right: *The 1st Leigh Scouts in the early 1950s.* Left to right, back row: *Philip Stallard, John Brooks, Allan Bowen, Brian Stallard, Eric Pritchard, Ken Jones, Stewart Atkinson, Francis Dee;* seated: *Donald Holmes, Michael Monk, Dennis Jauncey, Revd Moreton Jackson, Gordon Portman (Scoutmaster), Bob Green, John Shellam, Tony Clarke.* (COLIN PORTMAN)

Above: *Members of the 1st Leigh Scouts on a pot-holing expedition.* Left to right: *?, Edward Seymour, Peter Gardiner, Craig Barry, Guy Harvey, Paul Newall, Damien Barry, Paul or Andrew Milnes.* (PAUL ETHERIDGE)

Left: *Members of the 1st Leigh Scouts at the District Scout camp at Eastnor, 1978.* Left to right: *Roy Larder, ?, ?, Stuart Ainge* (standing), *Mark Sandford, Chris Morris, Garry Larder, ?, ?.* (PAUL ETHERIDGE)

Above: *Members of the 1st Leigh Cubs tidying up Bransford Chapel churchyard.* Left to right: *Michael Lampard, Matthew Cooper, Kevin Johnson, Kevin Brace, Richard Bradshaw, Simon Davies, Paul Crockford, Adrian Jones, Daren Sidney.* (PAUL ETHERIDGE/BERROWS)

Left: *Members of the 1st Leigh Cub pack after receiving their World Conservation badges, February 1982. This involved studying wildlife and learning how to assist in its conservation.* (PAUL ETHERIDGE)

Left: *Leigh Brownies, 1966.* Left to right, back row: *June Etheridge (née Symonds), Angela Swindell, Jeannie ?, Celia (?) Dee, Ann Vernalls;* centre: *Pamela Craske, ?, ?, ?, Leslie Lewis;* front row: *? Craske, Michael Dee, Nicole Edmonds, ?, ?. (Michael Dee was not a Brownie – he used to accompany his mother, who helped the Brownie leaders, Miss Sykes – a teacher at Leigh Hurst School – and Miss Cull.)* (PAT AND CECIL DEE)

Below: *Brownies' Silver Jubilee float, 1977.*
(ROSEMARY CHIDLOW)

Above: *Brownies' Easter Garden at Leigh Church, 1997.* Left to right: *Amy Downward, Hannah Davidson, Clare James, Joanna Green.*
(ROSEMARY CHIDLOW)

Right: *1st Leigh Brownies. The winning team (with certificates) in the 1990 Worcestershire Brownie Sports and the rest of the pack.* Left to right, back row: *Bev Smith, Lisa Worth, Sinead Lynch, Claire Randal, Lucy Stinton, Catherine Bradley, Nicola Jenkins, Catherine Price, Jenni Etheridge;* centre: *Joanne Betts, visitor, Charlotte White, Lucy Kelsall, Sophie Hampson, Ruth Barton;* front row: *Rosa Birch, Sarah Baldwin, Lisa Loundes, Carly Copson, Rebecca Taylor, Laura Hampson, Julia Hearnden.* (ROSEMARY CHIDLOW)

With about 70 members in all sections in 2002, scouting has been extremely successful, and the group is one of the largest in the district. They have a whole range of activities at their headquarters, including craft, football and other games. There are also activities which take them away, like camping, hiking, canoeing, climbing and orienteering. Finally, they are involved in community work – they organised the extremely successful Guy Fawkes bonfire and fireworks evenings for the last two years, and are joint organisers of the May Fair with the Village Hall Committee.

The Brownies were started by Mrs Moreton-Jackson in 1963, and in 1964 Miss Sykes, a teacher at Leigh Sinton School, took over as leader. She also ran the Guides, and both groups met in the school. In 1972, Angela Jones and Rosemary Chidlow took their children to join the Brownies and were persuaded to stay and help. By the end of the year Rosemary was the leader and Angela the assistant! In 1991, Rosemary handed over leadership to her daughter Zoe, becoming one of the assistants. All three left in 1999, and Shirley Ellis and Kaye James became the leaders.

151

The continued existence of the pack is a measure of its success. There are 24 members, drawn from the parish as well as from Alfrick and the edges of Malvern, and there is a waiting list for membership. Meeting in the Memorial Hall, their activities are similar to those of the Cubs, placing great importance on teamwork and social activities. Sport is important and they have won the Worcester Divisional Sports Shield six times since 1972, competing against 24 other packs.

The Guides have also been running since the 1960s and were again run by Miss Sykes, with the help of a friend, Miss Cull. The present Guide leader, Valda Cane, was a member during this period. The troop closed down for a while, but restarted in 1991 with Chris Durham as the leader and Valda Cane as assistant. Chris Durham left in 1998 and Valda Cane has been running it ever since.

They meet in the Scout hut and have a similar range of activities to the Scouts, except with a different emphasis. They have less sport and concentrate more on crafts and life skills. Their outdoor activities are similar and include abseiling, canoeing, caving, camping and hiking. They have recently been awarded two substantial grants to enable them to buy camping and hiking equipment rather than have to borrow it, so that they can now be much more independent in planning their activities.

Above: *1st Leigh St Edburga Guides at Leigh Church Fête, early 1950s. The Guide captain is Vera Griffiths, from Crowcroft, whose father was the baker. Glenda Merrell is sitting on the trailer on the right-hand side.* (GLENDA MERRELL)

Left: *1st Leigh Guide camp, 1970s. Miss Sykes and Miss Cull (from Worcester).* (ELIZABETH PORTMAN)

Below: *1st Leigh St Edburga Guides at a camp on Exmoor, 1953.* (GLENDA MERRELL)

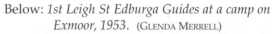

Villages Playgroup

This group was formed in 1976 by Jill Ellard and Katherine Brace. As the district nurse and health visitor, Jill saw a need for small children to be able to meet and play together, whilst Katherine, who had three children, had experience of playgroups in towns. Starting with a dozen children they met at the Memorial Hall, with a parents' committee to help in the running. Later the group became affiliated to the Pre-School Learning Alliance, and it is now a registered charity.

Children, who range in age from two and a half to five, attend for up to three two-and-a-half-hour sessions a week. The rising-fives can also attend for two extra one-and-a-half-hour periods. In addition to being able to play, the children are also prepared for school and there are a whole range of facilities to support these activities. The supervisor and her assistant are qualified and all the parents take it in turns to help. Parents are also involved in the decision-making over the school's conduct. There are currently 18 children attending, with an upper limit of 24.

There is also a Mothers and Toddlers Group that meets on Wednesday mornings.

Below: *Villages Playgroup, summer 2002.* Left to right, back row: *Owen Sanders, Sophie Armitage, Anna Watkins, Arthur Davies, Irma Strelczuk (supervisor) holding Frederick Grant, Lily Taylor, Chloe Dongworth, Ben Ager, Joanne King, Samuel Harcombe;* front row: *Sebastian Snowdon, Jonathan King, Jake Lawrence, Bethan Furniss, Zachary Webster, John Harvey, James Knightingale. Anna Watkins has just retired after 18 years as an assistant, and Mary Croad recently retired after nine years.* (PAULINE HARCOMBE)

Above: *Playgroup activity, 2001. Pauline Harcombe with* (clockwise): *Samuel Harcombe, Chloe Dongworth, Lily Taylor and Jonathan King.* (MALCOLM SCOTT)

Women's Institute

The Leigh and Bransford Women's Institute ('For Home and Country') was founded in 1934 by the diocesan architect's wife, Lavender Jones. Olive Emson and Nellie Gale were amongst its founder members and it has been meeting monthly every since. Over the years its activities have changed, and it is probably because of this that it has maintained its vitality. Although numbers dipped to around 30 a decade ago, at the time of writing there now 45 members, and Shirley Tasker is the president.

The evening normally starts with a business meeting, at which issues of local and national importance are discussed, followed by a talk or demonstration. Some of the speakers are local, whilst others are county or national figures. In addition, they have a wide range of campaigns. In the late 1980s they had a series of fashion shows, raising £650 for a local Scanner Appeal. In 1991, ploughman's lunches and other activities helped them to raise £1,200 for Cancer Research. More recently money has been raised for the Macmillan nurses and for the Cobalt Unit at Cheltenham. But not all the causes are local or national, recent ones having included making toys for Romanian children and clothes for children in the Gambia.

The WI has always been a campaigning and educational organisation, although this has not always been its image! It is also non-religious and non-political – which is why in 2000 the Prime Minister, Tony Blair, was slow hand-clapped at the Triennial General Meeting, some members feeling that he was hijacking the event to provide a political platform.

Membership card for Olive Emson, one of the founder members of the Leigh and Bransford Women's Institute, December 1934.
(OLIVE BISHOP)

Women's Institute event, 12 February 1960. Left to right, back row: *Mrs Wilf Pritchard, Mrs Handy (Powick), Maud Banner, Myna Hemming, Mrs Hemming (senior), Elsie Portman;* centre: *Hilda Wadley, ?, Florrie Roberts, Mrs Hughes, ?, Alice Sefton, Mrs Bowers, ?, Mrs Pithers, Pat Dee, Gladys Portman;* front row: *Olive Emson, ?, Mrs Wenden-Lambert (president), Nellie Gale.* (WI SCRAPBOOK)

A Women's Institute event, 1975. Left to right, back row: *Betty Eggett, Pauline Phillips, Mrs Sherriff, Christine Burston, Jennie Potter (?), ?, Mrs Earle, Jean Portman, Sally Stewart, Edith Booton;* centre: *?, Rosemary Chidlow, Mrs King (?), Ruby Davies, Myna Hemming, Hilda Wadley, ?, Dorothy Banner;* front row: *Mrs Bowers, Olive Emson, Mary Fynn, Elizabeth Portman (president), Ivy Weaver, Gladys Portman, Ethel Drew.* (SALLY STEWART)

Members of the Women's Institute planting an oak tree at the Memorial Hall, 10 December 1978. **Left to right:** *Pam Clarke, Marie Harrison, Nellie Gale, Mary Ralph (President, with spade), Derek Ralph, Mary Fynn, Gill Gale, Vi Handy, Peter Salmon, Mary Gale.* (ELIZABETH PORTMAN)

Above: *Women's Institute meeting on the theme of 'Herbs', June 1978.* Left to right: *Mary Ralph, Vi Handy, Elizabeth Portman, Mary Fynn.*
(WI SCRAPBOOK)

Above: *Judging the cake competition, Leigh and Bransford Women's Institute, 1970s.* Left to right: *Betty Eggett, ?, Elizabeth Portman, Mrs Colwick (the WI judge from Great Whitley), Sally Stewart.*
(SALLY STEWART)

Left: *Meeting of the Leigh and Bransford Women's Institute at the Memorial Hall, spring 2002.*
(MALCOLM SCOTT)

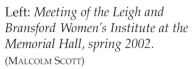

Right: *100 members and guests attended this cookery demonstration at the Leigh and Bransford Women's Institute meeting in the Memorial Hall, spring 2002.* (MALCOLM SCOTT)

155

BIBLIOGRAPHY

The main books which have been consulted in writing this history are as follows:

Articles in the *Worcester Herald* by 'A Stroller', April 1923 onwards.
Kelly's Directory of Worcestershire, 1884, Kelly and Co., London.
Post Office Directory of Worcestershire, 1868, Kelly and Co., London.
Directory and Gazetteer of the County of Worcestershire, 1855, M. Billing, Birmingham.
Proceedings of the Worcestershire Diocesan Architectural and Archaeological Society, 27 January 1893.
Transactions of the Worcestershire Archaeological Society for 1954.
Midlands Rivers, by John Drewett and John Roberts, Querus, Birmingham, 1996.
Littlebury's Directory and Gazetteer of Worcester & District, 1879, Littleburys, Worcester.
On the Ancient British, Roman and Saxon Antiquities and Folk-lore: Worcestershire, by Jabez Allies, J.H. Parker, London, 1852.
Worcestershire Within Living Memory, 1995, Worcestershire Federation of Women's Institutes, Countryside Books, Newbury & WFWI, Worcester.
A pocketful of hops, The Bromyard and District Local History Society, Bromyard, 1988.
Domesday Book Worcestershire, edited by Frank and Caroline Thorne, Phillimore, Chichester, 1982.
Worcestershire's Hidden Past, Bill Gwilliam, Halfshire Books, Bromsgrove, 1991.
Village Scenes, Charles Grant and Pamela Hurle, Charles Grant, 1997.
The Bromyard Branch from Worcester to Leominster, William H. Smith, Kidderminster Railway Museum, 1998.
A History of Malvern, Brian H. Smith, Alan Sutton and The Malvern Bookshop, 1964.
Collections for the History of Worcestershire, Volumes I and II, Treadway Russell Nash, 1782.
The Victoria History of the Counties of England: Worcestershire, Volume IV, pp101–11, St Catherine's Press, London, 1924.
Memories of St Johns, edited and compiled by Philip M. Adams, St John's Library Coffee Pot Club, 1997.
Henry II, by W.L. Warren, Yale University Press, 2000.
The Castles of Herefordshire and Worcestershire, Michael Salter, Folly Publications, Wolverhampton, 1989.
The Civil War in Worcestershire, Malcolm Atkin, Alan Sutton Publishing Limited and Hereford and Worcester Libraries and Arts, 1995.
Cromwell's Crowning Mercy. The Battle of Worcester 1651, Malcolm Atkin, Alan Sutton Publishing Limited, 1998.
The Parish and Church of Leigh, Worcester Diocesan Architectural and Archaeological Society, Vol XVII, 1882–4 edition.
Chronicle of Henry, Archdeacon of Huntingdon (c.1080–1160).
Coach Travel and Turnpike Roads, H.W. (Bill) Gwilliam (undated and soft bound).
Worcestershire's Historic Bridges, H.W. (Bill) Gwilliam (undated and soft bound).
The Buildings of England: Worcestershire, Nikolaus Pevsner, Penguin Books, 1968.
A History of Worcestershire Agriculture and the Rural Revolution, by R.C. Gaut, Littlebury and Company, The Worcester Press, Worcester, 1939.
The Mercian Maquis, Bernard Lowry and Mick Wilks, Logaston Press, Logaston, Herefordshire, 2002.
Rural Rides, William Cobbett, first published in 1830, published in Penguin Classics, 2001.
The Rambler in Worcestershire, or stray notes, John Noake, published in Worcester in 1848.

SUBSCRIBERS

Mr L.J. Alford, Leigh, Worcestershire

Kevin Allen, Malvern Wells, Worcestershire

B. and M. Atkinson, Leigh Sinton, Worcestershire

Bridget Bache, Malvern, Worcestershire

Banner (Godfrey) John, Leigh Sinton Road, Malvern, Worcestershire

H.L. Banner, Leigh, Worcestershire

Mr Lionel Banner, formerly of Leigh

Mr V. Banner, Defford, Nr Evesham

Geoffrey James Bartlett, Leigh Sinton, Worcestershire

Sarah Beaton (née Powell), Tauranga, New Zealand

Wendy J. Birch (née Banner), formerly of Leigh

Olive and Elizabeth Bishop, Leigh, Worcestershire

John E. Bishop, Henwick Park, Worcester

John C. Bosley, Suckley, Worcestershire

Ann Bowen, Leigh Sinton, Worcestershire

Patrick S. Bowers, Suckley Road, Leigh, Worcestershire

Derek and Carol Bradley, Alfrick Pound

Mrs Stella V. Braithwaite, Sparkford, Somerset

John and Joanna Brown, Leigh, Worcestershire

Alexandra Brown, Leigh, Worcestershire

William Brown, Leigh, Worcestershire

Revd Andrew B. Bullock, Leigh, Worcestershire

Joy E. Bunyan, Bransford, Worcestershire

Lance, Sarah, Joanna and Charlotte Cale

Rodney Cass, Brockamin, Leigh, Worcestershire

Mrs Anne Castle

Charles and Susan Chainey, Hopton Barn, Alfrick, Worcestershire

John T. Chapman, born Bransford

Mr and Mrs M.P. Chaundy, Ashfields

Jonathan and Diana Chilton, Smith End Green, Worcestershire

Edna F. Clarke, Rushwick, Worcester

Nella Clarke, formerly of Suffield Bransford

Desmond and Coral Clarke, Leigh Sinton, Worcestershire

Tony and Margaret Clarke

Neil and Lyn Coleman, Leigh Sinton, Worcestershire

Ivy J. Coley, Leigh, Worcestershire

Nigel and Linda Collis, Coles Green, Leigh Sinton, Worcestershire

Dr Linda Cotterill, Alfrick, Worcestershire

Sarah Cotterill, Alfrick, Worcestershire

Dennis and Dorothy Cottrell

Maggia and Fred Covins, Leigh Sinton, Worcestershire

Jane and Guy Covins, Leigh Sinton, Worcestershire

Steve and Sheila Cridland, Leigh

Maureen Croall, Clerk to the Parish Council

Ruth Curran, Worcester

John H. Davies, Leigh Sinton, Worcestershire

Mowey Davies, Worcester

Ken and Nancy Davies, Stocks Lane, Bransford, Worcestershire

John and Margaret Davison

Sally Davison (née Robinson), Leigh, Worcestershire

Anthony, Louise and Arthur Dawes, Stitchens Hill, Leigh Sinton, Worces

Cecil and Pat Dee, Bransford, Worcester

Mrs E. Dee, Leigh Sinton Road

Teresa Dongworth, Leigh Sinton, Worcetershire

Paul Dunmall, Brockamin, Worcestershire

Marilyn Dyer (née James), formerly of Leigh and Alfrick

Dorothy Dyson, Worcester (ex Bransford Service Station)

Ros and Terry Edden, Coles Green, Leigh Sinton, Worcestershire

Frances Emson, Alfrick, Nr Worcester

Mr Douglas Emson,

June and Paul Etheridge, Worcester

Philip B. Eve, Bransford, Worcestershire

John E. Farr, Leigh, Worcester

Margaret Farr (née Froggatt), Wheathampstead, Hertfordshire

Dr and Mrs H.S. Field-Richards, Leigh Sinton, Worcestershire

James Finn, Malvern

Catherine I. Forrester, Leigh Sinton, Worcester

David W. Fowler, Alfrick Pound, Worcestershire

Lucy and Graham Froggatt, Leigh Sinton, Worcestershire

Mary and Gill Gale, Bransford, Worcestershire

H.D. and W.A. Gardner, Worcester

Kevin and Jennifer Garrington, Bransford, Worcestershire

The Gatley Family, Alfrick, Worcestershire

Richard and Elain Goode, Leigh Sinton, Worcestershire

Bob and Sue Green, Bransford, Worcestershire

H. John Griffin, Ledbury, Herefordshire

Peter and Beryl Gwinnett, Smith End Green, Leigh Sinton, Worcestershire

Lawrence R. Haddock, Whitbourne, Teme Valley

N. and J. Hadley, Leigh, Worcestershire

Vi Handy, Leigh, Worcestershire

John and Pauline Harcombe

Leonard Frank Hardcastle, Brockermin, Leigh, Worcestershire

Bob Hatton, Leigh, Worcestershire

Derek and June Haworth, Brock Hill, Leigh, Worcestershire

Margaret Haynes (née Robinson), Leigh, Worcestershire

Patricia and Graham Hearnden, Leigh, Worcestershire

Susan Hibbert, Brynford, North Wales

R.H. Hickling, Malvern

Mr Roy Hill, Brockamin, Worcestershire

David G. Hill, Alfrick, Worcestershire

Neil, Susan, Mark Holbrow, Brockamin, Leigh, Worcestershire

Dick and Rose Holmes, Bransford, Worcestershire

June Hooper, Storridge, Nr Malvern, Worcestershire

Ian J. Hooper, Totnes, Devonshire

Wendy and Richard Howard, Brockamin, Worcestershire

Mrs Dorothy Hughes

Joe Hughes, formerly of The Norrest

Pamela Hurle, Storridge, Worcestershire

Kevin James, Bahamas

Barbara James (née Tredwell), formerly of Leigh and Alfrick

Sheila Jauncey, Llantwit Major, South Wales

Dennis Jauncey, formerly of Leigh, Worcestershire

Mr G.W. (Bill) Jauncey, Fernhill Heath, Worcestershire

Mrs Kathleen Jauncey, Worcester

Mrs Norah Jay, Leigh, Worcester

Brenda Johnson, Texas, USA

Mr R.W. Jolly, Leigh, Worcestershire

David Jones, Shrubbery House, Leigh Sinton, Worcestershire

Paul Jones, Shrubbery House, Leigh Sinton, Worcestershire

Graham and Susan Jones, Leigh Sinton, Worcestershire

Kenneth and Anne Jones, Shrubbery House, Leigh Sinton, Worcestershire

Roly and Marje Jones, Leigh, Worcestershire

Bib Jones, Leigh Sinton, Worcestershire

Gerald A.T. Jones, Leigh Sinton, Worcestershire

Gwendoline Jones (née Rowberry), Leigh, Worcestershire

Mrs Ivy Keeling

Carol Keniston, Leigh Sinton, Worcestershire

Mrs Sheila A. Kennard, Port Elizabeth, South Africa

Gary A. Kimber, Leigh Sinton, Worcestershire

Norman G. Kimber, Leigh Sinton, Worcestershire

James F. and Valerie J. King, Leigh, Worcestershire

Linda E. King, Leigh, Worcester

Iris Kinnard, formerly of Smith End Green

Joan and David Kirby, Alfrick, Worcester

Greg Kirby, Bransford, Worcestershire

Miss G.M. Lacey and Mr Terry Nightingale, Leigh, Worcestershire

Mr and Mrs J. Lapworth, Norrest Court, Leigh Sinton, Worcestershire

Seth Lawrence, Leigh Sinton, Worcestershire

Mr and Mrs K. Lee, Brockamin, Leigh, Worcestershire

B.H. Leeke, Deerhurst, Gloucestershire

Leigh and Bransford Primary School

E.N. Lewis, Bishop's Frome, Worcestershire

Janet H. Long (née Potter), Worcester

Barbara and Matt Lyons, Jasmine Cottage, Leigh Sinton, Worcestershire

James and Jenifer Marriott, Leigh, Worcestershire

Anne and Brian Martin, Alfrick, Worcestershire

Wendy Mason (née James), formerly of Leigh and Alfrick

Mr and Mrs McCallum

Jean M. McGowan, Leigh, Worcestershire

Mr Bosko Medakovic, Leigh, Worcestershire

Glenda Merrell, Drakes Broughton, Worcestershire

Margaret E. Merrick, Leigh Sinton, Worcestershire

Mr Jeremy Edmund Morfey, Dale Cottages, Brockamin, Leigh, Worcestershire

James and June Morris, Leigh, Worcester

Mrs Lilian Morris (née Pritchard), formerly of Smithsend Green

Paul, Jessica, James and Callum Nightingale, Leigh, Worcestershire

Janet Openshaw, Bransford, Worcestershire

Caroline Orgee, Leigh, Worcestershire

Dr C.A. Parsons, Woodford House, Knightwick, Worcestershire

Mrs B.G.M. Pass, Malvern Link, Worcestershire

Jayne Payne (née James), Malvern, Worcestershire

Lin Peet, Leigh, Worcestershire

Carole Peters (née Farmer), Barnards Green

Lady W. Pettit, Bransford Court Farm, Worcestershire

Mrs Pauline J. Phillips, Leigh Sinton, Worcestershire

Mervyn Philpott, Cranham, Gloucester

Mrs Elizabeth M. Plummer, New Zealand

Dr John Popert, Bransford, Worcestershire

Brian and Ann Porter, Bransford, Worcestershire

Harold Portman, Suckley Road, Leigh, Worcestershire

Colin R. and Barbara Portman, Nottingham

Gordon R. and Dora M. Portman, St Johns, Worcester

Derek Portman, Pear Tree Cottage, Hallow, Worcestershire

Merle E.A. Portman (née Banner), formerly of Leigh

Bernard and Olive Poultney, Stoke Prior, Worcestershire

Leslie J. Poultney, Droitwich, Worcestershire

Irene P.E. Powell, Somers Terrace, Leigh Sinton, Worcestershire

Nigel and Julie Price, Leigh Sinton, Worcestershire

SUBSCRIBERS

David and Sue Pritchard, Bransford, Worcestershire
Aubrey C. Pritchard, Powick, Worcester
Joyce H. Pritchard, Bransford, Nr Worcester
Kem Pugh, Broadwas-on-Teme, Worcestershire
Eileen Purvis, Leigh, Worcester
Mr and Mrs David Pye
The Rathmell Family, Leigh, Worcestershire
L. and B. Rawle, Hereford
Jane Raybould, Leigh, Worcestershire
Mr and Mrs F.W. Rayers, Leigh Sinton, Worcestershire
Caroline J. Rees, Leigh, Worcestershire
Sue Rickhuss, Worcester
John Roberts, 'Bri-Mar', Leigh, Worcestershire
M. Roberts, St Johns, Worcester
Brian Roberts, 'Bri-Mar', Dingle Road, Leigh, Worcester
June and John Robinson, Leigh, Worcestershire
Ian and Gill Ross, Leigh Sinton, Worcestershire
Doreen Rowley, Leigh Sinton, Worcestershire
Ruby A. Ruff (née Morris), Bransford and Leigh Sinton, Worcestershire
Mr and Mrs C. Salisbury, Leigh Sinton, Worcestershire
Malcolm Scott, Aubretia Cottage, Leigh, Worcestershire
June and Stephen Seymour, Leigh, Worcestershire
Mr and Mrs J. Sharkey
Mr and Mrs J. Sharp, Brockamin, Leigh, Worcestershire
Alex and Nicola Singleton, Leigh, Worcestershire
Sheila and Marshall Smart, Lynn Close, Leigh Sinton, Worcestershire
Geoff and Kate Smith, Leigh, Worcestershire
Lillian Somervaille, Aubretia Cottage, Leigh, Worcestershire
Peter and Thelma Spencer, Crowcroft, Leigh Sinton, Worcestershire
Mrs Joan Spencer (née Jauncey), Coventry
Guy and Debbie Sterry, Leigh, Worcestershire

Mr and Mrs Michael Stevens, Leigh, Worcestershire
Duncan Stewart, Leigh, Worcestershire
Barclay and Sally Stewart
Mr and Mrs D. Stewart, Leigh, Worcestershire
Jake, Netty and Lottie Stow, Leigh, Worcestershire
James R. Stubbs, Newland, Worcestershire
Des and May Symonds, Bransford, Worcestershire
Derek and Lyn Symonds, Whitbourne, Worcestershire
David K. Taylor, Leigh, Worcestershire
Stella M. Thornhill, Leigh Sinton, Worcestershire
David J. Throup, Powick, Worcestershire
Connie Tohtz, Leigh Sinton, Worcestershire
The Tolley Family, Alfrick, Worcestershire
William D. Tombs, Kings Heath, Birmingham
Dave and Val Tudge, Brockamin, Worcestershire
Margaret J. Tummey (née Chapman), Malvern, Worcestershire
Mrs Jacqueline F. Turner, Sandlin, Worcestershire
Pam and Frank Tyler, Leigh Sinton, Worcestershire
G. and V. Vos, Netherley, Mathon
Anthony G. Warburton, Stitchens Hill, Worcestershire
John and Anna Watkins, Bransford, Worcestershire
R.F. Wenden, Old Sandlin, Leigh Sinton, Worcestershire
The Wenden Family, Chirkenhill, Leigh Sinton, Worcestershire
Mrs M.B. West, Hanley Swan, Worcestershire
Bob and Prue Wilesmith, Tauranga, New Zealand
Tom C. Wilesmith, Whitianga, New Zealand
Gerald M. Williams, Leigh Sinton, Worcestershire
Peter, Zoe and Daisy Wood
Paul Anthony Worrall, Alfrick, Worcestershire
Miss Lisa Jayne Worth, Bransford, Worcestershire
Jason Philip Worth, Bransford, Worcestershire
Geoff and Sheila Wright, Brook House, Leigh, Worcestershire
Susan C. Youngs, Lechlade, Gloucestershire

Titles from the Series

The Book of Addiscombe • Various
The Book of Addiscombe, Vol. II • Various
The Book of Bampton • Caroline Seward
The Book of Barnstaple • Avril Stone
Book of Bickington • Stuart Hands
Blandford Forum: A Millennium Portrait • Various
The Book of Bridestowe • R. Cann
The Book of Brixham • Frank Pearce
The Book of Buckland Monachorum & Yelverton • Hemery
The Book of Carshalton • Stella Wilks
The Parish Book of Cerne Abbas • Vale & Vale
The Book of Chagford • Ian Rice
The Book of Chittlehamholt with
Warkleigh & Satterleigh • Richard Lethbridge
The Book of Chittlehampton • Various
The Book of Colney Heath • Bryan Lilley
The Book of Constantine • Moore & Trethowan
The Book of Cornwood & Lutton • Various
The Book of Creech St Michael • June Small
The Book of Cullompton • Various
The Book of Dawlish • Frank Pearce
The Book of Dulverton, Brushford,
Bury & Exebridge • Various
The Book of Dunster • Hilary Binding
The Ellacombe Book • Sydney R. Langmead
The Book of Exmouth • W.H. Pascoe
The Book of Grampound with Creed • Bane & Oliver
The Book of Hayling Island & Langstone • Rogers
The Book of Helston • Jenkin with Carter
The Book of Hemyock • Clist & Dracott
The Book of Hethersett • Various
The Book of High Bickington • Avril Stone
The Book of Ilsington • Dick Wills
The Book of Lamerton • Ann Cole & Friends
Lanner, A Cornish Mining Parish • Scharron Schwartz &
Roger Parker
The Book of Leigh & Bransford • Various
The Book of Litcham with Lexham & Mileham • Various
The Book of Loddiswell • Various
The Book of Lulworth • Rodney Legg
The Book of Lustleigh • Joe Crowdy
The Book of Manaton • Various
The Book of Markyate • Various
The Book of Mawnan • Various
The Book of Meavy • Pauline Hemery
The Book of Minehead with Alcombe • Binding & Stevens
The Book of Morchard Bishop • Jeff Kingaby
The Book of Newdigate • John Callcut
The Book of Northlew with Ashbury • Various
The Book of North Newton • Robins & Robins
The Book of North Tawton • Various
The Book of Okehampton • Radford & Radford
The Book of Paignton • Frank Pearce
The Book of Penge, Anerley & Crystal Palace • Various
The Book of Peter Tavy with Cudlipptown• Various
The Book of Pimperne • Jean Coull
The Book of Plymtree • Tony Eames
The Book of Porlock • Denis Corner
Postbridge – The Heart of Dartmoor • Reg Bellamy
The Book of Priddy • Various
The Book of Rattery • Various
The Book of Silverton • Various

The Book of South Molton • Various
The Book of South Stoke • Various
South Tawton & South Zeal with Sticklepath • Radfords
The Book of Sparkwell with Hemerdon & Lee Mill • Pam James
The Book of Staverton • Pete Lavis
The Book of Stithians • Various
The Book of Studland • Rodney Legg
The Book of Swanage • Rodney Legg
The Book of Torbay • Frank Pearce
Uncle Tom Cobley & All: Widecombe-in-the-Moor • Stephen
Woods
The Book of Watchet • Compiled by David Banks
The Book of West Huntspill • Various
Widecombe-in-the-Moor • Stephen Woods
The Book of Williton • Michael Williams
Woodbury: The Twentieth Century Revisited • Roger Stokes
The Book of Woolmer Green • Various

Forthcoming

The Book of Bakewell • Various
The Book of Barnstaple, Vol. II • Avril Stone
The Book of Brampford • Various
The Book of Breage & Gurmoe • Stephen Polglase
The Book of the Bedwyns • Various
The Book of Bideford • Peter Christie
The Book of Bridport • Rodney Legg
The Book of Buckfastleigh • Sandra Coleman
The Book of Carharrack • Various
The Book of Castleton • Geoff Hill
The Book of Edale • Gordon Miller
The Book of Kingskerswell • Various
The Book of Lostwithiel • Barbara Frasier
The Book of Lydford • Barbara Weeks
The Book of Lyme Regis • Rodney Legg
The Book of Nether Stowey • Various
The Book of Nynehead • Various
The Book of Princetown • Dr Gardner-Thorpe
The Book of St Day • Various
The Book of Sampford Courtenay
with Honeychurch • Stephanie Pouya
The Book of Sculthorpe • Garry Windeler
The Book of Sherborne • Rodney Legg
The Book of Southbourne • Rodney Legg
The Book of Tavistock • Gerry Woodcock
The Book of Thorley • Various
The Book of Tiverton • Mike Sampson
The Book of West Lavington • Various
The Book of Witheridge • Various
The Book of Withycombe • Chris Boyles

For details of any of the above titles or if you are
interested in writing your own history, please contact:
Commissioning Editor Community Histories, Halsgrove
House, Lower Moor Way, Tiverton Business Park,
Tiverton, Devon EX16 6SS, England;
email: naomic@halsgrove.com

In order to include as many historic photographs as
possible in this volume, a printed index is not included.
However, the Community History Series is indexed by
Genuki. For further information and indexes to
volumes in the series, please visit:
http://www.cs.ncl.uk/genuki/DEV/indexingproject.html